THE SEX OFFENDER HOUSING DILEMMA

The Sex Offender Housing Dilemma

Community Activism, Safety, and Social Justice

Monica Williams

NEW YORK UNIVERSITY PRESS
New York

NEW YORK UNIVERSITY PRESS
New York
www.nyupress.org

Portions of this book are adapted from Monica Williams, "Constructing Hysteria: Legal Signals as Producers of Siting Conflicts over Sexually Violent Predator Placements," *Law and Social Inquiry*. 2016. Epub ahead of print. doi: 10.1111/lsi.12265.

References to Internet websites (URLs) were accurate at the time of writing. Neither the author nor New York University Press is responsible for URLs that may have expired or changed since the manuscript was prepared.

Library of Congress Cataloging-in-Publication Data
Names: Williams, Monica (Sociologist), author.
Title: The sex offender housing dilemma : community activism, safety, and social justice / Monica Williams.
Description: New York : New York University Press, [2018] | Also available as an ebook. | Includes bibliographical references and index.
Identifiers: LCCN 2017034140| ISBN 978-1-4798-9711-7 (cl ; alk. paper) | ISBN 1-4798-9711-6 (cl ; alk. paper) | ISBN 978-1-4798-3649-9 (pb ; alk. paper) | ISBN 1-4798-3649-4 (pb ; alk. paper)
Subjects: LCSH: Sex offenders—Housing—California. | Sex offenders—Legal status, laws, etc.—California. | Sex offenders—Rehabilitation—California. | Community activists—California. | Sex offenders—Housing—United States. | Sex offenders—Legal status, laws, etc.—United States. | Sex offenders—Rehabilitation—United States. | Community activists—United States.
Classification: LCC HV6592 .W54 2018 | DDC 363.5/9692709794—dc23
LC record available at https://lccn.loc.gov/2017034140

New York University Press books are printed on acid-free paper, and their binding materials are chosen for strength and durability. We strive to use environmentally responsible suppliers and materials to the greatest extent possible in publishing our books.

Manufactured in the United States of America

10 9 8 7 6 5 4 3 2 1

Also available as an ebook

For Matthew,

without whom this book

would never have been possible

CONTENTS

LIST OF FIGURES AND TABLES

Introduction

In Washington State, Tammy Gibson beat a sex offender with a baseball bat after receiving notification that he had moved into her neighborhood.[1] Neighbors in Detroit assaulted a man suspected of raping a teenager,[2] and two people in Texas did the same to a registered sex offender there.[3] Such acts of violence have sometimes escalated to murder, as was the case in South Carolina when two people killed a registered sex offender and his wife.[4] Other, less extreme cases have involved not violence but property damage, such as the suspicious fire that burned down a trailer meant to house a man in California who was labeled as a sexually violent predator (SVP).[5] These kinds of stories focus public attention on extreme but relatively rare instances of physical violence, threats, and harassment against individual sex offenders.[6]

While media accounts would have us believe that vigilantes across the country lie in wait for sex offenders who move into their neighborhoods, responses to sex offenders more often involve collective, nonviolent political and legal actions. For instance, communities across the nation have built tiny pocket parks in neighborhoods where local ordinances prohibit sex offenders from living near schools or parks.[7] Residents in one Florida town protested a proposed sex offender village not by torching the proposed site but by attending town hall meetings, signing petitions, and rallying behind political and law enforcement leaders.[8] These types of responses to sex offender housing proposals may be more socially desirable than vigilantism, but they still pose severe challenges to sex offenders trying to reintegrate into society.

This book focuses on the problem of finding housing for sex offenders. The public has little sympathy for these offenders, but a lack of social supports and stable housing can increase the likelihood of reoffending.[9] For these and other reasons, many scholars have critiqued policies restricting where sex offenders can live as ill-founded and potentially counterproductive. For example, residence restriction laws in many states prohibit sex offenders from living within specified distances (usually five hundred to one thousand feet) of schools, parks, and playgrounds.[10] A growing chorus of voices has called for the repeal of or moratoriums on residence restrictions because empirical evidence suggests that they are not effective in decreasing recidivism rates.[11] Few sex offenders live in restricted zones to begin with, and residence restrictions have little to no impact on recidivism rates.[12] Far from ensuring public safety, residence restrictions can make it more difficult for sex offenders to reintegrate into society, which may in turn increase the likelihood of reoffending.[13]

Community notification laws exacerbate the situation. These laws require law enforcement to notify the public about some types of sex offenders, with the assumption that doing so will enable communities to keep themselves safe. Ironically, community notification may have the opposite effect. Those who receive notification do not appear to engage in self-protective behaviors.[14] Instead, people become afraid and have fewer social interactions with other community members. This in turn weakens the social integration necessary to support individuals returning to society after incarceration.[15] In addition to these negative effects on community members' sense of safety and well-being, notification laws do not appear to reduce the likelihood of reoffending.[16] These outcomes suggest that community notification laws serve largely symbolic functions that may be important for expressing societal disapproval of deviant sexual behavior but have little to no positive impacts on the behaviors of either identified sex offenders or the general public.[17] Instead, community notification laws appear to make it harder for those identified as sex offenders to find places to live.

Repealing empirically unfounded laws would be a step in the right direction, but sex offenders returning to society after incarceration would still face problems associated with their stigmatized status. The Tammy Gibsons of the world and the less violent but just as damaging people who band together to keep sex offenders out of their neighborhoods would continue to create major obstacles to reintegration. Beyond laws and policies, the everyday realities of trying to find housing for a highly stigmatized and feared group of people make the problem seem almost insurmountable. Where should these offenders go? How can we facilitate their successful reintegration into communities? How do we balance individual rights with public safety when trying to find housing?

Some have answered these questions by calling for individualized re-entry plans based on risk assessments and partnerships between communities, researchers, and policy makers.[18] These suggestions warrant serious consideration, but we cannot solve the problem of sex offender housing without looking closely at how and why communities oppose sex offenders in their neighborhoods. This book takes on this task by examining community opposition to SVP placements in California.

On the surface, local protests against sex offenders seem to reflect a simple "not-in-my-backyard" (NIMBY) attitude. Closer examination reveals more complex issues. As Tammy Gibson assaulted the sex offender in Washington, she reportedly told him, "If it were up to me, I'd kill ya."[19] This comment reflects a sense of powerlessness. Gibson, like others who harass individual sex offenders, acted not only out of extreme hatred but also from a sense of dissatisfaction with the institutions that regulate sex offender releases. Because justice was not "up to" Gibson to decide, she brought about her own version of justice. Others agreed with her actions. After the media reported on the case, Gibson received widespread support online. "I applaud her," said one commenter. "She was protecting her children from a predator!!"[20] "You go girl!" said another. "I'll buy you a lifetime supply of bats!"[21] For these individuals, justice required working outside of the law to protect children and other vulnerable populations from sex offenders, which suggests skepticism of how formal institutions deal with these offenders.

Similar concerns emerge in the more common, nonviolent community responses to sex offenders. One such response occurred one evening in April 2009 when community members in an unincorporated town in Monterey County learned of the proposed placement of an SVP in their town. I attended the community notification meeting to see how community members and local officials managed this potentially volatile situation. When I arrived at the local winery that was hosting the meeting, people milled about the gravel parking lot and reception hall discussing what they had heard about the SVP who might soon be moving into their neighborhood.[22] I sat in a folding chair next to a burly man who lived on the same road on which state officials had proposed the SVP placement. The man worked for a winery equipment business, and he told me that the community had never before faced anything like the proposed SVP placement.

After a few minutes, the county supervisor called the meeting to order by inviting the panel of local politicians, law enforcement officers, and a California Department of Mental Health (DMH) contractor to introduce themselves.[23] The audience generally quieted, but one man quickly interrupted the introductions, demanding that they "eliminate the bullshit and get to the questions." The county supervisor, trying to maintain order, assured him there would be an opportunity for public comment in due time. After a brief exchange between the two men, order prevailed. Panel members made their introductions and then provided some information about the placement.

When it came time for public comment and questions, one audience member questioned the legality of the judge's decision to place the SVP in the neighborhood. The supervisor answered that the decision was "probably" legal, but that he was not a legal expert and that we were not there to debate the judge's ruling. Instead, he said, the purpose of the meeting was to figure out how to move forward. After repeated attempts to continue asking the same question about the legality of the decision, the audience member picked up his young son and left the reception hall. After his abrupt exit, more questions about the decision-making process followed: How had the house been chosen? Why hadn't the public had the opportunity to comment before the judge made his decision? Why had the law even allowed for the SVP's release?

These were not the hysterical, irrational responses that I had expected based on pervasive popular stereotypes of community members as vigilante NIMBY crusaders. Concerns about the safety of children and other community members eventually crept into the conversation, but they did not constitute the bulk of the comments or questions. Instead, residents' concerns focused on the criminal justice and political decision-making processes that had brought a sexually violent predator into their neighborhood. While these concerns were rooted in resistance to a specific person moving in, they did not reflect the mindless, knee-jerk resistance often associated with NIMBY characterizations. Instead, these community members wanted to engage in serious conversations about criminal justice policies and practices.

Near the end of the two-hour meeting, a vigilante response finally emerged. A man with a breathing tube and inhaler made his way to the front of the room. Despite clearly struggling to breathe, he read a lengthy letter he had written to the editor of the local newspaper. After three pages explaining how the proposed SVP placement had come to their town, he reached a surprising conclusion: the community should gather torches, encircle the house, and burn it down, making sure that the SVP did not slip out the back door.

At first, I thought he was joking; however, the serious look on his face suggested otherwise. I waited for the reaction of others in the audience, while planning what to do next if they turned into the stereotypical angry mob of vigilantes. Finally, the man next to me chuckled. Across the room, I saw a woman roll her eyes. To my relief, the rest of the audience also rejected the vigilante proposal. While some may have secretly hoped for vigilantism, they took the socially acceptable path of nonviolence. Community members had had their chance to turn into a torch-wielding mob, but clearly they had no intention of engaging in vigilante violence.

The events in Monterey County resulted in more questions than answers. Community members shared with vigilantes an underlying desire for a voice in decisions about where to house sex offenders, but when a vigilante response could have emerged, audience members laughed it off as a ridiculous proposal. Then, they dispersed with few subsequent efforts to oppose the placement. Yet, according to media reports, communities in other California towns have resisted SVP placements by engaging with their local politicians, going to court, and mobilizing grassroots informal networks. If nobody wants a sex offender in their town, then why do communities in different places pursue different strategies of opposition? Why do some engage in vigilante violence while others mobilize politically or legally? Why don't similar concerns about sex offenders translate into similar strategies of opposition? To find out, I collected data on responses to SVP placements in three California towns. The data came from a vast array of sources, including in-depth interviews with residents and political officials, media articles, archival documents, and participant observation in each location. To add more context to these case studies, I also collected data on community responses to all SVP placements in California from 2003 through 2014.

As I discuss later in this introduction, I define community responses as those in which groups of activated residents oppose SVP placements in the name of their communities. In the community responses in California, the mere suggestion that a sex offender might move in ignited controversy over larger issues of perceived injustices perpetrated on communities by counties and the state. While residents held individual SVPs responsible for their crimes, these same individuals rarely blamed offenders for their geographic locations. Instead, activists focused on the political and criminal justice systems that targeted their towns for undesirable people and projects.

Contrary to the prevailing image of individual and collective vigilantism against individual sex offenders, the communities in my research and throughout California focused on mobilizing against formal institutions. For instance, in the case studies, local opposition more closely resembled political conflict than vigilante outrage, as residents often situated their anger in terms of their towns' histories of being neglected by county-level politicians rather than in terms of local crime rates or crime control efforts. These types of concerns were pervasive in all three communities, but they translated into different strategies for opposition in each place. Community members in the town I call Ranchito engaged in political mobilization; those in Deserton pursued legal routes; and in East City, community members engaged in a variety of largely disjointed strategies.[24] While these responses all centered on a perceived injustice perpetrated by political and legal systems, they took different forms in different places.

I argue that these differences in mobilization strategies stem from variation in local political and legal contexts. I characterize local contexts in terms of what I call "dominant community orientations" to political and legal authority. Later in this chapter, I explain how the concept of dominant community orientations to authority draws from and extends previous work on the role of local legal and political institutions in communities and collective action. Using this as a lens through which to understand variation in community responses to SVP placements, I show how relationships between communities and local politicians, political structures, law enforcement, and the courts manifest as community orientations to political and legal authority, which in turn shape local responses to SVP placements. This novel interpretation of local opposition to SVP placements opens new avenues for understanding not only how we might go about solving the seemingly intractable problem of where to house sex offenders but also the role of communities and expert decision makers in solving other complex criminal justice problems.

SVP Placements in California

As of 2013, twenty states and the federal government had implemented SVP statutes or sex offender civil commitment laws.[25] Processes for SVP placements vary by state, and most SVP laws have changed over time. California enacted its first sexual psychopath law in 1939 amid sensationalistic media accounts of sexual murder cases.[26] The law, which allowed the state to commit some sexual offenders to mental health facilities, underwent several revisions in the ensuing decades. In 1996, California became the fifth state to enact an SVP commitment program,[27] and in 2006, more than 70 percent of voters approved the most recent SVP statute.

In California, when a sex offender nears the end of his or her term of incarceration, the DMH conducts psychiatric evaluations and risk assessments to determine if the sex offender "has a diagnosed mental disorder that makes the person a danger to the health and safety of others in that it is likely that he or she will engage in sexually violent criminal behavior."[28] A judge or jury evaluates the expert evidence and determines whether a particular sex offender should be labeled as a "sexually violent predator" and committed to a state hospital. Although the SVP label lumps individuals with a variety of sex offense backgrounds and levels of risk into one category, the label itself implies a "worst of the worst" categorization that highlights some of the rarest types of sex offenses and neatly classifies a heterogeneous group of people as "outsiders."[29] By January 2014, California's sex offender registry included 774 SVPs,[30] and by December 2015, the state housed 886 SVPs in the state hospital.[31]

The SVP label applies even to those who have successfully completed inpatient treatment, further complicating the public's perception of these people. According to the SVP statute, the DMH must conduct annual evaluations of the SVPs in their custody. Those in custody can choose to participate in treatment, but many do not. By one estimate, more than 80 percent of SVPs in California's state hospitals chose not to participate for a variety of reasons, including not wanting to admit to the crimes they had been charged with and objecting to the treatment program as a "scam" to keep them indefinitely confined to the state hospital.[32] For those who do participate in treatment, annual evaluations determine whether they have made sufficient progress to be considered for conditional release, in which case individuals may "petition the court for conditional release to a less restrictive alternative or for an unconditional discharge."[33] Upon reaching this phase, hospital representatives, defense attorneys, and prosecutors appear before a judge to determine the appropriateness of and terms for conditional release. California began conditionally releasing SVPs in 2003. By October 2014, the courts had allowed twenty-six SVPs to enter into the conditional release program,[34] and by December 2015, twelve remained on conditional release.[35]

Even when conditional release is granted, sex offenders remain classified as sexually violent predators. Despite the continued signal of dangerousness implied by this label, the process of placing SVPs in communities has little statutory guidance. The statute states that "the community program director, or his or her designee, shall make the necessary placement arrangements."[36] It specifies neither the process by which those involved should "make the necessary placement arrangements" nor the role of surrounding communities in this process. This legal silence leaves it to decision makers to develop their own processes for siting SVPs in communities.

Despite state laws saying nothing about site selection processes, once a site has been chosen, the SVP statute mandates that the DMH notify local law enforcement and the district attorney at least thirty days before recommending a placement location to the court. Those entities have fifteen days to submit written comments to the court for consideration in determining the final placement site. While public notification is not required, the law enforcement agencies and district attorney's offices that are notified of proposed placements sometimes choose to invite public comment to include in their responses to the court. At this point, local siting conflicts begin as decision makers try to convince local residents that despite the implication that "sexually violent predators" are extremely dangerous, they can be safely released into communities. Predictably, community members resist this idea and start strategizing about how to exclude the SVP from their town. Local law enforcement officials, caught between correctional goals of reintegration and community notions of public safety, either join the community's opposition or emphasize their duty to protect both the SVP and community members from harm.

Local opposition to SVP placements has led in some cases to multiple placement attempts before finding stable housing. While California law mandates that SVP placements conclude within thirty days of a court-ordered release, they vastly exceed that amount of time in practice, with extreme cases having been drawn out for almost two years because of community opposition. These protracted placement processes allow the state to hold people labeled as SVPs in custody for prolonged periods after a judicial order for release. This complicates reintegration efforts and frustrates community members who are trying to control what happens in their towns. These outcomes may ultimately compromise public safety while also straining already fragile relationships between and among the public and government officials.

Moral Panic or Civic Activism?

Previous studies of negative societal responses to sex offenders have approached the phenomenon as threat-driven moral panic. National reactions to sex offenders have all the hallmarks of the archetypal moral panic: a heightened level of concern, hostility toward a perceived threatening deviant, general agreement about the seriousness of the threat, concern disproportionate to the nature of the threat, and episodic eruptions of moral outrage.[37] Latent anxieties about disruptions to social order contribute to a shared feeling of moral outrage against sex offenders, and interest group mobilization helps explain how and why these fears erupt into moral panics.[38] As one scholarly account put it, "Energetic advocacy by child welfare societies, social workers, psychiatrists and therapists, women's groups, prosecutors, law-enforcement bureaucrats, and members of the mass media" has shaped the ebb and flow of moral panic over sex offenders in the United States.[39] Political discourse has also fueled this panic by perpetuating irrational fears,[40] encouraging citizens to perceive themselves as victims,[41] and enacting legislation that addresses only the rarest, most extreme sexual offenses.[42] Local and national political activities help create panics over sex offenders and even encourage mobilizing emotions to achieve political goals.[43]

Moral concerns may explain some aspects of broad societal reactions to sex offenders, but according to a national public opinion survey, support for punitive sex offender policies also stems from a host of other factors, including concern for victims, sex offender stereotypes, and perceptions of crime trends.[44] Survey results also suggest a strong effect of conservatism on support for punitive sex offender policies and sex offender treatment. This finding implies that while moral concerns matter, we must closely examine citizens' relationships with their government to fully understand local reactions to sex offenders.

The focus on moral panic explanations has drawn attention away from the institutional and local roots of community opposition to sex offenders.[45] Despite the important role of communities in perpetuating and solving the sex offender housing dilemma, the moral panic perspective has contributed to framing the problem as one of recalcitrant communities that cannot and should not participate in reintegration efforts. For instance, one account of trying to find housing for those labeled as SVPs in Wisconsin described the public as an impediment to siting processes, in part because of a lack of education on issues related to sex offender threats, recidivism, and treatment.[46] In that case, the public's resistance interacted with a lack of political support for the placement process to ultimately thwart the siting committee's efforts to find housing. In this framing of the issue, the most obvious solution is to educate citizens and garner more political support for siting processes. These types of solutions may improve some aspects of the sex offender housing dilemma, but they fail to address the institutional structures that create the problems associated with sex offender housing and perpetuate community members' ongoing resistance to any mention of sex offenders in their neighborhoods.

This book takes a different approach. While community members may be misinformed about issues related to sex offenders, I begin with the assumption that successfully reintegrating these offenders requires recognizing community members as legitimate actors in reintegration efforts. This starting point provides opportunities to recast local opposition to SVP placements as locally contingent siting conflicts rooted in and shaped by communities' relationships with political and legal institutions. By this definition, community responses to SVP placements are more aligned with civic activism than with irrational, hysterical vigilantism.

To develop this new perspective on local opposition to sex offenders, I draw on insights from literature on siting unwanted facilities. In many ways, SVP placements resemble conflicts over other unwanted land-use projects such as attempts to site waste facilities, landfills, nuclear power plants, and prisons in communities. As one reporter put it, "Sexual predators are right up there in the NIMBY Top Ten, next to nuclear waste dumps, public housing and methadone clinics. In fact, those may be preferable to the sexual predator. A predator can turn on you at any second. At least you know a dump is always a dump."[47] In all these cases, communities resist what they see as risky projects imposed upon them, but, as the reporter's comment indicates, some key differences can heighten local opposition to SVP placements. First, SVPs are human beings, not inanimate facilities. They must have avenues for release from involuntary commitment, and there is always some potential for changes in their behavior once they are released. Second, other land-use projects often involve two sides, with proponents arguing that despite the potential risks, the facilities in question can benefit communities and broader society by promoting economic growth and collective public goods.[48] These potential benefits have even led some communities to recruit prisons,[49] waste management facilities,[50] and biohazard labs.[51] No one actively recruits sexually violent predators to their town.

Despite these differences, current understandings of conflicts over siting unwanted facilities can shed light on local opposition to SVP placements. For example, media reports and other sources often downplay local opposition to SVP placements and other kinds of siting decisions as knee-jerk NIMBY reactions. Yet, NIMBY concerns appear to play only a minor role in community responses to a variety of siting decisions. One study of a local protest against a public housing project in Australia reported that activists generally supported public housing, but they opposed a specific housing project because of an unfair decision-making process.[52] Others have documented similar dynamics in local opposition to renewable energy projects,[53] therapy communities for the homeless,[54] and biohazard labs.[55] In each of these instances, concerns over a lack of input in siting decisions fueled conflicts between community members and decision makers. Consistent with a procedural justice perspective,[56] these accounts suggest that community members resist siting decisions when they believe that the steps leading up to a decision have been unfair.

A city council member in Martinez, California, pointed out another common concern among those involved in opposing siting decisions. When explaining the community's opposition to a proposed SVP placement there, a newspaper article quoted him as saying, "This is not about Nimbyism. Our backyard's full. We've got the refinery, the dump and the jail and 47 people who are sexual offenders. It's time for other communities in the state to share the load."[57] Community members across the state shared this local politician's concern over the disproportionate siting of unwanted people and facilities in some communities. They believed that because these communities, particularly those marginalized based on their race, class, and geography, were relatively powerless to stop siting decisions, decision makers chose them more often as sites for unwanted people and facilities.[58]

These concerns recognize the realities of inequalities in both punishment in the United States and site selection for unpopular people and projects. Mass incarceration in the United States has disproportionately targeted inner-city black communities, with large proportions of black men being taken out of their communities. This practice can decimate families, increase local crime rates, and burden community members with supporting reintegration despite their lack of access to the resources necessary to do so.[59] These kinds of racial disparities in punishment and reentry appear in sex offender laws as well, with black men being required to register as sex offenders at higher rates than others,[60] and communities with higher levels of social disorganization housing more registered sex offenders.[61]

At the same time, decision makers choose the path of least political resistance when selecting sites for unpopular people and projects. They look to communities with little political power,[62] touting the benefits of proposed projects to gain local support in these marginalized communities.[63] As a result, low-income communities of color and rural communities disproportionately become sites for unpopular people and projects.

When disadvantaged communities point out the unfairness of unequal siting decisions, outsiders often perceive their resistance as simple NIMBYism, a characterization that makes it easier for the media, scholars, and the general public to ignore their claims. Instead, this book reinterprets community responses to SVP placements as civic activism rooted in local political and legal institutional contexts. As with most communities, those that oppose SVP placements do so to gain and maintain local control over local issues. They too desire a decent quality of life and safety for their most vulnerable members. Some of their concerns about SVP placements no doubt stem from resistance to the idea of sex offenders in local neighborhoods, but a sense of civic duty motivates them to mobilize in the name of public safety.

This interpretation of community opposition to SVP placements as local civic activism contrasts sharply with the image of weakening social ties and declining civic engagement that Putnam has argued characterizes contemporary public life.[64] While in the past civic engagement may have revolved around long-term volunteerism within community organizations, shifts in social and economic structures have precipitated new ways of participating in public life, including one-shot activism.[65] In the contemporary United States, this one-shot, short-term activism can involve addressing local crime-related issues, especially as crime has provided new ways for citizens to interact with local legal and political institutions.[66] For instance, politicians increasingly use "tough on crime" rhetoric to gain support for their political agendas,[67] creating new opportunities for community members to become civically engaged by interacting with the criminal justice system. As Garriott's ethnography of a rural community in Baker County demonstrated, this civic engagement may take the form of local residents working with law enforcement to solve a seemingly intractable crime-related problem.[68] In that case, local law enforcement educated community members about the realities of methamphetamine use and abuse and then recruited them to police and watch others in the community to identify suspected dealers and users. Through their attendance at community meetings and educational presentations, as well as their informal police work and surveillance, community members became active in trying to solve the local methamphetamine problem. In short, a collective focus on solving the drug problem activated community members to work with local institutions to increase public safety as well as their quality of life.

Similar processes occur in poor, urban neighborhoods where the structure of federal political and legal institutions can force residents to address crime problems locally.[69] While national political institutions tend to tout harsh punishment as the solution to crime problems, those who live in high-crime neighborhoods recognize that crime control requires attending to quality of life issues, harm reduction, and helping victims.[70] Without the narrowly framed messages that resonate at the national level or the resources to engage with national interest groups, residents in these neighborhoods attend local meetings, organize citizens' groups, and call their local political representatives. These types of activities more clearly fit a traditional definition of civic engagement than those of the residents in the rural community who worked with law enforcement to address their local drug problem, but both involve marginalized communities becoming active in solving a local problem by engaging with their local institutions. In a society in which safety is a key indicator of community well-being and crime is increasingly viewed as a joint problem for communities, politicians, and criminal justice institutions, civic engagement may well have shifted toward vocal participation in public safety issues.

This new perspective on civic activism provides a foundation for understanding the contours of community responses to SVP placements. Instead of the typical moral panic explanation, I focus on how urban and rural communities' relationships with local political and legal institutions facilitate and constrain the emergence of particular response strategies. In doing so, I show how the features of local contexts shape community responses to SVP placements, and in turn how we might include community members in solving the sex offender housing dilemma.

What Is a Community Response?

Previous studies of community responses to sex offenders have focused on community notification meetings as sites for potential action. One such study found that community members can find notification meetings useful when local law enforcement directly informs them of the meeting, the purpose of the meeting is clearly stated, and information is provided about legally legitimate means of self-protection.[71] Others have demonstrated that while notification meetings can be informative, they spur few changes in self-protective behaviors.[72] While these types of studies conceptualize community responses as individual audience members' perceptions of and reactions to notification meetings, I focused my study on the collective actions of groups of people who identified themselves as part of a community.

At the start of my research in 2009, twenty-one SVP placements had occurred or were in the process of being finalized in California. To understand the nature and extent of resistance to SVP placements in the state, I conducted extensive background research on all twenty-one cases. I gathered archival information from media and Internet sources; interviewed key informants at the DMH and Health Corp (a pseudonym for the company contracted to manage SVP placements); attended hearings, community notification meetings, and California Sex Offender Management Board meetings; and talked informally with local residents. These activities increased my knowledge of the population under study and helped me gain access to and develop rapport with those involved in SVP placements. I quickly learned that nearly every SVP placement in the state had incited some sort of local opposition. I reached the same conclusion when I later extended my background research to include all SVP placements in California from 2003 through 2014.

Throughout this book, I define community responses to SVP placements as reactions in which the community, as constructed by activated residents, emerges as a central actor in the opposition. Activated residents respond in the name of their communities by identifying themselves as part of a community, purporting to protect that community, and being recognized by others as community members. While some local residents may not share activists' conceptions of their communities,[73] community responses encompass the dominant messages and strategies for opposition that emerge within a particular place. This definition of community responses relies on an underlying conceptualization of communities as rooted in shared norms and ties to physical locations. When activated residents see SVPs or other sex offenders imposed on their local landscapes, they interpret these offenders as threatening community identity,[74] in part because they threaten shared understandings of a local way of life as well as the physical places in which community members live their everyday lives.[75] In short, community members can feel "invaded" by the new person in their midst, with little power to change the situation.[76]

With this conceptualization in mind, I examined my preliminary data for indications of community-based resistance efforts in which activated individuals asserted the interests of their communities in ways that resonated with their personal experiences and beliefs.[77] I found that individual perceptions of SVPs aligned with previous research on the public's fears and anxieties about sex offenders, but these common concerns resulted in different opposition strategies across places. Hypothesizing that local norms about acceptable ways of responding to collective concerns shaped community responses to SVP placements, I developed in-depth case studies of three such cases that represented a variety of mobilization strategies paired with a range of local political and legal contexts.

Studying Variation in Community Responses

While SVP placements across California almost always invoked local resistance, communities engaged in all sorts of opposition activities, including picketing, attending court hearings, writing letters to legislators and local newspapers, posting on Facebook pages, and more. To study the origins and features of this variation, I chose an inductive research strategy that emphasized building theory about how local contexts facilitate and constrain community responses to sex offenders. Aiming to build a theoretical model that would apply to other situations,[78] I chose my cases by looking for communities with different local political contexts and mobilization strategies.[79]

Four categories of SVP placements emerged from my preliminary research: easiest, easy, difficult, and most difficult. The "easiest" and "easy" placements occurred on the first attempt and involved high levels of support from local and regional officials, but had varying levels of public resistance. The "difficult" and "most difficult" placements required multiple attempts, involved high levels of public resistance, and had varying levels of support from local and regional officials. I chose cases in the first three categories because cases in the "most difficult" group (i.e., those in which community members and local and county officials both opposed a placement) represented a different set of circumstances than those I studied in which communities and local officials had conflicting goals.[80] The appendix provides more details on case selection and the characteristics of the three SVP placements.

The Three Cases: Ranchito, Deserton, and East City

In 2009, communities in the places I call Ranchito, Deserton, and East City all resisted SVP placements. At the time, Ranchito, an unincorporated town in Southern California, had just over twenty thousand predominantly white residents spread out over 150 square miles. It was a bedroom community where most people commuted forty miles each way to work in the city. Because of the mom-and-pop stores lining the main street, the friendly people, and the open spaces surrounding the tiny downtown core, some characterized Ranchito as a midwestern town in the heart of California. Residents there described themselves and their fellow community members as independent, individualistic people who believed in self-reliance and conservative family values. The self-described "countrified suburbia" relied on the sheriff's department for law enforcement. A locally elected planning group advised the county board of supervisors on land-use issues and mediated local political disputes over issues such as growth and city incorporation. While the planning group often sent recommendations to the county, it had little real political power.

One hundred sixty miles away, Deserton, a much smaller unincorporated town of 200 people, resembled a piece of the last frontier. In this predominantly white, rural outpost, residents generally had to fend for themselves. Most people knew each other, and a strong sense of independence permeated the local culture. Residents described Deserton as quiet, peaceful, and safe despite the presence of a handful of local drug users. While the sheriff's department provided law enforcement services, officers rarely patrolled the town before the SVP placement, and residents noted long response times when they called for service. Unlike Ranchito, Deserton lacked a formalized local political structure. Residents said that the board of supervisors seemed to have little interest in Deserton because the town's two hundred votes paled in comparison to the hundreds of thousands of votes in the rest of the county. Until the SVP placement, many residents were ambivalent about their relative political invisibility. Many had no interactions with their county supervisor, and others had given no thought to local politics.

Urban East City seemed a world away from the small towns of Deserton and Ranchito. This Northern California city consisted of nearly thirty thousand people packed into an area of only two and a half square miles. The urban core had a substantial proportion of racial and ethnic minorities, persistent poverty, and higher than average crime rates. Crime and gang activity had long afflicted the community, but these conditions had begun to improve by the time I began my research. Some working-class residents perceived East City as a city on the rise: crime rates were falling, drug dealers no longer sold openly on the streets, and new homeowners had begun to invest in local neighborhoods. The city had also had some success in attracting lucrative mainstream businesses and improving local schools and after-school programs. East City had its own municipal police department that historically had contended with rumors of corruption and abuse. While community policing strategies had started to alleviate some of the tensions between residents and law enforcement, some community members still did not trust the law to solve their problems. East City's formal political structure included a city council and mayor, but many in the community expressed ambivalence or even negativity toward city council members. The appendix provides more details on the demographics, geography, and political and legal structures of each place.

The SVP placements in East City (the "easiest" case) and Deserton (the "easy" case) occurred in relatively routine fashion: the judge ordered a conditional release, state and county officials worked together to secure housing, local law enforcement held a community notification meeting, and, despite protests, an SVP moved in shortly thereafter. The communities in Deserton and East City had both experienced political and legal marginalization, but their strategies for opposition differed. In Deserton, residents pursued a lawsuit against the county and gained national media attention for their cause. In East City, while residents talked about either appealing the placement decision or suing the county, neither legal strategy came to fruition. Similarly, sporadic protests and petitions never gained traction as a major part of the community's response to the placement. The placement in Ranchito (the "difficult" case) posed more problems. Local residents who composed the town's planning group found out about the potential placement and organized a meeting, which ultimately resulted in the landlord backing out of the rental contract. This forced the state to place the SVP in another town.

Data Collection

I compiled case studies of each SVP placement and community response by conducting semistructured, in-depth interviews with residents and local officials, searching online archives and media sources, and observing community meetings and protest events. During the summer of 2009, I attended community notification meetings and protests in Deserton and East City. Ranchito's town hall meeting occurred before I began my research, but interviews and media reports provided vivid descriptions of that meeting. From the summer of 2009 through the summer of 2011, I interviewed officials and local residents. Interviews generally lasted about thirty minutes to one hour, and I audio recorded and transcribed each interview for analysis.

Those I refer to as "officials" include individuals who represented the town or city politically, as well as prosecutors and public defenders, representatives from local law enforcement, and representatives from Health Corp and the DMH who were involved in the SVP placement process. Recognizing that individuals in these types of positions can be difficult to access, especially when discussing the politics behind controversial decisions, I employed a snowball sampling design in which I asked each respondent to recommend others who might be willing to speak with me about the SVP placement process. This approach yielded interviews with twenty officials (six in Deserton, eight in East City, and six in Ranchito) in a wide range of positions (see the appendix for position titles).

Each interview included questions tailored to fit the particular positions of those I was interviewing. Some had been involved in housing searches at the local level, others at the state level, and still others had not heard about the placement until after a house had been chosen. In all these interviews, I aimed to understand the roles of various people involved in the placements, how they viewed and experienced placement processes, how they chose particular towns for the placements, and their perceptions of the communities in the relevant towns. This diverse sample and in-depth interviewing method resulted in a rich, detailed portrait of site selection processes and other issues related to SVP placements in California. In this book, I draw on data from these interviews to situate community responses to SVP placements within their political and legal contexts. In particular, chapter 1 provides an in-depth analysis of site selection processes in California, including the political and legal factors that shaped these processes.

As with the officials I interviewed, I found local residents using a snowball sampling design. Initially, I identified potential respondents at community meetings, through media articles, and by contacting those who lived near the SVP's proposed placement site. Then, at the end of each interview, I asked those respondents to recommend others who might be willing to participate in an interview. Using these strategies, I interviewed fifty local residents involved in community opposition to SVP placements (twelve in Deserton, eighteen in East City, and twenty in Ranchito). The residents included direct neighbors to the placement location, those who had attended community notification meetings, picketers, school principals, parents, and, in Ranchito, the prospective landlord. The appendix provides more information about how I identified potential respondents and demographic characteristics of my sample of respondents compared with the population demographics in each place.

The semistructured interviews with residents began with respondents describing their communities and their relationships with local law enforcement and political officials. Then, we talked more specifically about the SVP placements in their towns. In this portion of the interviews, respondents told me their stories of what happened with the SVP placements, their initial reactions, how the community meeting went, and what activities they took part in or had heard of in response to the placements. The interviews ended with respondents telling me what they thought should be done with sexually violent predators.

To strengthen the external validity of the data, I included information from media and archival sources such as locally written histories and documentaries of Ranchito and East City. Across all three communities, I collected a total of forty-two related documents and seventy-three media articles to supplement the interview data. I also wrote thirty-six pages of field notes based on my observations at meetings and protest events in each place. These external sources of information helped put residents' answers into context and provided a check on my interpretations of each place as I compiled each case study. Overall, the broad range of data I collected provides a unique opportunity to examine how and why communities respond so differently to sex offenders moving into their neighborhoods and how local political and legal contexts shape those responses.

Dominant Community Orientations to Authority as Local Contexts for Mobilization

Throughout this book, I characterize the local contexts within which communities respond to SVP placements in terms of what I call "dominant community orientations" to political and legal authority. Unlike formal institutions, which govern behavior through official rules and sanctions, communities develop "group styles," or "recurrent patterns of interaction" that signal membership and shape social action.[81] When community members interact with formal legal and political institutions, their experiences contribute to prevailing local understandings of their relationships with different types of authority. Local norms that emphasize the use of informal methods of dispute resolution over turning to the law signal communities' independence from legal authority.[82] Similarly, the ways in which law enforcement and court actors handle problems can contribute to skepticism of the power of legal authority to resolve local disputes. When these experiences become part of communities' dominant narratives, they can result in community members stigmatizing the use of the law to resolve disputes.[83] The same can occur when community members interact with actors in political institutions.

Drawing on these insights, I define dominant community orientations to authority as community members' shared understandings of how formal authority impacts life in a community. Rather than representing the views of every person in a community, dominant orientations to authority reflect common themes in residents' narratives about their communities. While individual community members may have contradictory feelings about political and legal entities (e.g., trusting law enforcement but not the courts, or trusting formal political structures but not local politicians), their experiences with each entity inform broader community relationships with authority that allow for and incorporate these conflicting feelings.

Throughout the book, I define political authority as the power to govern,[84] which can be accessed through formal institutions such as local city councils, county boards of supervisors, and state agencies. Dominant orientations to political authority include activated community members' understandings of the role of formal political authority in local life (i.e., relationships with politicians in terms of how they treat the community and their perceived interests when making decisions) and the role of formal political authority in solving local problems (i.e., relationships with political structures in terms of the ability of local entities to make legally binding decisions). Specific local configurations of political institutions contribute to communities' orientations to political authority and their abilities to leverage political power to their advantage. For instance, local city councils may provide more access to formal political authority than a board of supervisors based in a county seat fifty miles away. At the same time, the city council may be less open to public input than a particularly receptive board of supervisors. Community members' experiences with these local political institutions impact how they relate to political authority when trying to resolve local issues such as unwanted SVP placements.

Legal authority encompasses the dual features of dispute-resolution and order-maintenance powers that are backed by statute and formal sanctions.[85] Experiences with the police and the courts inform dominant community orientations to legal authority, which include ideas about the role of legal authority in local life (i.e., relationships with law enforcement in terms of police presence in the community and who takes responsibility for crime control) as well as ideas about the role of legal authority in solving local problems (i.e., relationships with the courts in terms of the circumstances under which people go to court). Differences in communities' experiences with the police and the courts inform dominant community orientations toward legal authority, which in turn shape when and how communities try to leverage legal power in resolving local problems. For example, low-income residents in urban cities may have formal police departments that facilitate greater access to legal authority relative to those who live in rural towns, but perceptions of legal authority as oppressive can constrain efforts to call the police when crimes occur.[86] By contrast, those in remote rural towns who appear to have less access to the courts and law enforcement may perceive the law as essentially on their side, which can facilitate greater reliance on the law to solve local problems.

As these examples suggest, dominant community orientations to authority emerge through interactions between communities and political and legal institutions. The local structures of these institutions shape community members' interactions with political and legal authority, which in turn inform dominant orientations toward authority. The data presented in this book show how these orientations facilitate and constrain mobilization strategies as community members perceive political and legal power as more or less able to help them stop SVP placements.

The Plan of the Book

We have little hope of solving the problem of where to house sex offenders without a clear understanding of how and why community members oppose them in their neighborhoods. The chapters that follow examine the institutional contexts within which communities in California protested

SVP placements and how those contexts shaped local opposition efforts. They demonstrate that while community members shared concerns about the dangerousness of SVPs and the injustice of placement processes, differences in local contexts contributed to variation in response strategies.

Chapter 1 begins the discussion by analyzing SVP placement processes in light of a core contradiction in SVP laws, which classify some individuals as extremely dangerous and then require their release into communities. Drawing on data from in-depth interviews with decision makers involved in SVP housing searches, I develop the concept of "legal signals" to demonstrate how political and legal factors influenced SVP siting decisions that subsequently sparked local outrage against the placements. When this happened, legal signals about the dangerousness of SVPs and the role of communities in public safety shaped community members' concerns in similar ways across places. Despite these similar concerns, an analysis of strategies for community opposition to SVP placements across California demonstrates that communities engaged in a variety of opposition tactics, ranging from rare instances of vigilantism and inaction to more common political and legal actions that targeted potential landlords, housing decision makers, and criminal justice actors. Chapter 1 makes clear that political decisions made in light of interpretations of legal signals from the SVP statute and other sex offender laws essentially created the situations that prompted community responses.

Yet, these dynamics cannot explain differences in mobilization strategies across places. To examine how local contexts shaped response strategies, chapters 2, 3, and 4 provide in-depth analyses of case studies of community opposition to SVP placements in Ranchito, Deserton, and East City. Chapter 2 explains how in Ranchito, an orientation toward political authority as a source of entitlement and legal authority as a source of order maintenance contributed to the centrality of political mobilization in the community's opposition to a proposed SVP placement. Chapter 3 discusses how the community in Deserton related to legal authority as a source of protection and political authority as a source of invisibility, which facilitated the emergence of litigation as the main component of the community's opposition to an SVP placement. Chapter 4 argues that, in contrast to the local contexts in Ranchito and Deserton, orientations to legal authority as a source of control and political authority as a source of alienation contributed to the lack of a central strategy for opposition in East City. Together, these three cases demonstrate how, despite similar concerns about SVP placements across places, communities' relationships with formal political and legal institutions facilitated and constrained the emergence of specific strategies for opposition in each place.

Chapter 5 picks up this theme by comparing the orientations to political and legal authority in all three places in light of communities' racial, socioeconomic, and geographic characteristics. While all three communities struggled for local control over SVP placement decisions, the chapter shows how each community's unique configurations of privilege and disadvantage shaped its relationships with formal institutions, which in turn contributed to the types of opposition strategies that emerged in each place. This localized analysis of the three responses to SVP placements reveals the institutional roots of local opposition to sex offenders, which implies that solving the sex offender housing dilemma requires attending to the ways in which formal institutions contribute to the hostile environments that sex offenders face when trying to reenter society.

Considering these findings, chapter 6 concludes the book by offering practical suggestions for how we might solve the sex offender housing dilemma. The cases in the book demonstrate that we cannot reduce the problem to recalcitrant communities. Formal political and legal institutions create the problem of where to house sex offenders, and they also shape how communities respond to siting decisions. Ironically, we can attribute part of the problem of having no good place for sex offenders to live to local activists engaging in collective action to strengthen their communities. Instead of reinforcing the tendency to call for further isolating the public from criminal justice decisions, I argue that communities can help solve the problem of where to house sex offenders if they are allowed to be involved in all stages of decision making about where these offenders should live. Doing so would increase efficiency in sex offender reintegration processes, decrease local opposition, and provide criminal justice officials with more accurate information about the communities into which they expect these formerly incarcerated individuals to reintegrate. At the same time, communities would benefit from more opportunities for civic engagement, stronger ongoing relationships with powerful decision makers, and increased public safety brought about by enhanced social supports for sex offenders reentering society.

1

The Production of Siting Conflicts over SVP Placements

From 2003 through 2014, forty-nine community responses to proposed SVP placements occurred in thirty-six cities, towns, and broader regions in California. Thirty-nine of these responses emerged in places explicitly chosen as potential placement sites. The other ten communities began opposition efforts before a specific site had been chosen. A letter to the editor in the *San Diego Union-Tribune* perfectly summed up a common assumption about the underlying causes of these local protests against SVP placements. Responding to an article that the paper had published a few weeks earlier about opposition to a proposed placement in Soledad, the letter writer characterized those opposing the placement as "NIMBY types" and criticized the newspaper for potentially inciting "witch hunts and similar mass hysteria" in which local residents would take "improper and inappropriate action" against the SVP involved in the placement.[1] This characterization of local residents responding irrationally and hysterically to the mere mention of a sex offender has caused many to write off local opposition as nothing more than NIMBY-fueled vigilantism.

This chapter challenges the hysterical NIMBY assumption by analyzing the institutional contexts that produce controversial siting decisions and examining the vast array of strategies that community members have employed to protest SVP placements. Doing so shows that community responses to SVP placements emerge as part of a series of decisions and events that set the stage for local protest. From this vantage point, communities appear less as hysterical lynch mobs than as actors engaging in collective action to assert their rights to control what happens in their towns.

Institutional Contexts for Opposition

To examine how political and legal institutions shaped siting conflicts over SVP placements in California, I take a "sociopolitical" approach to decision making and local opposition to siting decisions. This approach stems from research on other types of siting conflicts, which shows that political concerns shape both site choices and local opposition efforts. For instance, decades of research on inequalities in exposure to pollution and other environmental hazards have documented the disproportionate siting of polluting facilities in racially and socioeconomically disadvantaged communities,[2] which may in turn motivate local opposition to siting decisions. Racial discrimination clearly plays a role in decisions to place environmental hazards such as garbage facilities in predominantly minority communities,[3] but sociopolitical explanations highlight how decision makers' desires to avoid local opposition shape siting outcomes.[4] From this perspective, authorities and industry actors recognize that racially and socioeconomically marginalized communities have less political power to resist unwanted projects, so they increase the odds of successful siting outcomes by siting hazardous facilities in those communities.[5]

When marginalized communities resist these unfair siting decisions, claims of "environmental injustice" play a central role in their opposition efforts.[6] For example, marginalized communities mobilizing against proposed biohazard labs[7] and landfills[8] claimed injustice in siting decisions based on historical legacies of siting unwanted facilities in their towns. From this perspective, siting conflicts such as those over SVP placements reflect a process in which those routinely excluded from local power structures try to claim their "right to the city," a self-governing political community in which all work together to govern themselves.[9]

Political factors provide a context for understanding siting decisions and local opposition to those decisions, but legal institutions also shape the perceptions of injustice and desires for local control over public safety that fuel local outrage over SVP placements. They do so through a mechanism that I call "legal signals," a concept that stems from Edelman, Leachman, and McAdam's conceptualization of the relationship between the law and social movements as overlapping fields that constantly interact with and inform each other.[10] From this perspective, the law operates not only as a tool but also as a "normative influence" on collective action.[11] Previous studies in this line of thinking demonstrate that state and national laws shape social movements by providing legitimate frames for articulating grievances,[12] legally acceptable identities for mobilization,[13] and tactics for bringing about social change.[14] Drawing on this previous research, I define legal signals as the implicit messages embedded in state laws that provide guidance for action or inaction. These messages need not be deliberately implanted in state laws by policy makers, and many legal signals may be unintended messages that inadvertently produce certain kinds of action or inaction. SVP placements provide an excellent opportunity to examine how legal signals impact siting decisions as well as communities' responses to them because SVP statutes require state authorities to "site" perceived dangers in communities within the context of highly publicized and sometimes contradictory state and national laws.

The examination of local opposition to SVP placements in this chapter demonstrates how legal signals help transform legal consciousness, or individuals' everyday understanding of the law,[15] into action. When people mobilize law in response to personal harms such as sexual harassment,[16] discrimination,[17] and other rights violations,[18] they are acting on their interpretations of legal signals about the nature of the harm and appropriate responses to it. Contradictory legal signals can produce conflict when different groups act upon competing interpretations of signals in order to make decisions and assert their rights, which is what happened in siting conflicts over SVP placements in California.

SVP Placement Processes

Decision makers' experiences in securing housing for SVPs in California and notifying communities of potential placements demonstrate how various political, legal, and public safety concerns played into site selection and community notification, which in turn set the stage for local opposition to these placements. Their stories, as related to me in interviews, reveal how they created their own processes in light of relatively few statutory regulations on SVP placements. At the same time, the decisions they made fueled community outrage, especially in light of legal signals about the dangerousness of SVPs and the role of communities in maintaining their own public safety. These dynamics illuminate how political and legal institutions shaped siting conflicts over SVP placements in California.

Housing Groups Find "Ideal" Hosts for Dangerous Subjects

Decision makers' first task in SVP placements was to find suitable housing. Upon a judge's order to enter an SVP into California's conditional release program, the Department of Mental Health notified agencies within the county in which the SVP would be placed and requested someone from the county to be designated to help with the housing process. Health Corp personnel then worked with the county's designee to form housing workgroups. These groups often included employees in public safety and social service agencies, attorneys involved in the case, and sometimes probation or parole officers. Much of what I learned about the internal workings of these groups came from telephone interviews with a former executive director at Health Corp, as well as with those who had been part of housing groups for the SVP placements in Ranchito, Deserton, and East City. These individuals told me that while housing groups sometimes found potential placement sites, they more often suggested general locations and evaluated the sites proposed by Health Corp. As the former Health Corp executive director explained, "In some situations, we have been able to work with the county to select facilities. [. . .][19] But, more times than not, we end up finding the housing units through people who are renting homes. On our own." She further explained that they looked for housing just as individuals do: through Craigslist ads and "driving around looking for rentals."

When Health Corp or the housing groups identified a potential property, Health Corp personnel contacted the landlord to gauge his or her willingness to rent to the state for the purposes of housing an

SVP. In informal discussions, the former Health Corp executive told me that these initial conversations involved explaining to the landlord who the tenant would be and what kind of resistance could be expected from neighbors (e.g., threats and angry phone calls). While candor in the initial conversations with landlords might have limited the number who agreed to rent their properties, the Health Corp executive explained, "There's no way that we can work with [landlords]" without being "absolutely up front" with them. Trying to hide the true intent of renting these homes would only exacerbate local outcry because landlords would eventually find out that they were renting to an SVP.

Housing searches often went on for months and sometimes even years. While a lack of available properties for rent could have posed problems in some areas, decision makers' descriptions of their searches for housing suggested that a lack of rental homes was not the primary problem. In a telephone interview, a deputy district attorney who worked on the placement that ultimately occurred in East City explained, "We're talking every day looking and looking and looking and most landlords won't let to one of these individuals, so most of these you just get turned away at the door. And then you find a handful of places and then most of them end up having issues." Another attorney in the same office elaborated: "We would get regular reports from Health Corp of all of the properties that they had investigated as potential placements for [the SVP] and none of them worked out. And they looked at over one thousand properties. [. . .] For every monthly meeting we had, Health Corp would attach a spreadsheet to the back of their report that would show just lists and lists of properties and the reasons that they had fallen through." The public defender involved in the case in Ranchito told a similar story. He said that meeting regularly with Health Corp and other actors to line up treatment and other services for the SVP was "the easy part." He continued:

The hard part is the housing. What would happen is we would get everything lined up except the housing. And then we would find ourselves meeting month after month after month, only to be told by Health Corp, "We still don't have any place." And they would look at hundreds of properties. They would come with these printouts of properties. And so, the problems included, number one, that people didn't want to rent to a registered sex offender, or number two, they didn't mind renting to a sex offender, but they didn't want the media attention they knew would come with it, or number three, again, after 2006, the law changed so that registered sex offenders are not supposed to live within two thousand feet of a school or park.

As in cases in other states,[20] these accounts suggest that while rental properties were on the market in the target counties, a lack of willing landlords and other issues with available homes extended housing searches for months and sometimes even years.

While those involved in housing searches for SVPs focused their discussions on the availability of housing in a given area, decision makers involved in siting other types of perceived hazards and unwanted facilities tend to choose sites based on the likelihood that surrounding communities will mount effective opposition.[21] As a result, low-income communities composed predominantly of racial and ethnic minorities house more garbage and hazardous waste facilities,[22] and areas with concentrated rural disadvantage tend to house more prisons.[23] A similar dynamic prevailed with SVP placements: decision makers knew that no community would welcome an SVP, so they searched for what I call "ideal" hosts, or those places that complied with legal requirements for sex offender housing and had communities that would ostensibly mount less powerful resistance than those in other areas. This concept of "ideal" hosts highlights how legal and political concerns influenced site choices such that some communities seemed better situated to receive SVP placements than others.

Legal Influences on Site Choice

Three legal mandates narrowed housing options to rural towns and the outskirts of urban areas. One section of California's SVP statute required SVPs to return to their county of last residence.[24] The law defined this as "the county where the person has his or her true, fixed, and permanent home and principal residence and to which he or she has manifested the intention of returning whenever he or she is absent."[25] SVPs had often been committed to the state hospital for years, making it difficult to determine their counties of last residence. To address this situation, the law also stated, "If no information can be identified or verified, the county of domicile of the individual shall be considered to be the county in which the person was arrested for the crime for which he or she was last incarcerated in the state prison or from which he or she was last returned from parole."[26] Because of these provisions, some SVP placements began with considerable debate in court over the appropriate county of domicile. For instance, in the case in East City, the SVP's county of domicile was unclear: he had committed his crime in a nearby county but had family in East City. Initial court hearings focused on this issue until the judge determined that East City's county would be considered the county of domicile. In this first narrowing of site choice, the law essentially designated the county in which the housing group would be formed and would search for a potential placement location.

Two other legal provisions further narrowed housing options. California's sex offender residence restriction stated that registered sex offenders could not "reside within 2000 feet of any public or private school, or park where children regularly gather."[27] The SVP statute did not specify whether individuals on conditional release were subject to the statewide residence restriction, but it did require that SVPs who had a history of victimizing children could "not be placed within one-quarter mile of any public or private school providing instruction in kindergarten or any of grades 1 to 12, inclusive."[28] As I discuss in the next section, these laws, in conjunction with political and practical concerns, contributed to an informal understanding of an "ideal" host community that, when put into practice, highlighted and reinforced regional inequalities between communities.

Political Influences on Site Choice

When Health Corp personnel finally located a potential property that seemed to comply with legal restrictions, they presented the site to the housing group. Although a judge had the final say, members of the housing group provided invaluable information about their county and local communities, which could in turn impact Health Corp's decision to recommend a specific property to the judge. While some housing groups' input related to the perceived potential for recidivism, other concerns focused on the political implications of placing SVPs in specific areas. In interviews, decision makers' discussions of placement decisions presumed that some communities made more political sense for SVP placements than others. In one particularly revealing telephone interview, the county mental health representative for assisting with SVP placements in the Ranchito area described his perspective on reactions in different communities:

> You could imagine in a very sort of well-heeled community that [. . .] they'd just call their political leader. [. . .] So, I think in higher socioeconomic areas, the ways that people attack it are gonna be different there. Because, you know, there's the pitchfork and torch, you know, from the Frankenstein movie, you know, "we're gonna go burn the monster." And then there's the more sophisticated way to burn the monster. So you can get picket signs and you can stand out in front of places [. . .] Or, you can be very sophisticated and put political pressure [on decision makers and other officials].

He went on to say that these differences figured into discussions about where to house SVPs because the "well-heeled" communities could potentially cause more problems. As his explanations imply, by constructing the "monster" to be released and then providing no guidance on site selection processes, the SVP statute implicitly guided decision makers toward sites in less politically powerful communities. In general, communities in relatively rural areas had fewer people, less political clout, and fewer resources to successfully fight an SVP placement; communities in urban areas with less political clout also posed fewer potential political problems than those in other areas.

During our interviews, decision makers never explicitly discussed how intersections of race, class, and geography played into their choices of communities; however, a brief look at the siting decisions in Deserton, Ranchito, and East City demonstrates how these factors influenced site choice. For the placement that ultimately occurred in Deserton, the housing committee initially identified a nearly ideal site in another town: it was within the required county, far enough from schools, and relatively close to treatment facilities. Yet, according to those on the search committee, county officials objected to the placement because local residents had recently protested a proposed jail site near their town. As the Health Corp executive explained, "There was already significant community opposition to the jail being built within ten miles of this community. So, they were trying to protect the jail site. And they didn't want it tainted with an SVP being placed in the same general area." The political infeasibility of that location contributed to the appeal of Deserton, a tiny, unincorporated rural town fifty miles from any other towns. Deserton had little to offer in terms of reintegration: the community of two hundred people was very close-knit, and the nearest treatment facility was in the next town over. Furthermore, the proposed site in the middle of the desert had no existing home, so the county would have to build a trailer on the bare land. Despite these issues, a judge ordered the placement there after a year of searching for properties and reviewing more than a hundred potential options throughout the county.

While the proposed placement in Ranchito seemed more compatible with reintegration goals, it still occurred in a relatively powerless community in the region. After a three-month search for housing in the required county, a local landlord agreed to rent his property to the state. The proposed home complied with residence restrictions, had few direct neighbors, and was relatively close to treatment facilities. Yet, the rural atmosphere of the town may have contributed to the siting decision. When asked about the features of the location that made it a good place to put the SVP, the Health Corp executive said, "It was fairly rural. And it was fairly . . . it wasn't nearly as rural as the place that was laid out in [another part of the] county, but it's not a populated downtown area." While her answer focused on the physical features of the place, the town, like many rural areas, was also unincorporated, which meant the community had less political clout in the region than the nearby metropolitan city.

Decision makers could not always place SVPs in rural areas. Relatively small and densely populated counties forced housing committees to settle for more urban areas, as was the case with the placement in East City. There, a countywide search lasted more than a year and resulted in reviews of more than one thousand properties. Few locations complied with residence restrictions, and landlords in legally acceptable areas often refused to rent their homes to the state. These challenges resulted in a site almost completely at odds with an "ideal" location: it was near schools in a densely populated urban neighborhood. According to those involved in the placement process, when the length of the search began to raise concerns about the constitutionality of keeping the SVP in custody, the judge reviewed a handful of homes that did not comply with residence restrictions and then declared the home in East City the most suitable for the placement. This outcome suggests that the geographic isolation and small populations of rural areas may have served as a proxy for a community's lack of political power to resist a siting decision. In this respect, the site in East City was an "ideal" location because the community of mostly lower- and working-class racial minorities had less political clout than nearby wealthier, whiter communities.

As these brief descriptions demonstrate, decision makers responded to legal signals about SVPs' dangerousness by adopting their own politically informed ideas about which sites would best address legal regulations and concerns about public safety. These decision makers chose sites based on considerations similar to those involved in siting unwanted facilities,[29] and communities with less political clout bore the brunt of their decisions.[30]

Geographic, Socioeconomic, and Racial Features of Sites Chosen throughout California

A broader examination of the characteristics of sites selected for SVP placements throughout California further supports the idea that decision makers chose sites in areas with particular geographic, socioeconomic, and racial characteristics. Thirty-three communities received or were proposed to receive SVP placements in California from 2003 through 2014.[31] Table 1.1 summarizes the geographic, socioeconomic, and racial characteristics of each of these communities.

TABLE 1.1. Demographics of Communities That Received or Were Proposed to Receive an SVP Placement in California from 2003 through 2014 ($N = 33$)

	f	%
Rural Communities		
Low SES, predominantly white	4	12.12
Low SES, predominantly Hispanic/Latino(a)	2	6.06
Medium SES, predominantly white	3	9.09
Medium SES, predominantly Hispanic/Latino(a)	1	3.03
High SES, predominantly white	2	6.06
High SES, predominantly Hispanic/Latino(a)	0	0.00
Total	*12*	*36.36*
Semi-urban Communities		
Low SES, predominantly white	0	0.00
Low SES, predominantly Hispanic/Latino(a)	4	12.12
Medium SES, predominantly white	1	3.03
Medium SES, predominantly Hispanic/Latino(a)	0	0.00
High SES, predominantly white	0	0.00
High SES, predominantly Hispanic/Latino(a)	0	0.00
Total	*5*	*15.15*
Urban Communities		
Low SES, predominantly white	2	6.06
Low SES, predominantly Hispanic/Latino(a)	3	9.09
Low SES, no predominant racial/ethnic group	1	3.03
Medium SES, predominantly white	1	3.03
Medium SES, predominantly Hispanic/Latino(a)	0	0.00
Medium SES, no predominant racial/ethnic group	1	3.03
High SES, predominantly white	6	18.18
High SES, predominantly Hispanic/Latino(a)	0	0.00
High SES, no predominant racial/ethnic group	2	6.06
Total	*16*	*48.48*

Note: Geographic classifications are based on U.S. Census categorizations. Socioeconomic status reflects U.S. Census reports of the percentage of the population that had completed high school (or equivalent) and median household income. Low, medium, and high SES classifications are relative to California's median educational attainment and household income in 2009. Medium SES means that a community either had higher educational attainment and lower household income than the state median or had lower educational attainment and higher household income. Racial composition is based on U.S. Census reports of the percentage of the population in each racial or ethnic group. No predominant racial/ethnic group means that no one group composed 50 percent or more of the population.

Site choices reflected a preference for rural and semi-urban areas, with just over half of the sites falling into these categories. Of the twelve rural sites considered, nine actually received SVP placements. While the rural sites tended to have populations with lower socioeconomic status (SES), the only three that did not receive SVP placements were predominantly white with medium to high socioeconomic status. Of the two predominantly white, rural communities with higher than average educational attainment and median household incomes, one successfully fought an SVP placement and the other did not. The first was Spring Valley, an unincorporated town in San Diego County where the DMH proposed placing an SVP in February 2014. After the county supervisor publicly stated her opposition to the placement and sent a letter to the judge and others involved in the placement process, local media reported that the DMH had retracted the proposed site based on its proximity to a high school and an in-home day care.[32] Three and a half months later, despite local protests and meetings, the SVP moved into a home in Borrego Springs, a more remote, predominantly white community with lower socioeconomic status than Spring Valley.

The other less-than-ideal rural community was unincorporated Jacumba Hot Springs, a tiny border town of 561 people. In 2008, a judge ordered two SVPs to live together in a home in Jacumba. About twenty residents spoke at the hearing on the placements, and after the judge made his ruling, one shouted, "How many (SVPs) are going to be released into our community after this?"[33] Both of the SVPs eventually violated terms of their conditional release, and one remained incarcerated as of 2016. In 2014, another SVP moved into the town despite significant local opposition in the form of a social media campaign, calls to the sheriff's department, written comments submitted to the San Diego County task force overseeing the placement, and appearances at the placement hearing. In February 2016, the state placed another SVP in Jacumba with little local opposition. By the end of 2016, both individuals still lived in the town.

While Jacumba's socioeconomic status made it a less "ideal" host than other places, its rural location, small population, and lack of a formalized local political structure aligned it more closely with the concept of an "ideal" host than might be suggested by its socioeconomic status. Thus, the rural communities chosen for SVP placements tended to fit with the notion of "ideal" hosts as those places with less access to political power and other resources to fight SVP placements. In the one case that did not fit this description, the community successfully stopped the SVP placement.

Semi-urban communities could also be "ideal" hosts, especially when they were not predominantly white and had lower educational attainment and household incomes than state averages. Three of the five semi-urban communities considered for SVP placements could not stop the placements in their towns. The two semi-urban communities that succeeded in their efforts were Ranchito (the lone semi-urban, predominantly white community with higher than average household incomes and lower than average educational attainment) and Holtville, a predominantly Hispanic/Latino(a) community with low socioeconomic status. Both communities successfully pressured local landlords into backing out of their agreements to rent their homes to the state to house SVPs. Holtville appeared to be a more "ideal" location than Ranchito because of its lower socioeconomic status and predominantly Hispanic and Latino(a) population. Yet, Holtville differed in one key respect: it was an incorporated city with a formalized municipal police department and city council. During the community's opposition to a proposed SVP placement there in 2007, the police chief publicly denounced the placement, and county officials vowed to fight the placement. A few days after the placement location became public, the landlord backed out of the rental contract, citing public outcry as one of the reasons for his decision.[34] Three months later, the SVP moved into a home in Seeley, a more "ideal" host in that it was a rural town of low socioeconomic status with a predominantly Hispanic/Latino(a) population. Once again, the choice of placements in semi-urban communities fits with the notion of "ideal" hosts. The community in Ranchito, the least marginalized semi-urban community, successfully stopped the placement there.

While urban communities may have been a last resort for both political and legal reasons, just under half of the sites chosen for potential SVP placements were in urban areas. The most "ideal" urban areas were those of low socioeconomic status with predominantly racial and ethnic minority populations. Surprisingly, just over a third of the sites chosen in urban areas were in places with predominantly white populations of higher socioeconomic status than state averages. These were arguably the least "ideal" sites, and, as might be predicted, three of the six communities in this category successfully resisted SVP placements in their towns. The other three ultimately received SVP placements, but the unique features of those placements demonstrate that the communities were more "ideal" than they appear at first glance. Residents in Otay Mesa, a community in San Diego, twice protested the placements of SVPs on the grounds of nearby Donovan State Prison. In both instances, SVPs moved into trailers on prison grounds. While this community may have enjoyed some of the privileges associated with being part of the city of San Diego, its status as a "prison town" meant it was more marginalized than the demographic characteristics of the broader San Diego area suggest.

This was not the case in Marin, where in 2004 an SVP moved into a motel five and a half months after a failed placement attempt in Martinez, a predominantly white, high SES, urban area. In Martinez, the landlord backed out of the rental agreement after intense pressure from city leaders and local residents. The same did not occur in Marin, in part because local residents found out about the placement only after the state had paid for the SVP to spend a week in a local motel. This type of housing is not entirely unusual. Across the country, motels have provided shelter for "social refugees" such as parolees and sex offenders,[35] but, as with SVP placements, housing sex offenders in motels has proved controversial. In one account, community members in "Dutchland" informally voiced their opposition to sex offenders living in a local motel by hurling insults at the motel occupants. The city tried to address the problem by passing a local ordinance against housing multiple sex offenders in one place. These measures reduced the number of sex offenders in motels throughout the city, but they also made it more difficult for sex offenders to find stable housing.[36]

Similarly, once the media began reporting on the SVP living in the motel in Marin, local protests prompted the motel owner to ask the SVP to leave after the prepaid week. State officials then moved him to various locations around the San Francisco Bay Area until, in 2005, he finally settled in Bay Point, a semi-urban area with a predominantly Hispanic/Latino(a) population with lower socioeconomic status. In this case, the strength of the community's outcry in less-than-ideal Marin ultimately changed the placement decision and resulted in a more "ideal" placement site.

The third urban, predominantly white, high socioeconomic status city to receive an SVP was Vacaville, a large city in Northern California. There, the SVP moved into town and stayed for a longer period despite residents trying nearly every possible means to keep him out. They signed petitions; attended protests; posted signs and flyers; attended court hearings, city council meetings, and press conferences; called the police; held vigils; and even vandalized the SVP's potential home. Their efforts might have worked against a less committed landlord, but in this case, the SVP had moved into a home owned by his wife. This family connection facilitated the placement in this less-than-ideal community.

As these cases illustrate, decision makers tended to choose more marginalized communities as potential sites for SVP placements. When they did not, local opposition sometimes forced them to look elsewhere for housing. Subsequent attempts to place the same SVP often resulted in placements in more marginalized communities. Where this did not occur, unique features of local contexts facilitated placements in less-than-ideal locations. At the same time, opposition in more marginalized communities such as Holtville sometimes successfully stopped SVP placements, countering decision makers' implicit assumptions that these communities would be powerless in their opposition efforts.

These dynamics of siting decisions emerged from the SVP statute's definition of SVPs as extremely dangerous, accompanied by legal silence on site selection processes and outcomes. This silence forced decision makers to adapt their own processes, which focused on abiding by state laws regarding sex offender locations while also addressing concerns about public safety, the potential political consequences of choosing specific sites, and communities' potential power to complicate a placement in a specific area.

Decision Makers Inform "Hysterical" Communities

After choosing sites, decision makers had every reason not to notify communities about impending SVP placements. Nothing in California's SVP statute or community notification law required public involvement in SVP siting decisions. Once a site had been chosen, the SVP statute required only that the DMH notify "the sheriff or chief of police, or both, the district attorney, or the county's designated counsel" in the community where the recommended site was located,[37] and that law enforcement "may notify any person designated by the sheriff or chief of police as an appropriate recipient of the notice."[38] These elements of the statute allowed local officials to notify the public but did not require them to do so. Similarly, California's sex offender community notification law required that the Department of Justice "make available information concerning persons who are required to register pursuant to Section 290 to the public via an Internet Web site" but did not require active community notification.[39]

Decision makers shared the widespread stereotype that communities would react with panicked vigilantism. These stereotypes came across in the very first interview I conducted and were repeated in interviews with officials throughout my research. In that first interview, I sat down at a busy coffee shop in Sacramento with the deputy district attorney assigned to the case in Deserton. About halfway through the interview, she brought up the public's "irrational fear," and then went on to explain that decision makers did not publicize the exact date when the SVP would move in because they "were afraid that somebody would show up and put a bullet in his head." About a month later, in the second interview I conducted, the vigilante stereotype appeared once again. This time, I met the sheriff's division chief for the Deserton area in a large hotel lobby in the city that served as the county seat. During the interview, I commented that I was interested in understanding more about what it is about sex offenders that causes so much concern. He responded by saying, "I think, it's the stigma that they carry that just creates fear. [. . .] You get this emotional reaction to stop it, you know, any way you can, leading to violence. And, and, you know, I'm, as I mentioned, I'm very surprised we didn't have any acts of violence [in Deserton], not directly at him, just, even at the trailer, and even when he was gone." His comments illustrate the stereotype that what he later characterized as "raw emotion" among community members would lead to vigilante reactions to SVP placements.

Surprisingly, despite fears of vigilantism and legal signals that active community input was not necessary, decision makers often felt compelled to hold community notification meetings. Their reasons for doing so demonstrate the predicament that the SVP statute put them in. The deputy district attorney for the placement in Deserton explained that those involved in the placement decision felt a "responsibility to tell people" because "we thought it would be really, it would be unethical and unprofessional to just slide him out there and not tell anybody. So we thought, 'You know what, we don't have to do it, but we do have to do it.'" This sense of ethical obligation stemmed from a recognition that communities needed to know about the potential dangers involved in SVP placements.

Others were less sure of the value of notification meetings, but they still emphasized the need for community members to voice their concerns. One of the deputy district attorneys involved in the placement in East City said she had "mixed feelings about the whole public notification." As she explained:

> Like, I understand why it is because you're saying "Look, this is one of the few in the small percentage who's the worst of the worst and he's getting out now." And I can understand why people want to know that. But, like I said, it increases anxiety and gives people this false sense of security that they were safe before the SVP got there. [. . .] I don't know that the public notification in just SVP cases really is all that helpful. Other than the fact that it gives the community an opportunity to be heard.

Her explanation demonstrates how an inherent contradiction in the SVP statute contributed to the perceived need for active community notification. Decision makers felt they had to notify the public because of the presumed dangers posed by SVPs, but notification meetings also highlighted these dangers and, in doing so, may have caused more problems than they were worth.

Nonetheless, notification meetings occurred in placements throughout the state. During my research, I attended three such meetings, including those in Monterey County, Deserton, and East City. Although these meetings took place after judges had ordered SVP placements, not all meetings occurred at this point in placement processes. For instance, the meeting in Ranchito, which I did not attend, was held during the fifteen-day comment period before the judge made the placement decision. Regardless of the timing, meetings proceeded in very similar fashion, beginning with a panel of local officials, law enforcement, and Health Corp representatives presenting information about the SVP and the conditional release process, and ending with a question-and-answer session.

In Deserton and East City, public comments and questions exemplified the types of substantive concerns that often come across in scholarly and media accounts of local opposition to sex offenders.[40] During the meetings in these two places, I watched as audience members expressed their beliefs that SVPs posed extreme dangers to their communities and asked what would happen in the event of a reoffense. In East City, one woman asked who would be responsible when the SVP "strikes again." The Health Corp representative responded that the SVP himself was responsible, to which audience members mumbled their disapproval. In Deserton, many residents asked how they should protect themselves, especially given their remote location and long response times by law enforcement. When the sheriff's division chief responded that they should only engage in legal actions, I overheard a man in the back of the room whispering to his friend, "What if something happens to him?" Similar suspicions about threats to the community prevailed in Ranchito, where one planning group member described the SVP slated to move there as a "time bomb" and another asked if there was any "guarantee that children will not be molested" as a result of the placement.

Predictably, protecting children was a key point of contention among community members in all three places. While the focus on children may have stemmed from a knee-jerk reaction to a perceived threat to a local vulnerable population, California's two-thousand-foot residence restriction law also shaped how these concerns played out. This law signaled that excluding identified sex offenders from some areas would increase public safety, and community members interpreted this to mean that placing SVPs in communities with children would lead to future sex crimes. As an elementary school principal in Ranchito argued in a letter to the judge, "[The SVP] must not be placed in such proximity to our school, to bus stops for our schools, or to any area where this repeated sexual predator can find access to the children in our community." For her, any "access" was unacceptable. Similarly, in Deserton, I often heard residents remark in interviews and informal conversations that having the SVP's trailer in a part of the desert where children regularly "hung out" and walked through on the way to the town's café would put those children in danger.

Even in East City, where the SVP had targeted adult women rather than children, residents wondered why the judge had placed him in a neighborhood with so many children. As I wrote in my field notes after the notification meeting, one woman said, "I am vehemently opposed to his release here. It's the worst place to put him. There's a day care on the corner, a prep school and other schools close by. He's surrounded by children." Empirical evidence contradicts this woman's assumptions that living close to children increases the chances of reoffending: family members and acquaintances perpetrate the vast majority of sexual offenses,[41] and residential proximity to children does not increase the likelihood of sexual offenses.[42] Yet, by signaling that protecting the spaces where vulnerable populations are likely to be will prevent recidivism, residence restriction laws provided an opening for this woman and other community members to oppose SVP placements on the grounds that the placements would endanger the community and children in particular.

Community members' discussions of SVPs during the public comment portions of notification meetings and in subsequent interviews revealed that the legal label of "SVP" contributed to their fears. In an interview, a white Ranchito woman in her early forties whose daughter attended an elementary school near the proposed placement location explained, "He should not be out because he's a *violent* sexual predator. He didn't just pat a little kid on the butt and try to see what kind of underwear they were wearing; he hurt children." In East City, a white resident in her late fifties who was active in neighborhood beat meetings sponsored by the police department surmised that the placement became such a big issue in the community "because of the violent nature of his crime." As these comments indicate, the "sexually violent" part of the legal label signaled the dangerousness of the person being placed in each town.

The "predator" part of the label reinforced the perceived danger by signaling that SVPs were not human and could not be cured. For instance, a planning group member and construction company owner in Ranchito compared SVPs to wild animals. "You know how some people like to take wild animals and make them pets and then they get killed?" he asked. "It's a wild animal. [. . .] [Y]ou can't control its instincts, right? Well, I think these pedophiles, or the extremes like this [SVP] character, the extremes, you never know when he's gonna go off." A Deserton man who had recently moved to the area made a similar analogy, saying, "They say you can't cure these pit bulls and they euthanize them when they bite people, well these people [SVPs] just continue. They repeat more than pit bulls do." While empirical research belies the notion that sex offenders have high rates of recidivism,[43] the "predator" part of the legal label invoked images of a dangerous wild animal instinctually preying on vulnerable populations, which in turn signaled to these community members that SVPs would reoffend if given the chance.

While most people did not explicitly compare SVPs to animals, the term "predator" still signaled a fundamental difference between these individuals and "normal" human beings, which contributed to their perceived dangerousness. In interviews, community members in all three places described the problem with SVPs as "something in their DNA" or "something [that] short-circuited in their brain," and they referred to SVPs as having "arrested development" and "a sickness." These perceived fundamental flaws in SVPs' biological makeup contributed to a belief that they could never be cured or "talked out of" their impulses to sexually abuse others. This theme emerged clearly in a telephone interview with a Ranchito woman who had been head of the local trails association. This white woman in her late forties told me, "You cannot rehabilitate somebody like that." Later, she explained, "There's something just wrong with them, be it chemically, psychologically, or whatever's going on. And it's not fixable. At all. Ever." For the local county mental health official involved in multiple placements in the Ranchito area, these types of perspectives on SVPs emerged at least in part from the SVP label. He summed up what he called the "incredible picture" created by the label as "these kind of fire-breathing guys with red eyes who are going to throw you to the ground, beat you, rape you, cut off your head." Thus, the legal label of "sexually violent predator" signaled that these offenders were not human and, in doing so, increased fears that they would reoffend when given the chance.

When these types of concerns arose during notification meetings, panelists responded as best they could. In these meetings, I watched those sitting at the front of the room listen patiently to audience members' concerns and emotional pleas, and then provide more information about the placement process while also trying to correct false assumptions about the SVP or the placement decision. For instance, my field notes indicate that the police chief responded to the woman in East City who was "vehemently opposed" to the placement by saying, "We believe [the placement is] a violation of Jessica's Law, but the question was if the law applies to SVPs whose victims haven't been minors. However, it was either that or homeless. There is no location for him to go in East City. Health Corp looked at over 1,100 residences." While these types of exchanges sometimes grew heated, those at the front of the room maintained their composure in the face of a sometimes hostile audience.

At least some community members appreciated panelists' efforts. During a Skype interview, I asked a man from Ranchito to tell me about what went well at their community meeting. He answered, "They weren't saying this guy's not dangerous. They weren't trying to blow smoke up anybody. They were acknowledging that he's a high-risk guy and they were in great detail about the plans to mitigate that. [. . .] But they never said, 'This guy's no danger.'" I too had been surprised at the extent to which those who led notification meetings honestly portrayed the SVPs' past crimes and did not try to dismiss audience members' fears about public safety. While some of these fears may have been unwarranted, most panelists seemed to recognize that the SVP label invokes fear and that dismissing audience members' concerns without further discussion would have proved fruitless.

Unfortunately, decision makers' honesty about potential dangers and their "plans to mitigate" the dangers did not assuage audience members' fears. An East City woman's comment explains why. She said, as I recorded in my field notes, "If you're so sure that he's ready to leave treatment, he wouldn't have all these conditions." With this statement, she clearly employed the inherent contradiction in the SVP statute to challenge the siting decision: if SVPs were as dangerous as the law made them sound, then they should not be let out into communities. Thus, while decision makers held notification meetings to increase public safety and mitigate local opposition, their actions inadvertently fueled siting conflicts as community members recognized and reacted to contradictory signals about the dangerousness of SVPs. From their perspectives, these dangerous individuals had no place in their towns. Nonetheless, the law required SVPs' release without any input from local communities. This inherent contradiction extended community members' concerns beyond a fear of the perceived dangerous individuals to claims of procedural injustices rooted in signals from California's community notification law.

"Hysterical" Communities in "Ideal" Locations Protest Perceived Injustices

Upon learning about notification meetings, community members expressed their outrage in terms of a right to know about potential threats. This perspective emerged clearly one afternoon when I interviewed a Ranchito woman and her husband in the living room of their home. The white couple in their early fifties lived near the proposed placement location, and both actively participated in the local Tea Party movement. Early in the interview, the woman commented that one of her frustrations with the proposed SVP placement in Ranchito boiled down to one question: "If we have dangerous people in our midst, how could we not be informed about it?" While she expressed other concerns throughout the interview, the lack of transparency in the placement decision remained one of her top issues.

In Deserton and East City, where SVPs actually moved in, protesters described their actions as "doing our part letting people know" and "mak[ing] the community aware of what was going on." In a telephone interview, a black East City activist in her early fifties who had worked on many community issues through a local interfaith alliance explained, "The whole purpose of [protesting] was to express our discomfort and to get out the information to the people of the community." A white Ranchito woman in her late forties who served as the chair of the board of a preschool near the proposed placement site summed it up by saying, "I don't want to live next door to a sexual predator on the one hand. On the other hand, if I know who he is and where he is, that's kind of a benefit to me, isn't it?" These community members assumed that knowing about an identified sex offender would reduce the chances that they or their children would become victims.

Community notification does not appear to reduce recidivism or increase self-protective behaviors.[44] However, as decision makers for SVP placements found out, making information available about identified sex offenders can increase local anxiety[45] and create and reinforce a sense of "information entitlement" in which community members believe they have a right to information.[46] Nationally mandated community notification laws such as the one in California further reinforce this sense of entitlement by signaling to communities that knowledge increases public safety, a theme reflected in community members' claims that they had a right to know about potential threats.

Community members also adopted a broader interpretation of the legal signal that knowledge increases safety. As with local opposition to public housing projects[47] and waste facilities,[48] community members claimed that they had a right to know about and be involved in decision-making processes, and that SVP placement processes had unfairly excluded them from siting decisions. When community members learned of proposed SVP placements, many were suspicious that decision makers were trying to "slide" an SVP into their town. For example, one afternoon in East City, I sat on the front porch of a house across the intersection from the SVP's home talking with the man who lived there. A black man in his late forties, he had lived in East City on and off for almost twenty years. He described his initial reaction to the placement as follows: "You just drop him in and there go your warning. That's it. I felt like that's . . . like we been raped." Similarly, the man who spearheaded the litigation in Deserton told me in an interview, "It was kind of like [the SVP] was being dropped out of space. We didn't know what was the process that led up to a selection of a residence for a person. We had no idea at all what was behind him coming." These and similar comments from other community members show that they believed they had a right to know not only about individual SVPs but also about the decision-making processes leading up to SVP placements. Although the SVP statute said nothing about community involvement in placement decisions, community members interpreted signals from California's notification law as affording them a right to know about identified threats and assigning responsibility to the state for involving communities in ensuring public safety.

Community members across California shared the concerns of those in Ranchito, Deserton, and East City. According to media reports, residents routinely referred to SVPs as dangerous monsters who should be kept away from "unsuspecting communities" and children. They also questioned decision-making processes, with the most common refrain being that officials treated the selected communities as "dumping grounds" for unwanted people and projects. As an editor of a local newspaper said, "These people don't have a voice. That's why the county treats them like a dumping ground."[49] In another case, a newspaper quoted a seventh grader as saying, "South Bay is not a dumping ground."[50] These types of comments often occurred alongside those calling for more accountability for those who placed SVPs in communities.

Underlying these claims of injustice were the inherently contradictory signals provided by the SVP statute. Local residents ardently believed that the people coming to their towns, people labeled as the worst of the worst type of sex offenders, could not and should not be allowed to reenter society. From this perspective, the law itself allowed for grave injustices to occur by requiring SVPs to be released into communities without any sort of local input. A white Ranchito mother in her midfifties who was active in a local Parent-Teacher Association (PTA) summed it up best by saying, "We just need to keep an eye on the government and make sure they're doing their job and keeping these people away from our children." As with perceptions of fairness in litigation efforts,[51] community members assessed the fairness of SVP placements in terms of both placement processes and outcomes. Their interpretations of legal signals from the SVP statute and other sex offender laws shaped their sense of injustice, which was rooted in perceptions of SVPs' dangerousness and communities' rights to know about and be involved in proactively protecting themselves.

Strategies for Opposition

When community members across California learned of potential SVP placements in their towns, they had many potential options for voicing their opposition. Civic activism, legal and political mobilization, mass media, social media, word of mouth, and vigilantism all had the potential to help communities fight SVP placements, but some strategies gained more traction than others. Figure 1.1 illustrates the percentage of communities that engaged in various opposition strategies. In most places, local opposition efforts involved multiple strategies, with the most common being civic activism. Thirty-four communities, or about 70 percent of them, participated in various forms of civic activism.

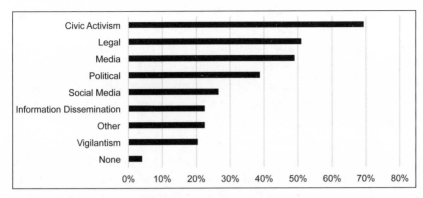

Figure 1.1. Percentage of Communities Engaged in Different Response Strategies (*N* = 49)

The most common were protests and rallies, followed by community meetings, petitions, letters to decision makers, and contacting potential landlords. Community members in two places produced and displayed buttons and colored ribbons to symbolize their opposition to SVP placements, and an activist in Soledad created a community group to provide information and education about sexually violent predators to children and their parents through community meetings, a telephone hotline, and a website.[52]

Perhaps because of community members' interpretations of SVP placements as political problems, the civic activism sparked by these placements dramatically contradicts the stereotype of community members as hysterical vigilantes out to "burn the monster" at all costs. In fact, vigilantism was the least common strategy, with only about 20 percent of local opposition efforts falling into this category. In these ten cases, vigilantism manifested most often as harassment or threats against the attorneys, landlords, and/or SVPs involved in each case. These threats transformed into action in only two places. In Lompoc, the media reported on an instance in which a neighbor "accidentally" shot at the vehicle of one of the SVP's security guards,[53] and in Vacaville, the SVP reported that someone had spray-painted his garage door.[54]

After civic activism, community members most often engaged with their local legal, political, and media institutions to voice their opposition to SVP placements. Just over 50 percent of communities protested SVP placements by attending court hearings, calling the police, litigating, and speaking to judges outside of formalized hearings. A slightly smaller percentage (almost 49 percent) of local responses involved contacting mass media outlets or attending press conferences. Community members in about nineteen places (39 percent) attended city council meetings, contacted their local politicians, passed city council resolutions or other formalized political action, and otherwise tried to apply political pressure to stop SVP placements.

Once again, these strategies contradict the stereotype of community members as irrational, hysterical vigilantes. They appear more in line with the image of engaged, informed citizens trying to gain control over local issues. Less common but still important strategies included forming social media groups (27 percent of communities), disseminating information through flyers and posting signs (22 percent), and other strategies of opposition such as taking personal safety measures, moving away, and informally watching the SVP (20 percent). Two communities had no clear response strategies reported in media outlets.

This brief portrait of response strategies across the state indicates that community members in California eschewed torches and pitchforks for less violent forms of opposition. While a few community members did engage in vigilantism, most focused on civic, legal, and political activism. Yet, the portrait is incomplete; it cannot explain why, given similar concerns across places, community members engaged in different strategies for opposition.

Similar Concerns, Different Strategies

While the emotions involved in controversies over sex offenders should not be discounted, this chapter has shown how political and legal forces intersect to set the stage for local opposition against SVP placements. In California, despite legal signals that SVPs posed an extreme threat to society, the SVP statute said little about how sites should be chosen or how communities should be involved. This legal silence allowed decision makers to adopt their own processes, which included selecting relatively powerless "ideal" hosts and then notifying those communities of upcoming placements. These decisions reinforced inequalities between communities and highlighted community members' exclusion from decision-making processes. Community members responded by pointing out contradictions in the SVP statute and drawing upon signals from other sex offender laws to mount their opposition. Their interpretations of the signals from the state's residence restriction and community notification laws contributed to a belief that siting decisions had been unfair. Ultimately, decision makers' and community members' interpretations of legal signals in light of state, regional, and local political contexts shaped SVP placements in ways that left vulnerable communities struggling to assert their rights to local control over local issues.

These dynamics occurred in SVP placement attempts throughout California. Similar substantive and procedural concerns across places may have been informed by similarities in placement processes throughout the state and broader societal discourses about the threats posed by sex offenders. Yet, communities engaged in a wide variety of techniques to oppose SVP placements, the least of which was vigilantism. Community members across California framed their concerns in terms of the injustice of having a perceived dangerous individual imposed upon their towns, but similar understandings of the issue across places did not always translate into similar responses to SVP placements. The next three chapters use in-depth case studies to show how local political and legal contexts transformed common concerns over SVP placements into different avenues of resistance. The cases in Ranchito, Deserton, and East City demonstrate that contemporary and historical relationships between communities and their local institutions facilitated and constrained the emergence of different strategies for opposition across places.

2

Political Mobilization in Countrified Suburbia

The thing is if you don't stand up and [. . .] fight against
things you don't want, things you don't believe in, things that
you feel would be destructive to your community, boy we'd
have all kinds of crap up here.
—Ranchito woman, former member of local trails and
transportation committee

When I visited the unincorporated town of Ranchito in 2011, it seemed
like stereotypical small-town America. A scenic two-lane highway ran
through the middle of town. The highway often clogged with traffic
during rush hour because of its connection to the sprawling metropolis
forty miles away. Chain restaurants and big box stores lined the highway on the outskirts of town, but the recognizable brands quickly faded
as the road turned into Ranchito's main street. In the small downtown
core, local businesses included a feed and grain supply store, a hardware
store, a small grocery store, antiques shops, the local history museum, a
few gas stations, and a couple of restaurants. Sporadic sidewalks made it
difficult to shop on foot, and visitors often passed through on their way
to more tourist-friendly towns farther up the hill. Residents described
the town as a "countrified suburban" bedroom community reminiscent
of Mayberry.

Those who lived in Ranchito had either grown up there or moved
there to get away from city problems and raise families in relatively in-
expensive homes on large lots. They enjoyed the self-described family-
oriented community, which boasted low crime rates, good schools,
youth sports programs, and hiking and equestrian trails. While drug
use and graffiti posed some problems, most community members noted
highway traffic as the biggest local issue. The sheriff's department provided policing services, and residents said that they valued their independence, privacy, and self-reliance. A strong Tea Party presence

reflected a pervasive distrust of big government in Ranchito, which also applied to regional and state-level politics. The town had no formal political body, but a local planning group advised the county board of supervisors on local land-use issues. The group had little political clout, and many residents I spoke with believed that the county supervisors paid little attention to the planning group's recommendations.

Despite community members' skepticism of regional, state, and national politics, they rallied around political mobilization as the centerpiece of their response to a proposed SVP placement in their town. The planning group chair, a white real estate agent in her midforties, organized a community meeting that culminated in the group passing a resolution against the placement. The next day, in a dramatic performance in front of television cameras, the landlord, a white man in his early seventies, withdrew his offer of housing by ripping up the rental deposit check and stating his solidarity with the community. After finding no other housing options in Ranchito, state authorities ultimately placed the SVP elsewhere. Later, despite their lack of access to formal political power and a profound distrust of big government (and the politics that goes with it), community members lauded the planning group's actions and described the town hall meeting as constituting their community's successful fight against the placement. In short, community members perceived the planning group as the voice of the community rather than a political body trying to gain status by catering to constituents.

This chapter explains how and why people in a community that prided itself on self-reliance and distrust of government came to embrace political mobilization as the centerpiece of their community's opposition to a proposed SVP placement. In some ways, Ranchito's story follows those of other communities that have opposed perceived unfair siting decisions. As in those other cases,[1] community members in Ranchito perceived the decision to place an SVP in their town as an inherently political problem in which state authorities were infringing on the community's "right" to govern itself. From this perspective, the SVP placement opened a "political opportunity"[2] for action in which the planning group saw an opportunity to act and framed the issue as a potential danger to the community, a framing that resonated with other local residents. According to traditional explanations, community members in Ranchito rallied around the planning group's efforts because, as with the general public and Californians in particular,[3] they trusted their local politicians more than those at the state and national levels. In the context of this trust of local officials, the community meeting facilitated the emergence of a collective identity based on a heightened sense of "us" (i.e., the community) versus "them" (i.e., state authorities who had proposed the SVP placement), which in turn encouraged support for political mobilization.[4]

The opening of a political opportunity for action and the formation of a collective identity contributed to the emergence of political mobilization in Ranchito, but neither factor fully explains how political mobilization became the centerpiece of the community's response to the SVP placement. The community lacked political capital, as demonstrated by the fact that Ranchito's planning group could only advise the board of supervisors, who, according to community members, often did not heed the group's advice. By taking a stand on a decision that they had no real political power to change, the planning group risked alienating themselves from the community. Had community members perceived their local leaders' actions as strategic tactics to garner favor with constituents, they could have rejected political mobilization as disingenuous or useless. Instead, community members rallied around the planning group's mobilization of political authority, perceiving this largely symbolic political move as the most important part of their fight against the SVP placement. The rest of this chapter explains how the community's relationships with politicians, formal political structures, and law enforcement bolstered support for political mobilization despite a lack of real political power.

Stopping an SVP Placement in Ranchito

In 2008, less than a year before the SVP controversy began in Ranchito, the deputy district attorney assigned to SVP cases in the county disseminated a two-page document that essentially translated California's SVP statute into eleven steps for conditional release, complete with commentary on each. After mentioning the document to me in an interview, she shared it with me, explaining, "I essentially took the statute and established a procedure. [. . .] The judge in our county, and to my knowledge in all of the counties now have pretty much accepted that procedure, even though my informal procedure isn't necessarily spelled out in the statute." It may have been an exaggeration that all counties had adopted her procedure, but the document did gain some notoriety, as evidenced by other officials who referenced it during our interviews. For instance, an attorney involved in the case in Deserton referred me to the deputy district attorney in Ranchito's county, explaining, "She is very knowledgeable about community placement of SVPs and has written a whole 'how to do it' for other DA's offices." Similarly, a housing consultant with the Department of Health and Human Services in Ranchito's county referred to its SVP placement process as "a model," adding, "I think we're very fortunate [in this county]."

Some of the commentary in the document could have partially mitigated community members' concerns about a lack of input into placement decisions. For example, steps seven and eight focused on the fifteen-day comment period, noting that a local task force "has agreed to accept and compile community input and present it to the Court," and that "community agencies may propose alternate locations for the court to consider" during this time. Prior to the publication of the document, the task force had been soliciting and compiling public comment to submit to the court, but having the procedure in writing solidified the role of the task force as an intermediary between the public and decision makers during SVP placements.

The document also clarified an ambiguity in the law as to when public comment should conclude. To this point, step ten addressed placement hearings, stating, "Courts have the discretion to accept community comment up to the hearing date and historically have done so. Courts also appear to have the discretion to take public comment at the hearing before issuing a ruling on the proposed placement." This broad interpretation of the law signaled that the public had multiple opportunities to respond and could do so up until the point at which the judge made a final decision. Indeed, the document noted that public comment could even influence siting decisions because, "based on community input, additional conditions might be imposed [by the Court]." In short, by clarifying the practical application of the state's SVP statute and providing implicit guidelines for those involved in SVP placements, the document formalized already established placement procedures in ways that signaled the importance of public input in placement decisions.

In January 2009, a few months after the document had been disseminated, the DMH recommended an SVP placement in Ranchito. In line with established procedures, the county task force put out a press release about the proposed placement. By this time, the task force had already handled six previous placements, including the conditional release of the same SVP slated to move into Ranchito. Four years earlier, he had been conditionally released to another site on prison grounds about fifty miles away. During that time, he gained notoriety in the region by participating in a one-on-one interview on a televised national news program. Approximately three months later, he violated a condition of his release and was returned to the state hospital.

When the state proposed to house the SVP in Ranchito after he had once again gained conditional release, no one involved in the process expected the community to remain silent. The Health Corp representative I spoke with explained that "because [the SVP] failed so miserably the first time around, it tainted the public's perception of him even more so than it would've if it was just his first time around." While this SVP would have created a stir no matter where he went, the prosecutor involved in the case expected particularly intense outcry in Ranchito. In a telephone interview, she explained, "The discussion went something like this: 'Look, we know that that may be the only guy who is willing to rent, but I know Ranchito. Ranchito is an extremely tight, rural community. And I think you're gonna have serious problems with any type of a placement in Ranchito, regardless of how far away that property might be from anything else going there.'" Despite the predicted outcry, "our responsibility," the prosecutor said, "is to channel [the community's] concern." Thus, while decision makers in the placement process expected local backlash, their somewhat formalized process attempted to "channel" that backlash to minimize its effects on the placement itself.

As expected, some Ranchito residents remembered the SVP's previous release and the televised interview. A PTA mother explained, "The name kind of rang a bell, but I wasn't exactly sure which child molester this was, so I Googled him and started looking at the pictures. I go, 'Oh no, not that guy.'" Others I spoke with also mentioned researching the SVP online and checking the sex offender registry to find out more about him. The chair of the board of a local preschool told me that when some parents heard about the proposed placement and then asked her to represent them at the upcoming community meeting, "I said I would. I went online, I researched [the SVP], I looked up what his crimes were." Generally, the more community members remembered about this particular SVP, the more they opposed his placement in their safe, family-friendly small town.

The weeks that followed the press release involved a frenzy of local activity. The woman who had been the head of the local trails association explained that she "told everybody I knew to tell everybody they know. I emailed it to every single person I could ever think of. Just to get it out there." While she also noted that she "didn't really even think about writing in the newspaper and that kind of thing," others wrote letters to local newspapers and the sex offender task force and also called in to a local radio talk show. One man, a white father of three who had lived in Ranchito for all of his forty years, took his actions a bit further by trying to organize the community. In our Skype interview, he said that he and his wife were

> talking about what to do about [the proposed placement]. And we had, recently, I had recently created a Facebook account. I said, "We've got this Facebook thing on there, we got a bunch of friends in Ranchito, let's just get the word out." So right then, on the spot, I made the Facebook group Don't Dump Your Sex Offender on Ranchito. [. . .] Within minutes of reading the article, we put that group up. And then, as, you know, Facebook's a wonderful tool for that, so I create the group, I like it, [my wife] likes it, now all our friends start seeing it. They all start liking it. People start posting stuff, and that was the genesis of my involvement in that issue.

Later, he referred to the group as an "electronic militia" trying to stop the placement in their town.

All these activities centered on the idea that the more people who knew about the placement, the stronger the opposition would be. As the PTA mother explained, "My initial reaction was that I was gonna have to mobilize the troops. That was the first thing that popped into my head was get the word out as fast as possible to as many people as possible." Similarly, the electronic militia leader said he "was confident that if enough people stood up and screamed, that somebody would make a different decision. And so my first goal was to get the word out as quickly as possible to as many people as possible." Despite differences in their immediate plans for action, these individuals wanted everyone to know about the proposed placement.

Regional and local political officials also mobilized in the weeks after the press release. The county supervisor who represented the area sent a letter to the court opposing the placement, and the planning group chair started to mobilize. To find out more about her actions before and during the SVP placement, I interviewed her in her real estate office one afternoon. She explained that upon hearing about the proposed placement, she began organizing a community meeting to disseminate information and raise "public awareness" about the issue. Technically, the planning group could only address land-use issues, but she argued that "[the SVP placement] was a land-use issue because it was all tied to where he was going to be able to live." Her comment shows how some people in the community perceived the SVP placement as similar to other types of siting decisions. As with siting potentially dangerous facilities, the SVP placement highlighted the state's power to put an unwanted element into a community with little public inclusion in the siting or placement processes. These parallels fueled local discontent.

At the same time, some individuals on the planning group disagreed that the SVP placement fell within their jurisdiction. According to the chair, a few members of the group believed so strongly that the planning group was overstepping its bounds that they refused to come to the community meeting. She explained that they "didn't think that we should be taking on this social issue." Nonetheless, the planning group proceeded with the community meeting because, as a longtime resident and planning group member who had served as a trustee for the local school district put it, "Something like [an SVP placement] really is outside of our purview unless we really want to stretch what it is, but because we have no governing body in Ranchito. [. . .] There's really nobody locally that somebody could come and say we don't want this in our community. So we took that stance." The planning group chair echoed these ideas, saying, "Ranchito, because it's not a city, doesn't have an elected official, or a venue for people to come and freak. [. . .] Or have their voice heard, or whatever." Thus, just two and a half weeks after the initial press release, the local governing body that was meant to deal with land-use issues held what it called a "community crisis management meeting" to allow community members to voice their concerns about the proposed SVP placement.

Local media publicized the meeting, with one editorial characterizing the proposed placement as a "state-sponsored threat" to the community. This framing of the issue as one of maintaining local control in the face of negative state-level decisions played well with Ranchito's politically conservative base. "We kind of find ourselves on the tail end of a lot of decisions, you know, so that frustrates people up here even more," said a white construction company owner and planning group member in his early fifties. "So, you get this 'us against them' mentality up here. So, whenever something like this [SVP placement] came up, that I think was the reason why there was a lot of people that showed up [at the meeting]." Others distinguished themselves from the "bleeding hearts." In a telephone interview, the owner of a gun store, a white man in his late fifties, explained his initial reaction to hearing about the proposed SVP placement. He said, "If the bleeding hearts want these guys to be released in the community, they need to let them go to their house and they can take care of them." His comment illustrates the political perspective from which some Ranchitoans viewed the proposed SVP placement. In a particularly revealing comment, the Tea Party activist I interviewed with his wife in their home near the proposed placement site argued that the government should segregate SVPs from society because "the government's job is to protect its people." This clearly illustrates that a general distrust of nonlocal government officials stirred local passions when it came to the issue of the SVP placement. The community meeting provided an opportunity to transform those passions into action.

Ranchito's Community Meeting

More than one hundred residents crammed into Ranchito's community center one Thursday evening in February 2009 to learn about and respond to the proposed SVP placement. The presence of the media, the prospective landlord, representatives from Health Corp and the offices of county and state elected officials, and a handful of officers from the sheriff's department added to the bustle of the meeting. Although the meeting occurred before I began my research, interviews, news reports, and official minutes provide details of what happened that evening.

By most accounts, even before the meeting started, the room hummed with a feeling of solidarity and togetherness. No one I spoke with could remember any other planning group meeting that had drawn so many people together. When I interviewed community members less than two years later, they still vividly recalled their experiences during that time. The Tea Party activist who lived next door to the proposed placement site explained that before the meeting, she "felt like it was kind of my problem. I was looking at it in a very personal way, like this is happening a few feet from my bedroom. [. . .] I was surprised that so many other people came out and even more [surprised] when I realized that they didn't know where it was. They didn't even know where they were talking about putting him, just that it was in Ranchito." For her, the size of the audience signaled that the placement would be a community issue rather than her personal problem.

Others reported similar perceptions of the meeting as bringing the community together. For instance, I interviewed a white father of three who had moved to Ranchito ten years before the SVP placement to start a family with his then girlfriend. He had been a teacher and was involved with the local school council and the PTA. He described the scene at the community meeting as "like a movie. [. . .] You just look across the room and you recognize people. And you're like, this isn't some earthquake in Japan where there's people in trouble who you see on the news, these are your neighbors." As these comments indicate, the meeting helped engender a sense of community among those who attended.

Many people I spoke with said that they went to the meeting because they believed the placement was a community problem that required a stronger response than they had engaged in for previous local issues. In a telephone interview, a white mother of four who had lived in Ranchito for almost three decades and served on the local design review board said that she had urged her neighbors to go to the meeting by telling them, "You know what, you need to voice your opinion and say something. And you need to stand up for this." She went on to say that even though she did not believe the community's input mattered in regional politics, she attended the meeting "because you gotta try somehow. You gotta try." Even though she was unsure about the power of local political action, she perceived the issue in terms of the community needing to fight a political decision through political avenues. The planning group's meeting provided her with the opportunity to be engaged in helping to solve that problem.

As with community meetings in other places, the meeting in Ranchito began with the Health Corp representative giving a brief presentation about the SVP, the conditions of his release, and the security precautions that would be put in place. Planning group members asked clarifying questions and then opened the floor for public comment. According to the meeting minutes, twenty-one people registered their opposition to the placement but did not want to speak publicly. Twenty-three residents voiced their concerns.

As in other places, people who attended the meeting in Ranchito expressed fear for the safety of themselves and their children. In an interview, the PTA mother recounted her involvement in the meeting:

> And I got up. And I had written a letter to the DMH protesting what they were doing. And I told the crowd, "This is the first time I've ever been to a planning commission meeting. My daughter is performing at the high school tonight. I am missing this performance to be here because it's that important to me. These are all my children. And I'm here to protect them like a lioness protects her cubs."

By describing herself as a "lioness," she gave the audience a clear visual representation of the danger she imagined the children of the community would be in and how she intended to protect those children from harm. She, like other audience members, had framed her concerns in terms of protecting one of the community's most vulnerable populations.

During the meeting, others framed their concerns about children's safety by bringing up the children who would be present in the preschools, at bus stops, and in open fields near the SVP's proposed location. In an interview, the principal of a nearby elementary school, a white woman in her late fifties, explained their logic. She said, "The space around a home doesn't necessarily mean that it's a secure place to put somebody. [T]here was a bus stop very close to that property. [. . .] [S]omebody could walk from that property across [the two-lane highway] and then through a lot of other open space to get to our school." The mother of a child who attended an elementary school near the proposed placement location expanded on the principal's explanation by saying, "If he sat on his front porch with a pair of binoculars, he could look down at my daughter's school. Although it was over a couple fields and—the distance was there—he definitely got a clear view of my daughter's playground and all 750 students that go to her school." Despite the site's distance from legally defined safe spaces, these and other community members still believed the SVP would find ways to victimize their children, either directly or indirectly.

In interviews, I asked each person why he or she thought the SVP placement became such a big issue in Ranchito. Many of the responses focused on threats to the community. For instance, the PTA father who had described the community meeting as being "like a movie" answered, "I think Ranchito felt like . . . Well, it's a very close-knit community, and it's very family-oriented. [. . .] It's really a stereotypical, nice small town. And, here's this guy coming into the community and it's like, 'This could affect any of us.'" The PTA mother also referenced the family-oriented nature of the community in her response to why the placement became such a big issue. She said, "This is a great place to raise kids. [T]he reason why a lot of people move to Ranchito is because of the great schools and the wide-open spaces and the low crime rate and that sort of thing. And anything that threatens that lifestyle, that way of life, is going to get some attention." The head of the local trails association summed it up by saying, "We can't have somebody dangerous like that in our community. [. . .] It's a threat to our way of living." Despite the reality that sex offenders already lived in Ranchito, the placement of someone in the community who was designated as an SVP represented a clear threat to the local "way of life" that prioritized families and children. The SVP label exacerbated the visibility of this threat, drawing a more intense local response than had been the case with other identified sex offenders in Ranchito.

While protecting children was a dominant theme among community members, some expressed more practical concerns related to the fairness of the placement. These individuals balked at the size and location of the home the SVP would be moving into. The large house sat on a hill just off the main highway. It boasted expansive views of the valley, and it included a swimming pool and hot tub embedded in a slate patio. Community members knew that taxpayers essentially footed the bill, and they did not want their money going toward such extravagant accommodations. "If the government's gonna supply someone with a home because they're too dangerous to be in society," said one of the Tea Party activists, "it shouldn't be pretty. It should be something [...] modest." Others echoed these sentiments, expressing reservations about someone legally labeled as a danger to society being housed in such a luxurious place.

These types of comments reflect broader public concerns about the conditions of confinement for inmates in the United States. Americans tend to believe that prisons are not harsh enough,[5] and public support for both educational and "luxurious" amenities in prisons declines when they are funded by taxpayers rather than inmates themselves.[6] Indeed, for some inmates, comfortable prison environments may at times lessen the perceived severity of punishment.[7] Thus, when Ranchito community members spoke incredulously about the proposed location for the SVP placement, they invoked a broader narrative about the use of taxpayer money to house a perceived dangerous individual in a generously appointed hilltop home with an expansive view of the surrounding area.

For some Ranchitoans, the injustice of the placement location went beyond a desire to punish the SVP by housing him in a more "modest" home. In a letter to the planning group, one woman who had attended the community meeting wrote, "He should not be living in luxury while the rest of Ranchito scrimps & saves trying to make ends meet." Another Ranchito resident, a white woman who had lived there for ten years and was active in her children's baseball league, echoed these concerns. She told me in an interview, "It was, like, I don't know, like a $5,000 a month house. Why does he need that? Why can't he have a trailer on a piece of property? You know, that the government is paying for. You know. I know a lot of people who work and live in little apartments. Why does this guy get . . ." She did not finish her thought, but the implication was that the SVP should not be provided such an expensive home while others in Ranchito made do living in apartments.

These concerns exemplify a sense of injustice born not solely out of punitiveness but also of evaluating the rights of an SVP relative to those of the broader community. For these community members, the state was pampering an identified sex offender while the rest of the community worked hard to live in more "modest" conditions. Despite the community's predominantly conservative, small-government leanings, some residents believed that the state should ensure that those they deemed less deserving did not receive better treatment than "respectable, law-abiding" citizens. When the state failed to do so by proposing the luxurious home for the SVP, community members saw this as fundamentally unfair.

Perceptions of unfairness also emerged in practical concerns about the distribution of sex offenders across the county. The PTA father explained that he had resisted a knee-jerk opposition to the placement. Upon hearing about the community's opposition to the SVP placement, he thought, "'Oh god, here's conservative Ranchito complaining about something.'" Nonetheless, he began researching the number of sex offenders throughout the county. "I started noticing a pattern that the [. . .] more rural you got, the higher the ratio [of sex offenders], meaning [our part of the] county was taking the lion's share of the county's sexual predators. And it was like, 'Well, wait a minute, that ain't right.'" He concluded that Ranchito had more than its "fair share" of sex offenders, and he brought statistics to the meeting to provide the planning group and the county an "actual reason" to oppose the placement. His actions suggest that at least some assumed that framing their concerns in practical terms would gain more traction with political officials than would concerns that appeared to be more knee-jerk emotional responses.

Underlying these practical questions of fairness was a general distrust of government. This played out in community members' concerns that if the placement was successful, the state would eventually house multiple SVPs in the proposed placement home. The baseball mother who had balked at the cost and size of the home explained this common sentiment by saying, "I think that they were probably going to rent that house and little by little move more in so they could have like a home. [. . .] And that's what a lot of people were saying [. . .] that they were gonna turn it into a home for sexual predators." The chair of the board of the local preschool echoed this sentiment when she said, "The home that they were planning to put him in was a four-bedroom home. Who were they gonna put in the other three bedrooms? [. . .]

They said 'Well, we don't have any plans at this time.' I don't doubt that, why would they have any plans, but if that opportunity is there and it's already established in the community, it's so much easier than putting him somewhere else." Thus, even practical concerns about the home and its location were linked to skepticism about the state's real priorities and intentions for the home.

These concerns funneled into the community meeting. With so many people packed into a small space to discuss such volatile issues, things could have quickly spiraled out of control. Indeed, during the meeting, the planning group member who owned the construction company highlighted the community's potential for vigilante violence. He explained to me that at the meeting he told Health Corp representatives, "Everybody that lives out here has a gun. And they've got multiple guns. [. . .] They're into protecting their neighborhoods. Do you really think a guy like [the SVP] will be safe in a community like Ranchito after what I just said?" The crowd responded with a resounding "No!" He went on to declare, "You put him in our town, and [. . .] this guy won't last. He won't stay living. He will be dead." Later, in our interview, he explained very matter-of-factly that for many of the men that he knew in Ranchito

> it would be no problem, no skin off these guys' . . . there's I mean, hundreds of them that I know—no big deal at all to just go over there and take a guy out no problem. [. . .] If they see a threat, they're gonna take the threat out also. And some of these people would even be, I shouldn't say it like this because I don't know this, but I would say almost like proud of the fact that they go around drinking, "Hey, I took that dude out." He'd be a hero, right? He'd be a hero. And the people of the town would back somebody like that.

His unapologetic description of some community members' propensity for violence made no judgement as to their right to use violence to protect themselves. Instead, he presented the information to demonstrate that some community members would retaliate against the perceived threat regardless of the moral or legal justness of their actions.

Similarly, I asked a mother of two preschoolers who was active in a local church community and had been featured in media coverage about the SVP placement what kinds of plans had been discussed after the community meeting. In response, the white woman in her early forties described a general sense that if "they bring him here, he won't live long. That was very obvious and I mean, nobody ever said that. There was never any indication, but that's the kind of town this is." She too brought up the potential violence against the SVP not to justify or condemn vigilante actions but to describe the atmosphere in the community around the time of the proposed SVP placement.

Comments about vigilantism might be expected in private interviews, but the fact that a de facto local political official brought up potential violence during a public meeting demonstrates community members' deeply held belief that SVPs did not belong in Ranchito and their conviction that they would take matters into their own hands if the state violated their perceived right to control what happened in their town. While threats of violence may or may not have transformed into actual violence had the placement proceeded, community members' general support for threats of violence as an opposition strategy suggests their belief that they would fight perceived unfair decisions in any way possible.

While some community members withheld judgment about potential vigilantism, the "lioness" PTA mother condemned the community's potential for violence in an interview. When I asked what she thought people in Ranchito could have done differently in response to the proposed placement, she answered that were an SVP to move into Ranchito, "I would be afraid that someone would take the law into their own hands, what we call cowboy justice up here. I would hate to see that happen because I am the kind of person who thinks that the pen is mightier than the sword, but I know that not everybody in this community feels that way." She went on to say that if such violence were to happen in Ranchito, "I would oppose any action that involved any kind of illegal activity. I mean, it's one thing to have a sexually violent predator in your neighborhood and picket their house. It's quite another thing to fire your shotgun through the window. So, I don't condone violence in any form and . . . but you have to do what you need to do to get your point across within the confines of the law." Considering her fierce opposition to the placement during the community meeting, her elaboration during our interview demonstrated a recognition that vigilante violence would not be a fair response to an SVP placement. Notwithstanding her renunciation of violence, community members I interviewed more commonly remained neutral about the SVP's lack of safety in Ranchito.

Despite threats of violence, the planning group maintained order throughout the meeting. While the chair had expected residents to "go nuts" on the landlord and the Health Corp representative, the audience was, as the electronic militia leader put it, "extraordinarily well-behaved." The PTA father further explained, "The planning group was very professional, almost annoying because they listened and they cut you off at the allotted two or three minutes of talking time. They kept it very unbiased. It was very straightforward." Many community members echoed these sentiments by commenting on the professionalism of the meeting. The group's ability to maintain order suggests residents' respect for their de facto local politicians and their willingness to participate in a local political process, even when they felt angry and betrayed by the county and the state.

Ultimately, the meeting ended when the planning group passed a resolution against the placement. The resolution noted the group's opposition to the placement based on seven concerns, including proximity to places where children gather, the cost of renting such a large home, the landlord's opposition to the placement, and the threat to Ranchito's children. The group sent it, along with sixteen letters of opposition from local residents, to the county's sex offender task force.

Some audience members left the meeting with a "wait-and-see" attitude. They believed that their local political body had done its job, and they hoped that would be the end of the proposed placement. The religious mother of preschoolers explained, "I am very proud of the community that we live in. Before that, like I said, I've never seen the community rally like that. To stand up to the government, to stand up to the state and say not our house . . ." This comment illustrates a common perception that the planning group's actions were really the community's actions. They had stood up to the state, and many said they felt proud of their community for doing so. "I remember walking back to my car," said the mother whose child attended the local elementary school, "going, 'There's no way this person is living in Ranchito.' I was proud to be a Ranchitoan. I was proud of the way people handled themselves. I was proud that nobody got out of hand." For her, "getting out of hand" would have undermined the real concerns of local residents and the strength of the opposition efforts. Although she did not elaborate, it also implies that she recognized the value in controlling emotions when fighting for change within this political arena.

While no one began immediately strategizing future actions after the meeting, a few discussed potential ideas. As the electronic militia leader explained, "There was a lot of pretty vague talk. But people were talking about, 'Okay, do we buy the house from the guy? Do we go raise money and just buy this house from the guy so that, you know, he's trying to sell the house, or he's trying to make money off it. Can we just buy the house from the guy so he doesn't have to sell it?'" Buying the home would have been a particularly unique nonviolent strategy for opposition, but other ideas proposed immediately after the meeting reflected strategies employed in protests over other social issues. For example, the electronic militia leader recounted the following instance in which some community members considered property damage as a protest strategy:

> There was a conversation, and this is a purely humorous thing, so I want to put it in context. It's a purely humorous thing. We have these bad Santa Ana winds here, and we have these fires here. And there was a conversation at one point, I think it was after the meeting, that said, well, and then the conversation went something like this: "Well, if he moves in, then I guess our next step is we'll just have a candlelight vigil just east of his house in October." And that was done purely in jest, but I thought it was interesting.

Despite the "humorous" context in which property damage emerged as a potential strategy in Ranchito, the incident demonstrates that some community members were willing to at least consider multiple avenues of resistance, even those that involved illegal activity. Engaging in illegal activity would not have been outside of the realm of possibility, particularly as activists in a variety of other social movements have used property damage and other illegal actions to gain the attention of those in power.[8]

Other types of protests might also have occurred if the placement had proceeded. The PTA mother explained, "I think if we had heard something different, that, well, it was probably gonna happen, there probably would have been a movement of some sort. [. . .] People would have gotten together absolutely. That's definitely what Ranchito does." When people talked to her about the meeting, she said that she told them, "'This isn't over. If he comes to Ranchito, we're going to picket the house.' And I said that over and over again until I had a lot of people say, 'Yeah, we'll join you with that.'" The situation never came to that because events the next day quashed the plan to place the SVP in Ranchito.

The Failure of the Proposed Placement

After the community meeting, one central actor in the placement decision had not yet exercised his power to stop the placement. During the meeting, the owner of the proposed placement home, whom I will call Cliff, began to state his case. He listened to community members' concerns and then stood, waving an envelope containing the rental deposit. He told the audience that he had not been given complete information before agreeing to rent the home to Health Corp. Minutes from the meeting stated that he said he was "unaware of the gravity of the situation when approached to enter into a contract" and that the proposed placement had "damaged his reputation." Despite his participation in securing the proposed placement site, he implored audience members to believe that he too was a victim of the state's siting decision.

As the meeting adjourned, the religious mother approached Cliff with eight-by-ten photos of her preschoolers. In a telephone interview, she described her actions to me. She said, "I went to him after the meeting and I showed him a picture of my children and told him, 'I am only asking you to think about what you're doing. Think about this, look at these children. These are the children in our community that are at risk. Think about putting them in this position.' And that's all I had to say. And I walked out. In tears." Although she hoped that the meeting and her plea would stop the placement, she "was very fearful that [it] wouldn't work." But it did work. The day after the town hall meeting, Cliff convened a press conference at the proposed placement site. With television cameras rolling, he tore up an envelope containing the rental deposit and said, "I love Ranchito. I love my neighbors. My intention is to have a residential care [facility] for the elderly and not a facility for sex offenders." Four days after the press conference, the state withdrew plans to house the SVP in Ranchito.

While many community members believed that Cliff had intended to proceed with the placement until he faced pressure at the community meeting, Cliff told me a different story. I visited his home one morning to interview him about his role in the SVP placement. During the interview, he explained that when he and his wife moved to Ranchito in 2004, they made a living largely by flipping homes: they would buy a home, live in it for two years while fixing it up, rent it for a few years, and then sell it. Unfortunately, the housing market crashed soon after they renovated the home that became the center of the controversy over the SVP placement, causing the home to remain vacant for much longer than they had anticipated.

Finally, in 2008, Cliff received a call from a representative of a medical corporation. After showing the home to this man, Cliff received a "one-page letter that was an agreement from a third party acting on behalf of the Department of Health and Human Services, they later told me. And it said that property was to be set aside and held for [the future tenant, whom he later learned was the SVP]. So we signed it, I signed it and sent it back; they promised to send a deposit." While Cliff was glad to finally have an interested renter, he adamantly explained to me that the letter "was not a contract. It was one piece of paper that said, 'This is related to [the future tenant's name], sign it and send it back. This will allow us to initiate the process.'" About a week after signing the letter, Cliff recognized his rental property on a television news report that an SVP with the same name as his future tenant would be moving into Ranchito.

Soon after the news broadcast, the host of a local conservative radio talk show called Cliff on air, boosting Cliff's notoriety in the community. According to Cliff, the talk show host "behaved as if I knew up front everything that was on the media. And I'll never forgive him for that because it was slander." After the disconcerting radio appearance, Cliff said he called the Health Corp representative, telling him, "'You're throwing me under the bus. What is this all about? Who put the media out? I wanna know who did it.'" According to Cliff, the representative said they had a signed agreement, and the deposit check arrived shortly after the confrontation.

By the time Cliff stood to speak at the end of the community meeting, he had in his hand the envelope containing the deposit. He said he meant to "make my points, which were 'Don't you know that I'm a citizen who's getting trampled?'" and then return the deposit to the Health Corp representative. Instead, when the meeting had "worn on too long" and "the noise and the crowd was getting out of hand," the planning group chair ended the meeting and Cliff "felt that I didn't get to finish my story." As he was leaving, the mother with pictures of her children approached him and "accused me of fostering that bastard." The next day, feeling that he needed a chance to "finish" telling his side of the story, Cliff called a press conference to denounce the placement. He summed up the issue by saying, "Had somebody used those words [sexually violent predator], or described what they were trying to accomplish, I would've immediately not even returned that stupid letter that said we're gonna send you a deposit."

When I interviewed community members, some said they believed Cliff's claims that he was railroaded by the state. The mother of a child who attended the nearby elementary school said, "My impression is that the poor person that owns the home got excited because they were willing to pay him above and beyond the rent of the home and probably they weren't too forthright with who they were gonna be giving it to, or let live there." Others agreed, with the chair of the preschool board stating, "I don't even fault the gentleman who owned the home who was just trying to make a living. [. . .] It's a really tough time in our country financially, and people are losing their homes all the time. And you make a living the best way you can. But . . . it just wasn't the best for Ranchito." These individuals placed more blame on the state than the landlord for the siting decision.

Others perceived Cliff as a "showboat" who had agreed to rent to the state because he needed the money but then had to publicly denounce the placement to save his reputation. The religious mother said in our interview, "[He] was also loaded with excuses, one excuse after another. Cry me a river." She went on to explain, "I didn't believe [Cliff's story] for one moment. You're a homeowner. You're gonna rent a property and you're not gonna ask the government, who wants to pay you at least two times the value of the monthly rent [who they're going to put there]?" From this perspective, Cliff had intended to rent his house for the SVP placement, but he was "shamed" into backing out. A Health Corp representative supported this view. When asked in an interview whether

Health Corp personnel had informed Cliff of the details of the placement, the representative stated, "It absolutely happened. There's no way that we can work with someone . . . we have to notify them of the pitfalls so that something like this does not occur. So, we had to be absolutely up front with him. And we were in this case, but, you know . . . he said that we were not, so . . ." While Cliff might have received the information, the Health Corp representative went on to say, "We told him that it was a sexually violent predator. I don't know if he knew the implications of that when he accepted our offer. And it became readily apparent to him at the community meeting."

Despite conflicting stories about the events leading up to the announcement of the placement in Ranchito, people I interviewed spoke of the community meeting and Cliff's subsequent refusal to rent his property to the state as the community's successful fight against a perceived threat and injustice. Although the planning group exercised little formal political power, these local politicians successfully facilitated and in some ways even created the community response. The next sections explain how and why political mobilization became the centerpiece of the community's response to the proposed SVP placement.

Community Orientations to Authority in Ranchito

Community members in Ranchito rallied around their local politicians' actions within the context of specific configurations of contemporary and historical relationships between the community and local politicians, political structures, and law enforcement. As I discussed in the introduction, I conceptualize these relationships as dominant community orientations to political and legal authority. The former reflects activated community members' understandings of the role of political authority in local life (i.e., relationships with politicians in terms of how they treated the community and their perceived interests when making decisions) and the role of political authority in solving local problems (i.e., the community's position within political structures in terms of the ability of local entities to make legally binding decisions). The latter include understandings of the role of legal authority in local life (i.e., relationships with law enforcement) as well as the role of legal authority in solving local problems (i.e., relationships with the courts).

In Ranchito, these understandings contributed to the community's dominant orientations to political authority as a source of power and an entitlement, and to legal authority as a source of order maintenance. These orientations reflect the interpretations and experiences of residents who actively opposed the SVP placement. They were disproportionately white, with higher household incomes and levels of education than the town's overall population. Other segments of the population, particularly the one-third of residents who identified as Hispanic or Latino and the half who had lower socioeconomic statuses, may have had different orientations to political and legal authority than those most active in opposing the SVP placement, but they did not represent the most activated community members. The following sections describe the historical development of the Ranchito community's dominant orientations to authority and explain how they emerged during the community's response to the SVP placement.

Political Authority as Entitlement to Self-Governance

Community members in Ranchito viewed political authority as an entitlement. From this perspective, the community should have been able to use political authority to govern itself with little outside interference. The belief in a right to self-governance aligned well with local values of self-reliance, independence, and distrust of regional and state government. Before the SVP placement, the community's relationships with regional politicians and the town's position within formal political structures emphasized political autonomy, which contributed to its dominant orientation to political authority. This orientation in turn shaped how residents responded to the proposed placement in their town.

RELATIONSHIP WITH POLITICIANS
Historically, Ranchito subsisted mainly on farming and agriculture-related business. The town's agricultural base began to shift in the 1970s when an out-of-town developer planned and built Country Acres, a pseudonym for a subdivision southeast of town that was marketed to city dwellers as affordable, resort-style living in the beautiful hills outside the region's major metropolis. Urbanites moved to the area, but this created new social and economic divisions between newcomers and those who

had lived in Ranchito for generations. The planning group member who had been a school district trustee described the situation as "a strange relationship" because "a lot of the original people who bought [in Country Acres] were a little bit of a snobbier nature and so they really didn't want to consider themselves part of Ranchito." Tensions flared around the issues of growth and incorporation, especially as newcomers ousted those who had historically maintained political power in the town.[9] Although both sides fought for their respective positions, they did agree on one thing: Ranchito residents needed local control over future planning and development issues.

A fifteen-member, locally elected planning group emerged in the 1970s, partly as the result of a failed attempt to incorporate Ranchito as a city. According to the former school district trustee, without the tax base to support an independent city, residents formed the planning group to "at least give the appearance of local voice" in land-use issues. At first, the board of supervisors would not recognize the group under its planning group pilot program. It finally acquiesced after three years of pressure from local residents.

The planning group occupied the lowest rung of the regional political structure: it advised the board of supervisors on land-use issues, but only supervisors could make legally binding decisions. The school district trustee described the planning group as "not even like a city council. [. . .] We hold no legislative power whatsoever. So whatever we decide that we're going to vote on, it depends on really whether it matches with what the county wants to do to begin with." Another resident echoed these sentiments. "The biggest problem with the planning group," he said, "is [. . .] they have no power. [. . .] They can scream at the board of supervisors, but not much else." The PTA mother explained that the planning group "does have some clout, but not necessarily a whole lot in the way of authority." As these descriptions suggest, the group exercised mostly symbolic power to influence county decisions.

Although the planning group had only symbolic power, winning the right to have a planning group suggested the potential for Ranchitoans to prevail against stronger regional political powers. Indeed, the planning group came to symbolize local autonomy. The planning group chair explained how this happened:

Over the years, I think Ranchito has started listening to the county, which is very different. Because what they were doing was saying, "It's our way or the highway," when we're advisory and [the county has] the power. [T]he county would say [. . .] these are our rules and our ordinances, and the elected people on the planning group would say, "Well we don't like that," and they'd want [the county] just to change it. Well, they can't. There's ordinances that they have to follow or they're gonna get sued. So, I think through education of our members on that group, we have been able to understand the limitations that we have to play in so that we can be effective [. . .]. It was more like a grab-your-pitchfork kind of thing before.

This account illustrates how the planning group's interactions with the county contributed to the community's dominant orientation to political authority. Instead of resigning itself to county regulations, the planning group asserted the community's right to local control by rejecting county ordinances and proposing, as the construction company owner put it, "some real crazy solutions to problems that drove the county nuts." As this strategy failed to help the planning group achieve their goals, they learned how to "play" the political game to maintain control over local affairs.

Ranchito community members saw the planning group as one of "us": empowered community members working toward the collective good. While the local voice presented by the real estate brokers, business owners, and local builders who tended to be on the planning group did not represent every person in town, group members' resident status aligned them more closely with the community than outsider politicians. Indeed, Ranchito residents who actively opposed the SVP placement often referred to planning group members as part of the community. As the electronic militia leader said, "They're all community members. We know all those people. We vote for them, we go to their meetings. They all have businesses in town and have livelihoods in town, so they're very much us and we're very much them." Later, he elaborated, "The local planning group, generally speaking, is made up of members of the community and will work with the community and respond to the community."

Community members did not always perceive the planning group in this way. Many told me that in the past, some group members focused on their own issues instead of making decisions based on collective interests. As the head of the local trails association explained, "Some people [on the planning group], I don't know why they get involved. Usually they have an issue like they don't want a street to be paved [. . .]. It's like one single thing instead of being community-oriented. And I think a lot of those people are now gone because [. . .] the community became aware of who they were and stopped voting for them." Others made similar points that the planning group's more recent iterations tended to focus on the community rather than on individual agendas.

Yet even those who believed that individual planning group members "ha[d] their own agendas" perceived the group as a whole as acting in the interests of the community. For instance, the preschool board chair reflected on her failed attempt to stop owners of adjacent land from splitting their lots to build more houses on each plot. She said, "So I'm obviously not thrilled with [their decision to allow the landowners to split their lots]. But, as the planning committee pointed out, I'm the only one who's not splitting [lots], so they're in tune with the community and I'm not [. . .]. I don't always agree with them, but I understand." Other residents echoed her sentiments, saying that the group tried to "meet in the middle" to do "what's good for the community as a whole." According to this perspective, local politicians exercised what little power they had to protect local collective interests rather than to advance their own political careers.

The planning group's position at the bottom of the regional political hierarchy facilitated perceptions that it was aligned with the community. This became apparent during an interview I conducted with the group's secretary. We sat at a small table by the window of my motel room, catching glimpses of the motel parking lot and the pink-purple sky outside. As the sun set, the white woman in her early fifties provided detailed descriptions of Ranchito's people, politics, and culture. When it came to describing the town's political structure, she explained, "[Ranchito is] an unincorporated area and right there, you don't have the governmentship that you would have in a city [. . .]. And that's part of the problem with the unincorporated area is [. . .] you don't have a city council [. . .]. It's just loose. Everything's just more loosely knit." Her characterization of the local political structure provides an apt analogy for understanding how the planning group's political position contributed to local residents' perceptions of the group. Rather than a strictly formalized local political system, the "loose" political structure separated local leaders from formal political power, making it easier for them to present themselves as concerned citizens looking out for collective interests. For example, planning group members could signal their affiliation with the community by speaking out against county-level decisions, such as the SVP placement, that could negatively impact Ranchito. At the same time, they had little political power to influence those decisions. Thus, without the backing of a formal political structure, the planning group seemed more removed from politics than the board of supervisors.

While planning group members were the most local politicians, community members perceived the county supervisor for their region as having a greater affiliation with the community than other regional politicians. The trails association president noted that the county supervisor "really knows our community well." The local gun store owner whom I interviewed described her as being "very familiar with the ... feelings of most of the people in this community because she's sort of a country girl herself." The PTA father went so far as to describe her as "the real deal. She cares about her community." Whether perceiving their supervisor as part of the community or as a community-oriented outsider politician, many believed that, like the planning group, she worked in the interests of the community.

By contrast, residents had a more contentious relationship with the board of supervisors as a whole. As the construction company owner explained, "What's good for places down the hill [in the larger city] is not good for Ranchito. But, as a county administrator, you can't pass a rule, right, that says everybody but you. [...] So they pass rules that affect us up here that don't apply to us. [...] Why are we being told to do this when it doesn't affect us?" This sentiment reflected those of others who pointed out the social and geographic distance of the board of supervisors from the community. The electronic militia leader described the board of supervisors as "a bunch of disconnected jerks who care about the [nearby city] and nothing else." In this political climate, the planning group appeared more closely aligned with local collective interests than with the board of supervisors as a whole.

Overall, regional politicians tended to grant the community in Ranchito some degree of autonomy in governing themselves, particularly in terms of affording the planning group some limited advisory powers. At the same time, local politicians learned how to appease the board of supervisors to achieve their goals at least some of the time. Community members' sense of planning group members as part of the community and their county supervisor as community-oriented contributed to their sense that political authority could and should help them maintain control over local affairs.

POSITION WITHIN BROADER POLITICAL STRUCTURES

Relationships between the community in Ranchito and local and regional politicians occurred within broader political structures that shaped community members' interpretations of their interactions with these politicians. While the planning group's low position in the regional political hierarchy contributed to a perception that it was less political than other regional bodies, the group's decisions were still political in that they mediated between parties on local issues. One issue in particular, an ongoing debate over incorporating Ranchito as a city, came up repeatedly in my interviews with community members. Their discussions of the issue highlight how the community's position within formal political structures contributed to its dominant orientation to political authority as an entitlement.

Incorporation would have created a new political structure in Ranchito by allowing the town to establish a formal city government that would control local resources and services. According to the construction company owner, some advocates for incorporation argued that the community needed more "local influence on what goes on in our town." The former school district trustee, an advocate for incorporation, said that Ranchito was "too large a community not to be self-governing." When asked if his view of incorporation had anything to do with his negative perceptions of the county, he went on to say, "Probably. It's probably one of the reasons why I have been in favor of incorporation is because greater local control is what I'm into. [. . .] I think self-determination is our, is what those of us who are in favor of incorporating are mainly into because we believe that if decisions are gonna be made about Ranchito, they should be made in Ranchito." His comments illustrate that skepticism of county government did not always translate into skepticism of political power. Instead, advocates for incorporation believed that they were entitled to exercise local control over local issues and that current local and regional political structures precluded them from doing so. They wanted to, as the electronic militia leader put it, "control our destiny."

Opponents of incorporation advanced two main arguments. First, some believed the local economy could not sustain an independent city. As the construction company owner explained, "I don't see [incorporation] working because of the fact that there's no money, there's no base. You have to have some type of income, some kind of business, where there isn't in Ranchito." From this perspective, incorporation would require something Ranchito did not have: a solid base of taxpayers that could support a city's infrastructure and services.

Others, especially an extreme group that the construction company owner called "antigovernment [and] very individualistic," argued that incorporation would change Ranchito's rural atmosphere. The Tea Party couple whom I interviewed explained this perspective in more detail. As we sat in their living room, the husband began, "It sounds like a great idea to incorporate Ranchito because then we can keep the local taxes local, but then eventually it builds. Ranchito's gonna build up like next door in [a nearby town] and then next thing you know, you're—." "[The nearby town] used to be rural," his wife interrupted. She continued:

> I grew up down there. And now it's just a cookie-cutter city. [. . .] [Incorporation] was, in my view, the beginning of the end because it used to be rural like up here, and then as soon as they became a city, then they get a redevelopment agency, and the redevelopment agency comes in and buys up, forcibly, all the mom-and-pop businesses because they're not pretty, and puts in affordable housing and all this crap and then [the nearby town] looks exactly like [another town], which looks exactly like [another town].

As her comments indicate, some believed that incorporation would bring more political and bureaucratic structures to Ranchito, which would increasingly interfere with everyday lives. This argument indirectly implies that the formal political structures that would come with incorporation would eventually encourage those who govern to act more like politicians than empowered community members.

The incorporation debate illustrates that the community's position within the political structure contributed to its dominant orientation to political authority. Cliff summed up both sides of the issue by stating, "The good news [about not being incorporated] is that you got a lot of freedom. The bad news is [that] you can't get the roads paved." The "good news" suggests that the loose political structure in Ranchito could handle local issues without county interference. The "bad news" countered that assertion by highlighting how the lack of local formal political structures increased the community's dependence on regional politicians to solve larger problems. In either case, residents asserted their belief that, if properly situated in relation to the community, political authority could empower the community in Ranchito to remain an autonomous, self-governing entity.

Taken together, the successful fight for a planning group, the perception of local political leaders as acting in the interests of the community, and structural constraints on the planning group's ability to exercise formal political authority all contributed to a sense of political authority as embedded in and aligned with the community. The planning group represented a local access point to formal political authority, but its position within the formal political hierarchy and local perceptions of its members as pursuing collective interests made them seem like part of the community. While the emphasis on political power as enabling self-governance may have led individual community members to different conclusions when confronting local issues such as whether to incorporate, the community's dominant orientation toward political authority as a source of entitlement underscored many of community members' arguments. For these Ranchito residents, political authority represented a community-based source of power that residents had a right to access and deploy in the name of self-governance.

Orientation to Political Authority during the SVP Placement

While many of those I interviewed in Ranchito viewed the board of supervisors as protecting the interests of those in larger metropolitan areas, they also enjoyed the relative lack of interference in their everyday lives as county politicians granted them some political autonomy. Yet this autonomy did not stretch far enough for some who believed that the county "dumped" undesirable people and projects on their community. When residents learned of the proposed SVP placement, many linked it to this larger problem of Ranchito being used as a "dumping ground." This perspective emerged clearly and succinctly one afternoon during an interview I conducted with a white woman in her early fifties who had lived in Ranchito for eleven years and had served on the local trails and transportation committee. We sat in her living room with her small dogs lazing on the couch and floor around us. Near the beginning of our conversation, I asked her to tell me about her initial reaction to the proposed SVP placement. She responded, "Are you kidding me? Are you kidding me? They want to put that guy up here? Freaking, no. Absolutely, freaking no. You know, it's like, enough's enough. Ranchito gets dumped on a little bit." She then went on to explain, "I just think that when you are not in the city, it's like they sometimes will push problems out in the outer communities." For her and other people I spoke with who shared this perspective, the SVP placement became yet another instance of the county "pushing problems" to more rural areas.

The community's general orientation to political authority as entitlement to self-governance informed these types of interpretations of the SVP placement. The former member of the trails and transportation committee went on to explain later in our interview, "It was just one more thing from the county. 'Really? You really want to do that to our community?' [...] It was a little invasive. [...] I guess it just makes you realize, 'Boy, we better pay attention. We better be on guard.'" Her comments suggest a belief that the county not only had tried to "dump" the SVP in Ranchito but also had "invaded" local turf by using its political power to impose an unwanted person upon the community.

Even those who did not explicitly name county politicians as the problem approached the placement as a political issue. According to minutes from the community meeting, one woman presented herself as "a small business owner [who] pays her taxes." By mentioning her status as a taxpayer, this resident presented herself as a legitimate political actor who deserved to be listened to. When I asked one of the Tea Party activists what points she brought up at the meeting, she responded, "I don't even blame [the SVP]. I blame our legislators. How could you put the public in jeopardy this way?" These types of comments highlighted the political nature of placement even when they did not specifically mention or target county politicians.

Regardless of whom community members blamed for the placement, they believed in their right to have a say in the placement process. In a telephone interview, a local elementary school principal described community members' general perception of the placement. She said, "I think that the community was upset that it was just kind of popped, you know, 'Surprise!' The feeling was I think that it was intended to be kind of a stealth 'Let's move him in' without letting the community know about it beforehand." From this perspective, the community meeting disrupted plans to slide the SVP into town without the community's knowledge. Cliff supported this point of view when he spoke of the placement as something being "foisted upon the community" and then suggested that I interview the governor to find out how the decision had been made to place the SVP in Ranchito. At the same time, some perceived the community meeting as giving them a chance to have a say. As the construction company owner said, "If the county just did it and didn't tell anybody and we found out afterwards, I think that that's when you [would] get people that really [would] go off." While his comment contrasts with those of others who saw the siting decision as a more covert process, it shows the importance of having a say in a decision affecting local residents.

The SVP placement challenged the Ranchito community's dominant orientation to political authority by violating its perceived right to self-governance. Residents' sense of autonomy had been violated by what they thought was the county's decision to place the SVP in their town. To them, the placement represented an intrusion of big government into their daily lives and reinforced a belief that only local political entities such as the planning group should represent local interests, even when those entities had little actual power to change regional political decisions. Interpreted in light of the community's previous interactions with local and regional politicians and its position within formal political structures, these features of the SVP placement reflected and reinforced the community's dominant orientation toward political authority as a source of entitlement to govern themselves.

Legal Authority as Order Maintenance

Community members in Ranchito never perceived the SVP placement as an issue for law enforcement or the courts. This was partly because the planning group's leadership highlighted the political nature of the placement decision and the issue was quickly resolved in the community's favor. As a result, in interviews, local residents said little about the community's relationship with local law enforcement and even less about the courts. Nonetheless, their scant references to these entities suggested a dominant community orientation toward legal authority as a welcomed source of order maintenance, which may have led them to turn to the law if political avenues had failed to stop the SVP placement.

RELATIONSHIP WITH LAW ENFORCEMENT

Ranchito residents relied on the county sheriff's department for most law enforcement services. Although the department operated a substation in the middle of town, many people believed it was understaffed given the large area it had to cover, which included Ranchito and other nearby towns. One man with extremely right-wing, conservative views who had lived in Ranchito for more than thirty years and had been on the planning group in the past explained, "One of [the sheriff's department's] biggest problems is that they're grossly undermanned, understaffed." The planning group chair explained that sheriff's deputies had "a very, very large territory, [. . .] like 104 square miles. That's just Ranchito. So if they have to do all of that . . . you know what I mean? But I think they do a really good job." Others echoed these sentiments, with the head of the trails association saying, "We could probably use a few more officers, but I think the ones that we have are great." Thus, these residents had positive perceptions of their local law enforcement agency, despite a belief that it should have a greater presence in the area.

Two community members I spoke with were more skeptical of the sheriff's department. The design review board member recounted a series of incidents including an assault and a neighborhood home break-in that had not been resolved to her satisfaction. She then remarked, "The sheriffs really don't do anything in Ranchito. [. . .] They don't follow up and they, you know, I think they screw around too much." While this statement suggests a negative view of local law enforcement, she expanded upon her statement later in the interview by saying, "They try. You know. I would not want to be a sheriff." This qualifier suggests that her negative perceptions were tempered by a recognition that not all experiences with law enforcement can be positive.

The only other person to question the department's performance was the chair of a local preschool board. She said that she was "not overly impressed with the sheriff's department." She explained, "I would imagine it's like any other place that some of them are very nice, and very good and very helpful and others are a little bit . . . they have control issues. [. . .] Some of them are not that good. Now, now, and others are really good. [. . .] It's funny, they're either really, really caring and good and step up or really not." In this case, negative perceptions stemmed from bad experiences with a few officers who, according to her, did not represent the entire department. Thus, even those who critiqued local law enforcement tended to lean toward supporting them overall.

Officers' efforts to be involved in the community contributed to community members' generally positive perceptions. According to the planning group secretary, "They're approachable and if there's a problem, they're not like dictating the law to you. They're approachable. They'll smile and answer your questions and they don't put a huge gap with jargon and stuff." Others echoed the sentiment that local deputies had good rapport with the community, with the head of the trails association describing the relationship as follows: "They'll pop into businesses and, 'Hey, how ya doing,' and chat with the customers. And you know, they'll just stop in a restaurant, not to eat, just 'Hey, how ya doing.' And if they're in there eating for some reason or a cup of coffee, they talk to people. They know people, a lot of people by name." Some of these deputies also lived in Ranchito, which further aligned them with the community. As the PTA mother explained, "I think the sheriff's department does a wonderful job, mainly because in this part of Ranchito especially, the east side of town, we have a lot of current and retired law enforcement living in the neighborhood. So these people aren't just nameless, faceless people in uniform, they're our friends and neighbors." Similarly, the elementary school principal explained that law enforcement officers who lived in the community had "a local investment" when dealing with local issues. All these comments demonstrate that, at least for those active in opposing the SVP placement, law enforcement officers maintained a welcomed, visible presence in the community.

Some of community members' experiences with local law enforcement suggested the implementation of a community policing model in Ranchito. According to the planning group secretary, "Because the leadership is kind of approachable, I think that it filters down [to] the deputies. And I've never felt that they ever want to be heavy-handed. I've never felt like that. Like if they're there as a presence, they're there as a presence." The perception of law enforcement as "approachable" and providing a "presence" in the community defines a key element of community policing initiatives, which aim to empower local residents to prevent crime by collaborating with police officers to identify and solve local problems.

The planning group secretary indicated the recent implementation of some elements of community policing as she described the relationship between the community and local law enforcement. "Now there's the sheriff's advisory group where it involves citizens, and that used to not be the case," she said. "I think that's really pretty cool. I think it's nice that they care." Community policing strategies may have increased local support for the sheriff's department, but not always because community members felt empowered to help solve their own problems. Instead, the head of the trails association commented, "[The officers] that we have are great. The ones that I've met personally, they're on it. They really watch this community." For her and other residents I interviewed, officers' presence in Ranchito contributed to a sense that they "watched" the community, not that they helped the community identify and solve its own problems. While this kind of police surveillance could have come across as overbearing, those I spoke with tended to interpret officers' presence as helping to maintain order within the community.

Ranchito's relatively low crime rate facilitated the order maintenance interpretation of police activities in the town. Community members active in opposing the SVP placement generally perceived Ranchito as a safe place with a "fairly low crime rate." When talking about their interactions with the police, they tended to focus on responses to public order offenses such as traffic violations, drunk driving, vandalism, and graffiti. The PTA father I interviewed on the telephone described the ways in which he thought the sheriff's department did a great job:

They keep an eye out on speeders in the neighborhood, people's kids and pets and that kind of thing. They patrol the area, make sure there's no drunk driving or . . . it's easy because there's not a whole lot of places, and so there's just a big presence here. And . . . there's not a whole lot of real major crime or anything. It's, I would say there's just a certain element in town where there's your drugs [. . .] and that's amongst themselves. I don't really see any gang activity or anything horrible like that. So, it's that kind of community.

His appraisal highlights the role of order maintenance and low crime rates in perceptions of the police. The sheriff's department kept an eye out for signs of disorder, and officers' visibility on patrols demonstrated to community members that they were doing a good job of keeping the "horrible" crimes at bay within Ranchito. While vehicle break-ins and gang and drug activity also occurred in Ranchito, residents typically did not perceive these as chronic problems that indicated a failure of local law enforcement.

Some used stories of law enforcement responses to more serious crimes to describe the effectiveness of the police in the community. The planning group chair, whose office was in downtown Ranchito, recounted the following experience: "There was a nasty drug haven that was going on. And we knew when school was out because the kids from high school would come, park in our parking lot, walk down the alley to get drugs and leave. So [the sheriff's department] cleaned it all up and now it's been completely removed." Rather than blame the existence of the "nasty drug haven" on a failure of law enforcement, she lauded the sheriff's department for cleaning up the drug problem.

Her story also reflects a broader tendency among community members to let the police take care of local crime problems rather than solve them informally. For instance, a white woman in her midsixties who worked at a property management company described a situation in which her assistant's car was broken into and they called the sheriff's department for help. She said, "They were two little skateboarders, just went in and grabbed her purse. And we saw them. We knew they were right here in the neighborhood and we called the sheriff's department." Rather than approach the two thieves who were "in the neighborhood," they relied on the police to solve the problem. The electronic militia leader related a similar story in which he had relied on the police rather than informally resolving a problem with neighbors. He explained, "We had some neighbors frankly who were kind of out of control, when we moved into the house that we live in now. And we called the sheriff's [department] with some frequency on them for probably five or six years." Even in this situation, where the problem was "out of control" neighbors, the solution was to call the police rather than address the problem without law enforcement's help. All of these scenarios suggest that community members tended to leave the responsibility for order maintenance, and crime control more generally, to formal law enforcement.

Overall, community members supported and respected local law enforcement. Within the context of a relatively low crime rate in which public order crimes were the most pressing, residents' experiences with sheriff's deputies emphasized order maintenance. The police force maintained a presence in the community, and many community members perceived law enforcement officers as responsible for dealing with the relatively minor crimes that occurred in Ranchito. These relationships reflected and reinforced a sense that legal authority could and should be used to maintain order in the community.

RELATIONSHIP WITH THE COURTS

The relationship between the community in Ranchito and the courts is difficult to determine. No local historical issues involved high-profile court battles, and only four of the community members I spoke with even mentioned judges or the courts more broadly. While law enforcement and the courts both operate within the criminal justice system, it would be inaccurate to conclude that overwhelmingly positive perceptions of the sheriff's department translated into the same perceptions of judges and/or the courts. For instance, the preschool board chair who had been "not overly impressed with the sheriff's department" quickly followed her statement by saying, "The court system up here and the court in Ranchito, it's really good. We have a local court, and the judge there is very fair, very good." By offsetting her critique of local law enforcement with a positive appraisal of the courts, she demonstrated that negative perceptions of the police did not always apply to the courts and/or judges.

Two community members I spoke with were skeptical about the role of politics in judges' decisions. One of the Tea Party activists said that they had held a community event on "judges legislating from the bench." The man who spent most of our interview detailing his right-wing, conservative views about state and national government explained, "The only way we're gonna correct things is we have to change the makeup of the state legislature because the state is radically left-wing. And until we change the state legislature, which would eventually change the state courts because the judges are appointed by the governor, nothing's gonna change. It's gonna get worse and worse and worse." Both of these individuals expressed skepticism about courts and judges in general, but neither discussed their views of local courts or judges.

The other individual who mentioned the courts spoke more specifically about the situations in which community members tended to interact with local courts. The electronic militia leader explained, "We will band together when people need help, but there's also a healthy respect for privacy. So there's not a lot of, [. . .] not as much busybody stuff going on. There's not as much 'I'm gonna take you to court and sue you because your yard doesn't look the way I want it to.' There's just not much of that that goes on really." This comment shows how the community's values of self-reliance and independence translated into a general reluctance to take public order issues to court. Community members may have relied on local law enforcement to help solve these types of problems, but they did not necessarily bring them to court.[10]

The second example of interactions with the courts that the electronic militia leader gave implies a generally positive perception of how local judges resolved traffic violations. He said, "[Highway Patrol officers] issue tickets, but the tickets frequently get overturned in court because the guy goes down there, he says, 'Look, your honor, traffic's backed up half a mile. I'm trying to make a right turn, [. . .] there's no turn lane there, so I have to sit in traffic for [. . .] fifteen or twenty minutes to make a right turn to go into town and I'm the only car trying to make a right turn.'" The way that he recounted this story suggests his perception that local judges listened to community members' concerns about traffic tickets and then responded fairly.

These few comments about judges and/or the courts suggest that generally positive perceptions of law enforcement did not necessarily translate into the same perspective on the courts. Community members had conflicting views of the courts, some of which were tied to their broader perspectives on state and national politics. While the community tended to perceive legal authority as a source of order maintenance in their everyday lives, they did not necessarily rely as heavily on the courts for order maintenance as they did upon law enforcement.

Orientation to Legal Authority during the SVP Placement

Community members recognized that the courts played an important role in the final placement decision. Many sent letters to the judge to protest the proposed placement location, and one letter writer stated, "I am prepared to voice my opposition publicly at the hearing, and anticipate that there will be a substantial number of parents and other community members at that hearing." Had the hearing actually occurred, perceptions of the law as a source of order maintenance may have shaped how the community interacted with the courts. However, Cliff's refusal to rent his property precluded the hearing, and local residents never interacted directly with the judge.

While community members never blamed law enforcement or the courts for the proposed placement decision, their orientation to legal authority shaped how they interacted with and perceived local law enforcement during the brief controversy over the SVP placement. Sheriff's deputies attended the community meeting, and the planning group chair explained that she had "asked them to come to that meeting to keep the peace." For her, the sheriff's department had to be at the meeting to maintain order. While her role as the planning group chair was to maintain order in public meetings, she also recognized that more contentious meetings such as the one about the SVP placement required the support of formal law enforcement. As she went on to explain, "Whenever we've had the sheriffs come to any of the meetings, it has only been to maintain civil order if I can't. [. . .] I don't think if they weren't there that [people in the audience] would have listened to me at all." These comments suggest a perception that order within the meeting may have been jeopardized without law enforcement presence.

Just as community members generally welcomed law enforcement's presence in the community, they also appreciated the presence of police at the meeting. The electronic militia leader characterized the deputies at the meeting as "professional." He went on to say, "They were at the meeting in terms of keeping order. They were clearly, they were not there to affect people's opportunity to voice their opinion, they were there because the sergeant said they had to be there, so they were very professional at the meeting." A mother whose daughter attended a nearby elementary school agreed, saying, "They were prepared for whatever was gonna happen. And like I said, I went in there thinking there was gonna be torch-wielding citizens." These comments demonstrate that these audience members interpreted the law enforcement presence as key to order maintenance rather than a heavy-handed display of police power.

Community Orientations to Authority and Political Mobilization

In Ranchito, dominant community orientations to political and legal authority facilitated an emphasis on political actions in the response to the proposed SVP placement. When the placement emerged as the latest political battle, residents came together around the institutional authority that symbolized their right to maintain control over local affairs. The community may also have pursued legal strategies, but the short-lived nature of the issue meant that, as one of the Tea Party activists put it, "It backed off before it went into the court. Before [the judge] made a call on it, they pulled everything away." Considering the local context in which community members generally perceived the law as a source of order maintenance, they never came to see the issue as a problem that legal institutions had created or that required legal mobilization to resolve. Instead, for them, the proposed SVP placement in Ranchito represented another attempt by outside politicians to unfairly wield their power. Rather than rejecting political authority, the community rallied around the planning group's symbolic use of power to stop the placement.

Political mobilization may have been interpreted quite differently in a community with a different racial makeup and socioeconomic status. Poor, urban minorities often find themselves and their interests organized out of political structures.[11] When they do become involved in formal politics, they must fight to have their voices heard. These kinds of interactions can increase skepticism about the benefits of political mobilization because such actions rarely work in favor of community interests. For the community in Ranchito, a community with a history of

interactions with politicians that emphasized the use of political authority to retain autonomy (even in the absence of actual political clout) and
a local governing body loosely connected to a formal political structure,
political mobilization fit with local understandings of political authority
as a potentially useful tool for retaining local control over controversial
issues.

Community members' strong support for the planning group's actions reflected their belief in the legitimacy of political authority when
deployed locally. For instance, the former member of the trails and
transportation committee explained:

> The thing is if you don't stand up and [. . .] fight against things you don't
> want, things you don't believe in, things that you feel would be destruc-
> tive to your community, boy we'd have all kinds of crap up here. And
> people would just have their way. People that did not have our best inter-
> ests at heart. See, we have our best interest at heart. Did those people that
> were gonna put him up here? No. That's because that's not their focus.
> Their focus is where are we gonna dump this guy, basically.

According to this resident and others who shared her perspective, they
had successfully fought other undesirable people and projects by mobilizing with those who "have our best interest at heart." This perspective
illustrates that rather than reject political authority as useless for achieving collective goals, community members embraced this authority as a
power that could work in their interests despite a relative lack of formal
power at the local level.

The political reality of a relatively powerless political body representing the community did not dampen community members' belief in
the use of political authority to stop the SVP placement. The electronic
militia leader explained, "In essence, [the planning group] knew they
were powerless, so they were all supportive because they knew that they
couldn't do anything to keep [the SVP] out. [T]hey could pass a resolution saying [the SVP] should not be here, but . . . so they were all in
favor of it because there was 350 people there that had pitchforks and
torches." Later in the interview, he went on to say that the community's
response to the placement "validated everything I know" about the planning group. Thus, despite skepticism of the planning group's actions as

essentially powerless and simply meant to placate an angry audience, he retained his belief that these local politicians would and should work in the interests of the community to stop the placement.

As a political entity, the planning group's efforts to organize a collective response could have failed if residents had perceived these actions as a ploy to further the political careers of the group's members. Instead, the people I spoke with perceived the planning group's actions within the context of their previous relationship with the group as part of the community. Looking back on the meeting, many described it as the community's successful fight against an undesirable political project. "The community did it," said the religious mother. "If there's a hero, the community is." The planning group secretary expanded on this view when she said, "I thought it was really an amazing thing to not get him placed up here, that they decided not to do it because of the community outcry." These kinds of comments make no distinction between the planning group's political actions and the community, suggesting the close connection between the two.

The planning group's relative lack of formal political authority further facilitated its actions becoming the centerpiece of the community's response to the SVP placement. The elementary school principal supported this perspective by saying, "They're not a decision-making body for something like that, but I think that they, the planning group, saw themselves as a group that could pull something like this together." By "pulling together" the meeting, the planning group provided physical and discursive space in which the community (rather than local politicians) emerged as the central actor in the response. At the same time, providing a space for audience members to publicly assert their right to self-governance allowed the planning group to become even more embedded in the community after the SVP placement issue. As the head of the trails association described, community members "gave a little bit more credence and credibility to the planning group. [. . .] Because the planning group agreed with the community. [. . .] We all feel the same way. All of us." Thus, despite the planning group's symbolic reliance on political authority to maintain status within the community, it represented the community and its collective interests during the SVP placement, which further entrenched planning group members in the community after the placement fell through.

When I interviewed the planning group chair, she described that group as being more like other local groups than a political entity. For instance, when asked if she thought the same kind of response would have occurred had some other group held the meeting, she responded:

> I think if the chamber [of commerce] would've put it on, I think that if a real estate firm would've hosted it, they would all come. Because it would've been the one thing that, you know, the voice, the people could be heard. And get information on. [. . .] It wasn't about it being the planning group, it was because we stepped up and did it. All the other entities were scrambling around and saying, well, how do we react to this and what do we do and what do we say, well, I can't get the people here . . . [laughs].

While these remarks downplay the role of political capital in bringing residents together, they suggest that the planning group presented itself as a community group in Ranchito. This self-presentation may have contributed to the extent to which community members perceived the community meeting and the planning group's resolution as a key part of their response to the proposed SVP placement.

Community members may not have perceived these actions as central to their response to the placement had they not had a sense of political authority as a source of power that should and could help them solve their local problem. Allowing residents to "have a voice" through the community meeting certainly spurred the collective response, but the planning group's unique position as loosely connected to formal political power and part of the community contributed to the sense that the meeting itself was the community's response. In a context in which the community felt entitled to leverage political authority to maintain its autonomy from outside political forces and had previously done so through the planning group, the community meeting represented a gathering of peers working to resolve a local issue rather than a group of self-interested politicians trying to gain favor with their constituents or position themselves for higher office.

In many ways, Ranchito's planning group acted in the same way as other local politicians who have spoken out against SVP placements in their areas. While community members usually agree that SVPs should not live in their neighborhoods, not all communities embrace their local politicians' actions. Skepticism of political power can lead some to perceive local politicians as career-oriented and simply saying what they must to further their political careers. Similarly, the community in Ranchito could have written off the planning group's attempts to address the SVP placement as political maneuvering by politicians interested in maintaining their local status. Instead, community members rallied around their local political leaders, whom they perceived as representing the community's interests even in the absence of any real power to do so. Having access to a local political entity and building a collective identity as a community contributed to the emergence of political mobilization in the response to the SVP placement, but the events in Ranchito suggest that the community's dominant orientations to political authority shaped the centrality of political actions to its response.

The Aftermath

Ranchito residents dealt with the placement issue for little more than three weeks. During this relatively short period, they came together to oppose what they believed was an unjust decision to place the SVP in an unsuitable home. The chair of the preschool board described the aftermath as "a huge sense of victory and accomplishment for them. Or should I say, for us. They felt like they spoke their minds and they were heard and it made a difference. And that's the whole basis of being an American. That one person can make a difference." Both the local elementary school principal and the religious mother said they gave a "collective sigh of relief" after the placement fell through.

While many celebrated the local opposition efforts, they also noted few long-term effects on the community. The religious mother said she felt "closer to the community" for a short time after, but then she went on to explain that "after everything was said and done and the news died down and it wasn't in our faces and [. . .] we were victorious, I think after all of that [. . .] everybody kind of went back to [. . .] our normal small-town, laid-back routine." The electronic militia leader tried to maintain his group, but the collective energy did not translate into activism on other local issues. He explained, "I started another [Facebook] group called Ranchito Electronic Militia, and the idea was to maybe try to harness some of that energy for other issues. But it turned out that that energy just dissipated faster than it arose." Perhaps winning the battle reinforced perceptions of the strength of the community and thus created no lasting changes.

As in other cases in California in which rental arrangements fell through in proposed SVP placements, the housing search committee in Ranchito's county resumed its search, continuing to work with Health Corp and the judge to identify a suitable placement location. As the deputy district attorney assigned to the case described it, "All of us involved in this process knew that Health Corp was probably between a rock and a hard place [when the placement in Ranchito fell through]. [. . .] [A] judge might, as has happened in other counties, release a patient as a homeless transient sex offender here in the county. And nobody wanted that." Instead, some of those on the search committee "encouraged Health Corp to reconsider the possibility of working with the Department of Corrections" to house the SVP in the trailer he had previously occupied on state prison grounds.

From Health Corp's perspective, the trailer presented some problems. A representative explained, "The Department of Corrections wasn't eager to have any more SVPs placed on their property. They didn't want to be a dumping ground for SVPs. [. . .] We really needed to try and find him housing in the community because this was community reintegration, not isolation on a prison somewhere." Despite these drawbacks of placing the SVP on prison grounds, Health Corp eventually struck a deal with the California Department of Corrections and Rehabilitation to house him in the trailer. Seven months after his second release, the SVP returned to court on allegations that he had violated his conditions by failing to disclose sexual thoughts to his therapist. Almost three years later, after no further incidents, the SVP was released unconditionally. As of February 2017, he was living in the large city near Ranchito, and no other SVP placements had occurred in Ranchito.

Conclusion

In some ways, Ranchito's story is straightforward: residents perceived the SVP placement as a political issue, and they rallied around political mobilization to fight their battle. Yet, they did so despite a lack of formal political power held by their local political body. Although community members may have deployed other strategies for opposition had the placement proceeded after the community meeting, their dominant orientation to political authority facilitated political mobilization becoming the centerpiece of their response. In a place in which political authority seemed like a useful tool for self-governance, community members perceived political mobilization as a community-based response. In other words, Ranchito politicians leveraged their tenuous connection to political authority to serve as activists within and for the community.

The planning group inhabited a unique space between individual community members and formal political structures. In responding to the SVP placement, the planning group negotiated its position within the community by drawing on its largely symbolic political power to pursue a perceived collective good. But what if the community had had none of these local political activists? How might a community in a place with no formal political body or any other local political ties fight an SVP placement? The next chapter attends to this situation by examining the community response to a proposed SVP placement in Deserton, a place where social and geographic isolation from formal political institutions precluded political mobilization and contributed to a very different strategy for opposition.

3

Litigating in a Rural Outpost

Well, if you want to oppose something like this, you probably well know that you have to do it legally. You can't just
make telephone calls and so on and so forth.
—Deserton woman, owner of a local trailer park

The previous chapter described the situation in Ranchito, where the
community's orientation toward political authority as a source of
entitlement and legal authority as a source of order contributed to the
centrality of political mobilization in its response to an SVP placement.
While the community in Ranchito benefited from its political relationships, other communities lack ties to formal political institutions. Such
was the case in Deserton, an unincorporated rural town in Southern
California that one resident described in a television interview as "an
economically depressed and politically impotent area." In contrast to
the Ranchito community's sense of entitlement to political authority,
community members in Deserton experienced political isolation: they
could not leverage political authority because they had no political ties.
Instead, when a judge ordered an SVP placement in Deserton in 2009,
the absence of local politicians and isolation from formal political institutions dampened prospects for political mobilization and indirectly
bolstered support for legal mobilization.

At the time of the controversy over the SVP placement, Deserton
looked like little more than a dusty collection of buildings that had seen
better days. A former prison town, it was physically and socially isolated
from nearby communities, and the two hundred predominantly white
residents went about their lives without much outside interference.
Twelve miles southeast of a defunct mine and prison site, Deserton's
main street boasted a café and post office, but other shops and the town's
only gas station had long been closed. All that remained of the town
were a small residential neighborhood, a market, two cafés, and the post

office. To buy groceries and other household necessities, residents had to drive fifty miles to the next town over.

A strong sense of independence permeated the tight-knit community. Community members described Deserton as quiet, peaceful, and safe. There were no local formal political structures, and the sheriff's department tended to provide only minimal law enforcement services. When residents learned of the proposed SVP placement, they banded together to support a lawsuit against the county. Although they ultimately failed to stop the placement, many community members judged their efforts as successful because the lawsuit gave them a voice in a local political arena in which they were usually invisible.

At first glance, Deserton's legal mobilization may seem to be a simple case of community members turning to the law when they could not leverage political power to make their claims heard. This explanation echoes other research on the circumstances under which individuals and groups bring their disputes to court,[1] but it cannot fully account for why litigation became the central response strategy in Deserton. Community members had many reasons to be cynical about the power of law. First, a judge had ordered the placement even though Health Corp representatives had expressed concerns about Deserton's geographic isolation and lack of services. The judge had to balance these concerns with the SVP statute's requirement for release, a placement process that had taken almost a year, and a lack of other feasible sites. The order for the SVP to move to Deserton, along with a community meeting spearheaded by law enforcement officials and, more broadly, state law allowing for the release in the first place all indicated a failure of the law to protect the community in Deserton. For these reasons, the SVP placement could have resulted in increased legal cynicism among community members in Deserton.[2] Instead, they rallied around litigation efforts.

Considering the law's failure to protect the community, why did legal authority seem to be a viable alternative to mobilizing political authority? How did legal mobilization emerge as the central strategy in the community's response to the SVP placement? The answers to these questions lie in understanding the community's relationships with the public faces of formal political and legal institutions. This chapter explains how the Deserton community's orientations to political and legal authority shaped its opposition to the SVP placement. In particular, the community's orientation toward political authority as a source of invisibility and toward legal authority as a source of protection legitimized litigation as a strategy for opposition. Instead of legal cynicism, residents perceived political and legal authority as separate forms of power, with political authority as biased and unable to help them, and legal authority as basically unbiased and a useful tool for achieving their collective goals. Some have described this phenomenon as a sense of the law as being above politics; whereas politics is the messy, value-laden business of governance, the law is a higher power that governs without the biases of human beings.[3] Deserton's story expands upon this perspective by showing how local relationships with the public faces of formal institutions can protect against legal cynicism and foster a sense of the law as a tool to achieve collective goals, even in a community that is geographically and socially isolated from those formal institutions.

Organizing against an SVP in Deserton

In June 2009, sheriff's deputies began distributing flyers that announced the impending release of an SVP in Deserton and gave information about an upcoming meeting. One woman, a waitress at the truck-stop café who had grandchildren living in a nearby town, recounted in a telephone interview how she first heard about the placement. "Well, I was one of the first ones to hear because I was at work at the store," she said. "And the police came in and handed me a flyer and told me that they were gonna be having a meeting at the [community] hall because they were placing this sexual predator here." What, I asked her, was her initial reaction, her very first thought upon receiving the flyer? "Seriously," she responded, "you're not kidding me are you? There's gotta be some kind of a joke. Who in their right mind would put a violent sexual predator in the middle of this little small community where there's no police? Where there's no law enforcement? Where he can't be watched or monitored?" Upon hearing the news, she "got on the phone and started calling everybody."

According to other community members, the café waitress, a white woman in her fifties, often served as a source of information about local news. When she began "calling everybody" about the SVP placement, local social networks exploded with the news. Within a few days, most people had heard that a sexually violent predator might be moving into town. Many were stunned that someone had chosen their tiny town—a place where kids spent their free time playing in the desert, and law enforcement rarely visited—as a suitable location for an SVP. Unanswered questions began to circulate. Who had made the decision? How had they decided on Deserton? What was a sexually violent predator? Was he even from the area? What was the best way to stop this from happening? According to a white retiree in his early seventies who had moved to Deserton six years earlier, the community went from "zero to one hundred miles per hour."

In the ensuing two weeks, residents began to strategize about the best way to voice their opposition during the notification meeting. They began to list reasons why Deserton would be an unsuitable location for the placement: a lack of jobs, no public transportation, no anonymity, and no local law enforcement. In a telephone interview, a white mother in her early forties who had been born and raised in Deserton and had recently returned after a ten-year absence explained some of these concerns. She said she was "shocked and appalled" by news of the placement because it violated "all of [the SVP]'s rights, to be honest with you." When I asked her to expand on her statement, she explained, "Well, I used to work for the prison and I worked in the medical field and he, he's supposed to be able to be in a location where he can get a job and get medical help because he's got a mental illness. And access to things and be able to get back into society. You don't come out here to learn to conform to society. There is no society out here." This perspective, while not expressed by most community members I spoke with, demonstrates that at least some residents considered the placement from the SVP's perspective.

Along these same lines, another person I spoke with mentioned the cruelty of confining the SVP to a trailer in the middle of the desert without any chance for social interaction. I visited this white woman in her late eighties one afternoon in the trailer park that she owned. We sat in her office for an informal conversation. I did not record it, but later that day I wrote in my field notes: "She reiterated many times throughout the conversation that it wasn't fair to him to be out there all by himself. 'It's cruel' to keep him out there, she said." Her comments, like those of the

woman born and raised in Deserton, framed concerns about the placement in terms of the SVP's potential experiences living in Deserton.

As in Ranchito, these two women and others believed that emotional
pleas would not sway the panel of law enforcement and political officials
who would be at the notification meeting. Instead, they urged fellow
community members to think "logically" about the issue. The woman
born and raised in Deserton explained, "We tried to keep people as calm
and focused as much as we could and make them look at it from a logical
perspective because getting hysterical wasn't going to do us any good."
A clerk in the general store, a white woman in her early fifties who had
previously worked as a prison guard, echoed these ideas when she said,
"We talked about what some of the issues were, what we wanted to ask
because they told us you're only limited to three minutes or a minute to
talk or something, so we kind of had a game plan together as, 'Okay, you
ask this question, you ask this question.'" By organizing in this way, community members explicitly tried to challenge the stereotype of communities as vigilante mobs hysterically trying to keep SVPs out at all costs.

Even so, some in Deserton periodically brought up the possibility of
burning down the trailer or engaging in some other physical action to
prevent the placement. The café waitress explained, "I absolutely think
that every time that they did something to put [the SVP] in somewhere,
[the house] should've been sabotaged in one way or another." She went on
to say, "When they had that big tank for the water put in, shoot a couple
of gun holes in it. Make them have to replace it. When they got the wires
put in for his electricity out there, go out there and cut it a few times. You
know?" One man in his early thirties who described himself as white and
"Indian" had moved with his wife to Deserton about five years earlier.
He mentioned similar protest tactics when he explained that during the
placement issue, he thought, "'Hey, everybody's angry about this, if that
thing caught on fire, we got 126 residents out here, you got 126 suspects.
[. . .] If it burns down, are they gonna do another one?' Probably not
because at that point, how do they bring him there? [. . .] That's showing
that, 'Hey, these people are angry, it's not safe for the guy to be here.'" In
a rural outpost such as Deserton, community members could easily have
engaged in property damage as a protest strategy, just as activists elsewhere have done in response to a variety of other social issues.[4]

Yet, neither vandalism nor violence occurred in Deserton. When asked why not, some pointed to the community's overt efforts to quell such impulses. For instance, the waitress followed her comments about sabotaging the placement location by explaining, "Believe me, there was a few people around here that were crazy enough. [. . .] And they would have done it. And we had to talk them out of doing it. [. . .] We had to say 'No, you can't do that. No matter how much we would stand behind you if you did it, we don't want you going to jail or doing it.' Because there are a couple crazies out here that were more than willing." At another point in the interview, she reinforced these ideas by saying, "We as a community decided that we were not gonna do anything illegal to put any of us in danger of going to jail over this. It wasn't worth any one of us going to jail." The general store clerk made similar comments during our interview, saying, "It's like, 'Hey you know what, he ain't worth going to jail for. Because he's gonna screw up. He's gonna do it to himself.'" While community members may have felt taken advantage of by those in power, they chose not to risk being held liable for illegal actions against the SVP or his placement in Deserton. Instead, even though legal actors had proposed the SVP placement in their town in the first place, community members united to find legally legitimate means to stop the placement.

The emphasis on legal actions may have shifted had the SVP reoffended in the community. A man who had expressed his "disappointment" in people for not acting on their talk of vandalism qualified his statement by saying, "But, am I gonna risk getting in trouble and losing my family for that? No, because they're not the victim at that point. Would I risk it if he did something to them? Absolutely." If his family had been victimized, he said he would have enacted his own version of justice. "Let me get him," he said. "You know, that sounds bad, but . . . all they're gonna do is give him a good time again. He's [in] jail, that's what he wants. Maybe that's not what he wants, but he'd want that better than I guess [. . .] my justice. [He laughed.] I don't mean to be bad about it, but it's the truth." His comments demonstrate that while community members may not have wanted to go to jail when opposing the placement, they may have considered violence to achieve justice if the SVP had victimized their family or friends.

With the community generally set on eschewing violence and vandalism for legal strategies to oppose the placement, one man whom I will call Jack began researching California's SVP statutes. Jack, a white man in his early sixties, had lived in Deserton for about five years. At the time of the proposed SVP placement, he lived in a local trailer park, but he had recently purchased property across the road from the proposed placement location. He recounted how he found out about the placement and then quickly realized that it was near his newly purchased plot of land:

> [The trailer park owner] handed me the flyer. Because the sheriff, I think it was the sheriff's deputies, had come around to distribute the flyer about [the SVP]. They were going up and down the roads here handing them out to people. So, she told the sheriff's deputy, "I need two because I need to give one to my neighbor." That would be me. She comes up and hands me this thing and I'm looking at it and I'm thinking, "What's this? Is this some guy who used to live here who's coming back after spending twenty years in jail?" I had no clue who he was. And then I looked at the address where he was supposed to live and I said, "Wait a minute, that's right across the road from my property." And then that was when I first found out. I think it was four o'clock on a Thursday afternoon.

As with other community members, Jack had never heard of an SVP, much less the process by which the state placed these individuals into communities. He had had some experience as a contract writer for the government, so he used his skills in interpreting legal statutes to pore over California's SVP law. After much research, he decided that the law restricted counties' involvement in placement decisions, and that officials in his county had had too much influence in the decision in Deserton. Upon reaching this conclusion, he began planning legal action against the county. By the time the community notification meeting rolled around, he had a solid legal plan.

Deserton's Community Notification Meeting

The community notification meeting occurred late on a warm summer afternoon in June 2009. Residents who had arrived early sat in rows of folding chairs facing a panel of people, including the county supervisor's director of communications, a deputy district attorney, and a representative from Health Corp. Others, including myself, stood along the back wall of the community hall. To ensure order, a field operations chief from the sheriff's department moderated the discussion. Audience members passed their names to the chief, who then called each person to the microphone at the front of the room. Sheriff's deputies lined the perimeter of the room, providing an additional law enforcement presence.

The meeting unfolded much like those I had attended in other places. Audience members asked the usual range of questions, from those involving procedural issues such as how the site had been chosen to practical concerns such as how residents should defend themselves in the event of a reoffense. One man asked about the decision-making process and ended by telling the panel: "Don't dump your trash here." Others declared that the men in town would protect the women in any way possible, "even if they have to go to jail." One woman said that her son would protect his sisters by any means necessary. While these statements contradicted those of people who said they did not want anyone to go to jail over the issue, they also indicated the volatility of the situation.

Some approached the microphone with more place-specific concerns that involved tales of doors that usually remained unlocked, children allowed to roam the desert or walk alone to the café in their free time, and unsupervised early-morning waits at the school bus stop. Others explained how their previous victimization experiences made them especially fearful of the upcoming placement; one abuse victim said that she had moved away from a bigger city to minimize her risk of becoming a victim again. With these types of comments, community members intended to "logically" prove that Deserton was not a suitable place for a sexually violent predator.

The people on the panel responded to the audience's concerns by emphasizing that the law required the SVP's release. Panel members said that the SVP would be strictly supervised and that the sheriff's department would work closely with Health Corp personnel to ensure public safety. The field operations chief frequently stated that one purpose of the meeting itself was to enlist community members to be the eyes and ears of the department. He urged residents to call 911 if they saw the SVP doing anything "suspicious." Communities in other rural towns have had similar experiences in which law enforcement officials urge local residents to report signs of criminal activity.[5] This strategy can have unintended consequences, as recounted in Garriott's ethnography of one rural community's efforts to combat drug problems. In that community, law enforcement's encouragement of informal surveillance ultimately created and reinforced implicit divisions between community members as they categorized each other based on signs of suspicious behavior. Daily interactions became tinged with legal implications, which provided new meaning to law enforcement in the town. While the SVP placement in Deserton differed from combating drug problems in that it involved the state essentially importing a problem into the community, in both cases, asking local residents to watch for and report suspicious behavior highlighted the role of the community in its own protection. This in turn implied some local responsibility for residents to keep themselves safe.

As the meeting in Deserton progressed, community members grew increasingly dissatisfied with the sometimes vague and noncommittal answers from people on the panel. At one point, rumblings of dissatisfaction boiled over when a man stood and demanded to know why the district attorney's representative shrugged her shoulders and rolled her eyes whenever people in the audience asked questions. She responded, "I'm sorry you don't like my mannerisms, but that's just how I am." To this, audience members mumbled their disapproval. The man who had initially challenged her said she was not answering the community's questions and asked if she wanted to be there. After a moment's hesitation, she affirmed that she did.

The meeting adjourned after an hour and a half. The audience filtered out of the community center, and a few people lingered in the gravel parking lot to discuss the meeting and the proposed placement. I stood with them, listening to their conversations. Some implied that they might tamper with the land on which the SVP's trailer would be installed by, for example, pouring cement into the well to obstruct the water supply. According to the field notes I wrote later, one woman stated, "As soon as he messes up . . . I don't want to say he's a dead man, but . . ."

While these were extreme reactions, residents shared a common sentiment that the meeting had been a waste of time. In an interview, one man, a retired "ex-cop," referred to the meeting as "an afterthought," saying that "the decision had already been made." The general store clerk agreed, saying, "What we didn't know [before the meeting] was that the decisions had already been made. It didn't matter what you said to them, he was coming out here. 'Too late, the judge already made the decision, you're it.' And that's what it all boiled down to and that's when people really got upset." Others said that officials could have achieved the same result by simply mailing an informational letter. When I interviewed a local environmentalist, a white woman in her midfifties, she described her reaction: "'Why are you even having a meeting? Send us a letter that we're gonna get a pervert.' It's just that they say, 'Oh, we went and talked to the community. The community knew what was gonna happen, so we sure covered all our bases.' Big deal." In short, residents felt ignored and belittled by a decision that had been made before they had even had a chance to give their input.

Community members' dissatisfaction with the notification meeting reflects and contradicts previous research on such meetings in other places. Two elements should have contributed to satisfaction with the meeting: local law enforcement directly disseminated information about the meeting to residents, and the meeting included information about legally legitimate strategies for self-protection.[6] These two elements may not have facilitated satisfaction with the meeting in Deserton because law enforcement and other officials failed to clearly state the purpose of the meeting beforehand. The flyers distributed to community members simply stated information about the SVP and the time, date, and location of the upcoming meeting. Thus, residents went into the meeting expecting to have their legitimate concerns accounted for; when they realized the decision had already been made, they became even more upset. This experience suggests that all three elements—direct notification by law enforcement, information about self-protective strategies, and clearly stated purposes—may be critical to ensuring the public's satisfaction with notification meetings.

Despite residents' discontent, the notification meeting in Deserton served an important function of bringing community members together and providing them an opportunity to plan further actions. Indeed, the days and weeks after the meeting brought a flurry of conversations about actions they might take to stop the placement. "We kinda rallied together," said the mother born and raised in Deserton. "Everybody picked their little assignments and everybody started doing research. We were trying to get the media involved, we were pushing for the media to be involved in what was going on out here." From these various activities, two main strategies emerged as the most prominent: protests across the street from the proposed placement site and litigation against the county.

Protests

The first collective responses after the meeting came in the form of protests. Jack allowed community members to use his recently purchased plot of land across the highway from the proposed placement site for their protests. He explained, "What I was telling people was don't [protest] on [the SVP]'s side of the highway. [. . .] If you're on [the SVP]'s side, you may get into trouble with the sheriff and besides that, you've got a very narrow area to be on and it's also dangerous because cars go by sixty-five miles per hour. So I said come on, [protest] on my side." At first, about twenty residents gathered on his property by the side of the highway, holding signs with slogans such as "Honk for no sexual predators!" They had two main goals: to let the county know that they would not accept the placement without a fight and to raise awareness among passing motorists who often made pit stops in Deserton on their way to other places. According to the café waitress, "People would stop and ask us questions. We were passing out flyers to cars as they went by." The general store clerk explained, "We didn't do anything illegal. We were not on the road, we weren't impeding traffic, we were not on the property. We were just out there letting people know with our signs up that there's a pervert that's living over there." For both women, the protests served as a legally acceptable way to increase visibility for their cause.

Although the protests may have caught the attention of passing motorists, they likely had little, if any, impact on county officials. Indeed, Jack noted that he never believed the protests would change the placement decision, but he still encouraged the protesters to use his land because, as he put it, "I thought that it would be good for the community to have a way to protest. [. . .] It was an outlet. 'If you want to express yourself, here's how you can do it, you'll be safe, and you won't get hit by a car.'" The local environmentalist I interviewed concurred, saying, "It's very cathartic to just scream your head off and [have] it be socially acceptable. [. . .] It felt like people had a little bit of control over what was happening. Even though we had no control, it felt like there was some control that we were doing something." Community members knew that they had to find ways to express their concerns in ways that political authorities might recognize as legitimate while at the same time allowing residents an opportunity to vent their concerns without breaking the law.

Eventually, the protests died down. Community members returned to their daily lives as summer temperatures rose and it became clear that protesting would not keep the SVP out of their town. While the protests had given them a chance to band together against the placement, achieving their goals would require a new strategy to put more pressure on county politicians.

Litigation

Throughout California, litigation emerged as a potential strategy for opposition to SVP placements; however, in many places, residents discussed legal strategies without ever moving forward with a formal lawsuit. In these communities, the complexities of the legal system and the monetary costs associated with filing a lawsuit outweighed the slight chance of a victory in court. For this reason, communities often limited their court engagement to the invited public comment portions of formal court hearings.

In some ways, the litigation in Deserton emerged from participation in one such public comment period. Jack attended a hearing to inform the court of potential violations of county land-use ordinances. He had been trying to develop his own vacant parcel of land, and he had had difficulties obtaining the required building permits. From this experience, he surmised that the county had not undergone the proper permitting process to make the placement site habitable. In court, he argued that the land on which county officials had planned to install a trailer to house the SVP was neither zoned nor ready for residential use. He won. The judge ordered the county to bring the land up to code before placing a dwelling on the site. As a result, the placement was stalled for a few months. This minor victory may have bolstered community support for further litigation against the placement.

After his first victory in court, Jack continued to litigate. He was convinced that California's SVP law was "a good law" that had been improperly implemented. In our conversations, he consistently cited his concern that the county had had "undue influence" on the siting decision. While he understood that SVPs had to be placed in their counties of last residence, he believed that county politicians had had too much sway in the decision to put the SVP in Deserton. From his perspective, politicians had lobbied for the placement in Deserton to minimize the political impact of the siting decision.

Jack may have been right that the county was more involved than usual in the decision to place the SVP in Deserton. The county's public information officer refused to speak with me, but others involved in the placement process suggested that the location of the placement reflected the county's preference. According to one insider, "It was unusual to have the county as involved in this as they were in this case. The county was really involved in this. [T]here were representatives from a number of different departments at the hearings and involved in the [judge's] chambers conferences, which is unusual." While the extent of the county's involvement appeared unusual, it remains unclear whether it was illegal.

Jack initially attempted to obtain information about the placement decision directly from the county, but he had little faith that county officials would produce the requested documents. At one point, he forwarded me an e-mail that he had sent to county officials urging them to respond to his request for information. He wrote to me, "I don't expect the County to answer either of the messages below—however, when I go to court they will be exhibits attached to the complaint." When the county repeatedly refused to provide what Jack believed to be public information about the placement process, he sued.

In a letter to the county counsel and the county's public information officer, Jack stated that considering the county's lack of response to his request for information, "our only recourse now, in defense of our community, is to litigate the County's role in the placement of [the SVP] at Deserton." Pursuant to the California Records Act, a judge eventually ordered the county to release the requested information. Jack received censored documents, so he brought the case back to court. This time, the judge decided that county officials had done their due diligence and refused to order them to produce uncensored documents. Undeterred by the court's decision, Jack appealed. Eventually, the case made it to the California Supreme Court, but the court declined to review the case.

Deserton residents could have written off Jack's lawsuit as frivolous, with no potential to stop the placement. A judge's order had brought the placement to Deserton in the first place, so community members had little reason to believe that a judge would side with them over regional and state-level decision makers. Furthermore, while Jack's time and motivation to pursue the lawsuit contributed to its viability as a strategy for opposing the SVP placement, he had no intention of organizing the community. As a relative newcomer without much social capital, Jack was not a local leader, and many people in the community had never worked with him before. Nonetheless, as the man who had recently retired to Deserton explained, "[Jack] was just the catalyst, but he couldn't have done anything by himself without the community standing behind him, of course. [. . .] It was a community effort; he was just the one with the brains and the ability to put it all together and put it to words and action." While community members left the legal interpretation and writing to Jack, they supported his efforts by holding fund-raisers for court fees and gas, providing secretarial assistance, and accompanying Jack on the fifty-mile trip to the county courthouse.

Some of those I spoke with said that they referred to the lawsuit as the only legitimate community response when they were trying to dissuade fellow residents from engaging in vandalism or violence. As Jack explained:

> We intended from the beginning to control reactions to this so they were not in themselves criminal. [. . .] We collectively got the word out, those of us who were trying to do it the right way, we got the word out as best we could that this should follow the legal process. Nobody should do anything on their own. And nothing [illegal] happened. There was no effort by anybody to do anything illegal.

Once again, community members focused on legally acceptable strategies for opposition. With this mind-set, litigation quickly became the centerpiece of the community's response to the SVP placement.

The local opposition efforts gained media attention when a regional newspaper picked up the story. They then made it into a national newspaper, and a well-known national news program sent a reporter to cover the story on location. When the reporter arrived in Deserton, community members gathered at the café to talk with her. In the resulting television broadcast, one person said on camera that small, politically irrelevant communities like Deserton "just get the dregs of society heaped on them." Another said he believed that the judge had thrown a dart at a map and chose Deserton as the best placement site. With these and other snippets of conversations with local residents, the news program portrayed the community as a group of concerned citizens trying to protect their small town from an "unwanted neighbor."

Although the residents I spoke with agreed that the SVP did not belong in Deserton, the news program televised only some of their concerns. One woman I interviewed, a mother of six children who had moved to Deserton less than two years earlier to accommodate her husband's job on the border patrol, was disappointed in the broadcast because it portrayed only concerns that were "all fears and not built on facts and reality." In contrast, she told the reporter she was not worried about her children's safety and that everyone "deserves a second chance." At the same time, she believed that Deserton could not provide the necessary supports for successful reintegration. None of her statements made it on air. By leaving these perspectives out of the broadcast, the news program reinforced the notion that community members had a knee-jerk NIMBY mentality that failed to recognize the realities of sex offender reintegration.

After the broadcast aired, Jack "exchanged a couple of e-mails" with the district attorney. In one, he asked the DA to assess the possibility that another SVP would be placed in Deserton. According to Jack, the DA assured him that he would oppose any future SVP placements in the town. Jack explained, "And so I just have to believe that the huge uproar and the months of legal action and ultimately getting into the national media, I just have to think that that's our best safeguard against getting another person like [the SVP] put out here." Although the DA could not have been sure he could stop future SVP placements in Deserton, his promise symbolized a political actor's acknowledgment of the community. After the California Supreme Court refused to hear the case, the DA's promise and the media coverage of the community's response provided enough recognition of the problem that Jack decided not to continue with the lawsuit.

While Jack's individual motivation may have instigated the lawsuit, the community's historical and contemporary relationships with legal and political authority contributed to the centrality of the lawsuit in their response to the SVP placement. As I explain in the next section, the appeal of litigation as a central part of the community's response to the SVP placement in Deserton stemmed from the community's contemporary and historical relationships with local law enforcement, courts, politicians, and political structures.

Community Orientations to Authority in Deserton

The community in Deserton had unique orientations to legal and political authority that stemmed from the town's isolated, rural location, small population, and racial and class status. Legal authority had historically been deployed to protect the community, but political authority had often kept the community politically invisible. When the conflict over the SVP placement occurred, political mobilization seemed like a dead end. Instead, the community's positive orientation toward legal authority as a source of protection contributed to its support for fighting this particular political battle through legal mobilization.

Legal Authority as Protection

The community in Deserton had a strong stake in the protective aspects of the law. Residents' relationships with law enforcement and the courts reflected a hands-off, on-demand approach to keeping order within the community. As in other rural communities,[7] people in Deserton did not usually turn to the law to resolve local problems, but they generally had a positive view of the law as a power that could protect them when necessary. The community's dominant orientation to legal authority as a source of protection emerged from local relationships with law enforcement and the courts, which in turn contributed to their pursuit of litigation to stop the SVP placement.

RELATIONSHIP WITH LAW ENFORCEMENT

At the time of the SVP placement, Deserton's recent past had been characterized by dramatic swings in population size due to the construction of a mine in the late 1940s and, more recently, a prison. After the mine began production, Deserton's population swelled to roughly four thousand residents, with mining company employees sustaining the local economy. As the environmentalist I interviewed recalled, "When we first moved here, this was a lovely community," but after the mine closed in the early 1980s after thirty-five years in operation, "things really started tumbling downwards." The trailer park owner said that when the mine closed, "it was a great loss to the community, financially and otherwise. The town [. . .] was very active. They had a couple of churches up there, they had a full shopping center up there, [a bank] and everything up there. When the [mine] closed—it's all boarded up up there, there's a big chain-link fence all the way around it—that killed the whole area, really."

In 1988, the area experienced a brief revitalization when a private company built a minimum-security prison at the site of the old mining company town. The defunct mining town became a center of social and economic activity once again. One woman, a white mother of three in her early forties who had been a Girl Scout leader, described the town during this time: "Well, when I first moved here, we had the private prison and it was a very family-oriented place. There was always something going on. The kids were top priority; we were always doing something for the kids. You know, little Halloween fairs, just everything centered around the kids. We had Girl Scouts and Boy Scouts." When the prison closed after only five years in operation, everything changed. She explained that after the prison closure, "There was a loss of population of course, we lost a lot. We lost a lot of support, we lost a lot of families. And we just keep losing and it's, it used to be, if you were involved, you used to be a lot more supported and now, it's not like that anymore." By the time the SVP placement occurred, the mining and prison operations had been boarded up, and Deserton's population had dwindled to just over two hundred people.

When I visited Deserton in 2009, much of the town's population lived about halfway between the main street and the mine/prison site in a residential resort that catered to snowbirds who lived part of the year in Deserton. In the resort, houses sat on culs-de-sac roughly arranged around an artificial lake, and amenities included a community center, golf course, swimming pool, library, and small fire department. Despite the relative oasis, Jack described this time as "pretty much rock bottom" for the community. The mother who had grown up in Deserton had recently returned to find the town going "in kind of a negative direction." She explained, "It's just the town's run-down and things are falling apart, and I think people were just kind of getting complacent. [. . .] If you don't actually encourage people to come in and do business here, there's not gonna be anybody left. It'll be just as much a ghost town as [the mine/prison area]." While the prison had been closed for over a decade, her comments indicate a tendency among those I spoke with to compare the current state of the town with the vibrant community that the prison had sustained. For these residents, the short-lived prison era evoked hope of what their community could become once again. In some ways, the prison symbolized protection of the community itself: with the prison, residents had a viable community; without it, the town inched toward becoming a "ghost town."

Although most of those who worked for the prison in Deserton had since moved away, local residents still had ties to the prison system. Throughout my time in Deserton and the subsequent telephone interviews, I frequently heard community members refer to the handful of residents who worked or had worked as guards at the state-run prison in the next town over. These continual references contributed to a sense that Deserton's physical isolation from formal law enforcement did not translate into social distance from the protective aspects of the law. Instead, a shared sense of prison employees as active community members symbolized and constituted alignment with the protective aspects of the law. The retired ex-cop put it best when he noted, "There's some guys out here who work at the prison, so there's already kind of a law enforcement presence." While those who worked at the prison were not responsible for local law enforcement, their presence in the community further aligned it with the protective aspects of the law. As a result, community members who opposed the SVP placement were accustomed to being on the side of law enforcement, the side that emphasized protecting citizens from crime.

While the current and former guards tied the community to formal legal authority, sheriff's deputies rarely patrolled the town before the

SVP placement. Instead, they left residents to live their lives with minimal interference unless specifically called for. As the sheriff's field operations chief for the area put it, Deserton was "out of sight, out of mind" to law enforcement officers. Community members shared this perspective, with Jack describing the situation as follows: "There's no police protection. We'll take care of ourselves and our families if that's what we have to do." The man who had recently moved to Deserton with his wife echoed this perspective when he told me in an interview, "I mean, what it comes down to, 'Yeah, we got law enforcement,' but it's a small enough town it can police itself really." The lack of formal law enforcement presence and the resulting need for residents to police themselves reflected the dual realities of physical isolation and low crime rates. According to Jack, "As far as a person here walking down a street, nothing's gonna happen to them. There is absolutely no street crime here." Similarly, others described Deserton as the kind of place where people left their doors unlocked and keys in their cars.

Although no one I interviewed explicitly discussed the role of race in the community's relationship with law enforcement, law enforcement's hands-off, on-demand approach to crime control in Deserton may have stemmed from the racial makeup of the town. According to the U.S. Census, Deserton's population was overwhelmingly white in 2010, with 80 percent of residents reporting white as their only race. The United States has a long history of using the law against people in racial and ethnic minority groups through practices such as slavery, segregation, redlining, and mass incarceration,[8] and a community composed predominantly of individuals in racial and ethnic minority groups may have invoked more suspicion among legal and political officials.[9] Indeed, recent research has shown that order maintenance efforts in urban cities tend to target racial and ethnic minority populations as symbols of disorder,[10] and increased concentrations of minority groups can increase perceptions of neighborhood disorder.[11] Suspicion of these communities is also reflected in research showing that the police stop minority populations more often than whites, even after accounting for rates of involvement in crime.[12]

Racial and ethnic minorities may also be more wary of invoking formal legal authority to solve local problems than white individuals, particularly if they live in poor or high-crime areas.[13] While negative perceptions of the police have been associated with frequent, negative

interactions with them,[14] Deserton residents could have become cynical if they perceived law enforcement as neglecting their town. Instead,
community members believed they could rely on the sheriff's department when necessary. The waitress at the café explained, "Any time that
any one of us had problems, it might take them an hour to get here, but
they're out here." Other residents recounted an instance that occurred before the SVP placement in which a man with a gun arrived at Deserton's
elementary school. The school went into lockdown, and administrators
called the sheriff's department, which responded as quickly as possible.
While response times may have been longer than residents would have
liked, a positive outlook infused their retellings of the story. Community members also mentioned calling the sheriff's department for problems such as a local parolee giving the café waitress "a hard time" after he
wrote a bad check, an unfamiliar car driving on a residential road late at
night, property crimes, and domestic disputes. Although slow response
times were a common concern, community members trusted the sheriff's department to provide protection when they arrived. In short, for
those involved in opposing the SVP placement, interactions with formal
law enforcement tended to occur in the context of calling for protection
rather than feeling controlled by the police.

The relationship between Deserton residents and the sheriff's department, combined with Deserton's history as a prison town and the presence of prison guards within the community, fostered a sense of legal
authority as a source of protection. In some ways, the very viability of
physical and social life in Deserton was linked to the protective aspects
of legal authority. Historically, the prison had sustained and enlivened
both the local economy and local social life. More recently, jobs in the
state prison had provided residents with resources and a sense of protection. At the same time, physical and social distance from the sheriff's department and the racial makeup of the town allowed community
members to maintain their unique local community with minimal outside interference. In these ways, the community's dominant orientation
to legal authority was rooted in the protective powers of the law.

RELATIONSHIP WITH THE COURTS

The orientation toward legal authority as a source of protection extended
beyond the community's relationship with local law enforcement

officials to the its previous experiences with the courts. In the late 1980s, the county proposed converting the old mine pit to a landfill. Unlike the SVP placement, the dump proposal divided the community. According to an account on the town's website, "Our community was suffering from a near fatal blow, [the mining company] had declared bankruptcy and families, the lifeblood of our community were pulling away in U-Hauls and trucks, leaving behind nothing more than memories." In addition, county politicians promised free garbage services to residents as an incentive to support the landfill. Aside from the general undesirability of living near a garbage dump, those opposed to the project focused on its potential environmental impacts and questioned the process of procuring the land where the dump would be located. The environmental activist I spoke with mounted particularly fierce opposition to the project. She recounted the community's response:

> Once this dump thing started happening, elected officials started coming and having little private parties in everybody's houses and promising the moon if they wouldn't object to the dump. And at that point, I would say 99.9 percent of the people who lived here were against that dump. They didn't want any part of it. But once they started getting promises of free assessments and so much money every year to run this and free garbage. I mean, free garbage almost got me to sign off on it. You know, it's just incredible. They all jumped like rats off the *Titanic* [in support of the dump].

She and her husband eventually led a lawsuit against the county, and their litigation efforts became the centerpiece of the opposition.

Similar to the litigation in response to the SVP placement, those who sued over the dump did so without a lawyer. The environmental activist described the initial process to me in the following way: "I bought a how-to book from some fellow in [a nearby county]. I didn't even have a computer then. We wrote all of our legal briefs on a typewriter and we argued in superior court and won. [. . .] It was amazing." While the lawsuit successfully kept the dump out of Deserton, litigation did not unify local residents as it did with the SVP placement; however, even those opposed to the lawsuit witnessed the power of mobilizing legal authority. Furthermore, people on both sides of the debate acted to protect the community despite differing definitions of the collective interest. Their actions perpetuated the idea that legal authority could be leveraged as protection. As one of the key strategies for opposition, the successful use of litigation to oppose the dump signaled a belief in legal authority as a source of power for opposing perceived injustices and legitimized litigation as a strategy for opposition. Both of these effects of community members' encounter with the courts contributed to a sense that the law could help protect the community.

Orientation to Legal Authority during the SVP Placement

The SVP placement had the potential to upset the community's orientation toward legal authority as a source of protection. Legal authorities had essentially let local residents down by facilitating the placement of a potentially dangerous person in their town. Furthermore, during the notification meeting, the community's dominant orientation toward legal authority could have shifted when residents encountered sheriff's deputies lining the walls of the community center. Consistent with my own surprise at the law enforcement presence, community members bristled at the number of uniformed officers. As the general store clerk explained:

> And we get to the meeting and they've got the building basically surrounded. They've got cops everywhere, [. . .] standing there with their arms folded looking like we're criminals. And that didn't intimidate me, it actually pissed me off more than anything. Because just the way they were treating us—I didn't go in there upset, I knew what I wanted to say, but their demeanor ticked me off. [. . .] And I think part of it was I'm used to being on the other side. Working in the prison, how they were treating us is like how, like, when we're expecting something bad to happen on the yard and all the cops are just standing there waiting for it to happen. You know, so I was feeling like I was a criminal that night.

Others expressed similar reactions to the heavy police presence. The mother born and raised in Deserton said, "And we realized, once we got inside, that they weren't there for our protection, they were there because the people on the board were afraid that they needed them to protect them from us. So we were very insulted by that [. . .]. Especially when there's a big chunk of the population that are [corrections] officers where we work in the prison in some capacities, so we were very insulted by that." For both women, the community's history of "being on the other side" of law enforcement efforts contributed to dissatisfaction with the show of police presence at the meeting.

Community members' anger may have stemmed in part from deeper historical tensions between police and corrections that pit the latter as not "real" law enforcement;[15] however, residents' resistance to feeling controlled rather than protected also suggests that the sheriff's deputies' strong presence at the meeting ran counter to the community's dominant orientation to legal authority. Rather than being the protectors and protected, residents who attended the meeting interpreted the law enforcement presence as the sheriff's department relying on legal authority to assert control in a potentially hostile situation.

In an interview, the sheriff's field operations chief cast a different light on the law enforcement presence. As he prepared for the notification meeting, he believed it was very important to signal solidarity with the community. He explained, "I was expecting that the folks, the community would see how serious I was, representing the sheriff, how serious we were going to take that case. [. . .] I didn't mean for it to be an intimidation factor, but I wanted those people to see, 'Hey, you know what, this is how serious we're gonna take this. These are the guys who are going to maintain, manage, and solve this problem. [. . .] This is your sheriff's department.'" In light of the community's historic isolation from law enforcement, the field operations chief brought deputies to the meeting to show the community that the sheriff's department would provide protection in the event that the SVP exhibited risky behavior.

This same perspective became evident in the weeks and months after the meeting, when the department stepped up its patrols of Deserton. The field operations chief described the increased law enforcement presence as an attempt to improve relations with the community. He said, "That was one of the things that I picked up on very strongly at the [notification] meeting was that we were not representing ourselves very well in the community." Yet, after the placement, many community members were frustrated by the increased police presence in their town. The mother and former Girl Scout leader explained, "All of a sudden we had law enforcement all over, all the time. And if you didn't use a blinker, you were being stopped. If you were walking down the street, you were being asked for ID. So then the complaint was there's too much law enforcement and that we were being harassed." "Some people got mad and irritated," said the café waitress, because they had been pulled over for having a taillight out, speeding, or other infractions.

The general store clerk picked up on the inherent contradiction in the community's relationship with the sheriff's department that these events emphasized. In our interview, she explained, "We complained that we wanted them out here [more]. Now that they're here, they're gonna do their job. And it's not out of spite, it's because they're here to do their job." While community members generally seemed content with the lack of law enforcement presence in the town before the SVP placement, some had occasionally wished for more police presence; yet, as the preceding comments indicate, when the sheriff's department increased their visibility in Deserton and began to "do their job," community members began to complain because they were used to being left alone.

In short, when law enforcement officials tried to signal the very protection of the community that residents believed they should receive, residents perceived the new proactive measures within the framework of their history with law enforcement as a reactive force. Not accustomed to finding themselves targets of the controlling aspects of legal authority, they became angry and frustrated. While the SVP placement changed the nature of community members' interactions with law enforcement, stories about the police presence at the meeting and subsequently being pulled over for minor infractions were offered as exceptions to the norm. As such, these stories and interactions reinforced the community's orientation to legal authority as a source of protection.

While local contestations over issues such as the SVP placement and the dump had the potential to shift the community's dominant orientation to legal authority, both reaffirmed the idea that the law was a source of protection. As in other rural communities,[16] working with criminal justice institutions to solve a local problem changed community members' everyday interactions with these institutions; however, the outcomes in Deserton demonstrate that changes in everyday interactions do not necessarily alter broader understandings of the role of legal authority in solving local problems. Instead, these community members interpreted their interactions with criminal justice institutions within the context of their community's dominant orientations to legal authority, which proved more stable than their short-term perceptions of actors within the criminal justice system.

The limited police presence in Deserton and community members' related sense of policing themselves, along with their historical use of litigation to assert collective rights, facilitated both the emergence of litigation as a potential strategy for opposition and the centrality of that strategy in the community's response to the SVP placement. However, their orientation to political authority also played a role in their decision to litigate. As I explain in the next section, despite perceptions of the SVP placement as a political issue, the community's relationships with regional politicians and its position within broader political structures delegitimized political mobilization as a viable strategy for local opposition.

Political Authority as a Source of Invisibility

In stark contrast to the role of legal authority in local life in Deserton, the community had had relatively few interactions with formal political authority. Historically, residents had been politically apathetic, and their relationships with politicians and political structures emphasized the irrelevance of political authority to local life. Deserton was an unincorporated town like Ranchito, but Deserton residents had no local political body before the SVP placement. While leaders such as Jack sometimes spearheaded local efforts, no one rose to the status of de facto mayor or town council. As the former Girl Scout leader explained, "We don't really have a local government [. . .]. The board of supervisors is as local as we get." Community members in Deserton tended to characterize their relationship with "local" politicians as one in which the county generally left residents alone with few negative consequences. The community was politically irrelevant, distanced from political decisions, and had no formal political structures. Political authority in effect allowed the community to remain invisible to outsiders, except when county officials needed a politically convenient "dumping ground."

The community's perceived political invisibility did not mean that political authority had no influence on residents' lives. Instead, the absence of formal political actors and structures in the town allowed community members to cultivate and enjoy a community built on values of self-sufficiency and freedom from outside interference. Political authority did not appear to affect them either positively or negatively, and when problems arose, they tended to find informal solutions that did not require formal political decision making. In some instances, political decisions violated the interests of the community, but more often political authority seemed irrelevant to residents' everyday lives. These dynamics contributed to a sense that political authority allowed the community in Deserton to remain relatively invisible, but, as the SVP placement issue illustrates, the community's invisibility sometimes created problems.

RELATIONSHIP WITH LOCAL POLITICIANS

From community members' perspectives, before the SVP placement the board of supervisors treated Deserton as if it did not exist. With the county seat so far away, the county supervisor for the area rarely visited, and Deserton had little to offer the county by way of money or political support. The former Girl Scout leader characterized the relationship with county politicians by saying, "We weren't anything; we were nothing and we weren't important." The mother born and raised in Deserton expanded on this when she said, "We're so small in population that really, our vote really doesn't count. We don't have the tax revenue out here because we're so scattered and there's not any industry, so they're not really making any money off of us. It's just . . . we're here and that's it." For these residents, their community seemed politically irrelevant.

The lack of attention from political officials allowed community members to conduct their lives with little outside interference. Accordingly, most had little to say when asked about their views of county politicians. They knew that no local politicians represented their community's interests, but they also did not believe that county officials actively tried to work against local interests. As Jack put it, "[County supervisors] do things and nobody ever pays much attention to them, so they never get questioned." This comment and others made by community members I spoke with reflected a sense of isolation from the board of supervisors in which the board made decisions that sometimes may have impacted those living in Deserton, but usually had no effect on local life.

POSITION WITHIN BROADER POLITICAL STRUCTURES

Life in Deserton generally proceeded without any consideration of local or regional politics. Before the SVP placement, the town had no political structures, and the community had no motivation for a voice in local politics. Most community members had little desire to create a local political structure because they had rarely had major complaints that could have been mitigated through local political channels. The general store clerk explained, "We really haven't had anything to deal with [before the SVP placement]." Others mentioned at least three regional political issues that had impacted the community. These included proposals to build the garbage dump, a raceway, and a solar panel farm in Deserton. Each of these proposals caused some controversy within the community, but stories about the dump dominated residents' recollections of a major issue in which the county had interacted with the community. Those opposed to the dump lamented their lack of political voice but ultimately did not push for the creation of local political structures to stop it from being sited in the community. Instead, as discussed earlier in this chapter, they funneled their opposition through the courts.

Orientation to Political Authority during the SVP Placement

Had the community in Deserton had a local political group akin to the planning group in Ranchito, it may have mobilized politically against the SVP placement. Instead, political mobilization would have required relying on county politicians to protect the community's interests. Given the local context in Deserton, this would not have been feasible. The ways in which community members talked about their dissatisfaction with county politics in terms of a lack of votes, tax revenue, and political clout reflected their sense that the board of supervisors acted in its own political self-interests. Residents believed that county politicians did not care about communities in unincorporated desert areas because catering to the interests of these communities would not get politicians elected.

From community members' perspectives, their political irrelevance contributed to county politicians' belief that they could "dump" unwanted people and projects in desert towns without political consequence. Referring to both the controversy over the dump and the SVP placement, the environmental activist I interviewed explained that she would like to see "a little more respect toward this community from our elected officials who just seem to believe that this is just a sink for all of urban externalities." For her, the SVP placement was one of those instances in which the county used the town as a "sink" for those unwanted "externalities."

Many of those I spoke with agreed that the county had placed the SVP in Deserton because it was the least politically dangerous place to put him. During one of my early visits to Deserton, before I started conducting formal interviews, I met up with a white woman in her midforties who lived on a farm that was their family's business. She had moved to Deserton less than two years earlier with her husband and two young children. As we sat at her kitchen table discussing the SVP placement, she told me, as I recorded in my field notes, that the county placed the SVP in Deserton to "brush him under the rug" so that he would be "off the radar." This kind of recognition of the political realities of SVP placements also came through in my telephone interview with the man who had recently retired to Deserton. "If I was a politician who was running for office and was making these decisions," he said, "I would do the same damn thing." He went on to say that Deserton made the most political sense as a placement location because, as he explained, "We don't have the political clout and we don't have the money."

The controversy over the SVP placement fueled latent discontent about the community's relationship with county politicians. According to some, the SVP placement became such a big issue in Deserton in part because of the community's previous history with county-level political decision making. Jack characterized the reason for the community's response as a "sense that the county doesn't care about us except when they want to dump somebody like that on us." The ex-cop agreed, saying, "People are a little tired of 'It's just the desert, just dump him out there. Nothing ever happens out in the desert. Don't worry about it, nobody lives out there anyways.'" These comments reflect a sense that the county generally overlooked Deserton except when a politically unpopular decision had to be made. As a piece of land, Deserton was not completely invisible to the county, but political decision makers often presumed a lack of community in the town. In this context, when the SVP placement highlighted the community's lack of political power, residents mobilized not politically but legally, invoking a source of authority that they saw as more accessible and more likely to work in their interests than political authority.

Community Orientations to Authority and Legal Mobilization

The community response in Deserton suggests that legal mobilization emerged from unique configurations of local relationships between the community and political and legal authority. In particular, community orientations toward political authority as a source of invisibility and legal authority as a source of protection contributed to the centrality of litigation in the response. The community's relationships with regional politicians and formal political structures emphasized the role of political authority in keeping the community politically invisible, while its relationships with law enforcement and the courts emphasized the potential for the law to protect the community from perceived threats and injustices. Together, these orientations to formal authority shaped the form of community opposition to the SVP placement.

Until the SVP placement, many Deserton residents were unconcerned with their political invisibility. When the SVP placement issue arose, community members banded together in part because of a latent concern over their lack of political voice. While Jack initially tried to go through formal political channels to request information about the decision-making process, neither he nor other community members were surprised that the county ignored his requests. Aside from the formal request for information, the community had no other way to leverage political authority.

The community had historically been isolated from both political and legal authority, but the latter had been used to protect it in the past. Despite the law's failure to protect the community in allowing the SVP placement in Deserton, legal authority represented a legitimate way to become visible in the perceived political battle. Reflecting on the community's response, the trailer park owner said, "Well, if you want to oppose something like this, you probably well know that you have to do it legally. You can't just make telephone calls and so on and so forth." The importance of litigation as a legitimate response strategy was also indicated by community members who referred to the lawsuit as a tool for informal control of those who might have engaged in vigilante violence. These residents legitimized nonviolent community responses and contributed to the centrality of litigation in the response.

Ultimately, community members believed that their opposition would never have had the powerful voice that it did without the lawsuit. The environmentalist explained, "I think the litigation that [Jack] put [county officials] through [. . .] put a little bit of egg on people's faces, and they said 'We will not place anybody there anymore.' If they hold true to that, then that's wonderful. They would never say anything like that if [Jack] hadn't taken that legal route." As her comment suggests, invoking legal authority through the lawsuit gave the community a voice against an opponent backed by political authority—a source of power against which community members had little direct recourse. As the retiree put it, "Just because a community may look kind of ragtag and out there and not have a lot of political clout and stuff, that doesn't mean they don't have opinions and aren't willing to work on them." For community members in Deserton, getting their opinions out was political power. In doing so, they believed they fulfilled their mission to let county officials and others know that they would not stand by and let decisions impact their town without a voice in decision-making processes. Litigation appealed to residents not only because they believed in the legitimacy of legal authority but, more important, because they perceived legal authority as a source of protection that could be leveraged to achieve their collective goals in a political battle.

The Aftermath

Despite lawsuits and other protests, the SVP ultimately moved into Deserton. He lived in a mobile home surrounded by the desert land between the highway and the main residential neighborhood. Some community members said that when they drove past his home, they honked their horns just to let him know they were watching him. Almost nine months after he moved in, he violated a term of his conditions when, during a bus ride in a nearby city, he asked a woman who turned out to be an undercover police officer to visit his home. He was subsequently recommitted to the state hospital, where he remained as of February 2017. As of that time, no other SVP placements had been attempted in Deserton.

Even though community members failed to block the placement, they judged their opposition efforts as a success, with many of them emphasizing the national media attention that they believed undercut county politicians' credibility. "It was amazing to be on [the national news program]," said the café waitress. Jack concurred when he told me in our interview, "So, we actually were successful because the county tried to keep this thing quiet. [. . .] However, the story got out anyway and it got out to the national press and television." These kinds of comments indicate that gaining publicity for their cause symbolized success, even though they ultimately did not stop the SVP placement in Deserton.

Some evidence suggests that the board of supervisors became more responsive to the community after the SVP placement. In June 2013, the board approved the use of funds from a local solar project to refurbish Deserton's community center. In March 2014, the board solicited public input into how to use more of these funds within the community. While these actions may reflect only symbolic concern about the community, they suggest that the people living in Deserton had gained some political visibility.

This increased visibility may have stemmed from events that occurred soon after the placement. Life after the SVP placement mostly returned to normal, but in one important respect the community had changed. Many saw the SVP placement as a wake-up call: they could either let their town slip further into decay or they could revitalize their community. They chose the latter. In May 2010, Deserton residents, recognizing the value of an organized body that could represent them, formed a chamber of commerce. As the woman born and raised in Deserton explained, "When [the SVP placement] happened, people started talking about we need [. . .] some town government [. . .]. I found out that the chamber is actually the quickest and easiest to get started and they do hold some small level of political pull." While the chamber was not explicitly a formal political body, it stemmed from motivations to improve the state of the town and increase the community's political clout by attracting outside businesses and representing their interests within the region.

Forming the chamber of commerce achieved a secondary goal of increasing the town's political visibility. The Deserton native explained that the chamber gave residents "a place to meet so we could start working on getting the county to get us a town council appointed." Community members envisioned a community council as their political voice in local matters. They pressured their county supervisor to appoint residents to a community council that would advise the supervisor on locally relevant political issues. The county supervisor explored the possibility of such a council, but he ultimately concluded that the population was too small to support such a group. By the start of 2014, the idea of a community council had died and the chamber was dormant.

Conclusion

In some ways, the community response in Deserton reflects a classic legal mobilization story: a community pushed away from the political arena turned to the law to gain a voice in a perceived political battle. Yet this is not a simple tale of closed political opportunities and open legal opportunities. The law had failed the community by allowing for an SVP's release; the judge had failed residents by putting the SVP in Deserton; and law enforcement had traditionally left them to their own devices. Considering these marginalizing forces, community members could have become just as skeptical of invoking legal authority as they were of leveraging political authority. Instead, they perceived political and legal authority as separate entities, allowing the legitimacy of legal authority to remain intact while political authority came under intense scrutiny. Perceptions of formal institutional authority in Deserton emerged from the community's orientations toward political and legal authority, in which they viewed the law as a source of protection and political authority as a source of invisibility. These orientations created a unique local environment in which litigation appeared to be the best way to achieve their collective goals.

The communities in Deserton and Ranchito both sought to leverage formal authority to stop the SVP placements in their towns. In both cases, communities' relationships with formal political and legal institutions created local contexts in which community members believed in the power of a formal institutional authority to aid and protect the community, despite the failures of these powers to protect them from SVP placements in the first place. While both communities had positive perceptions of at least one type of formal institutional authority, others that are marginalized from formal institutions may develop political and legal cynicism. How would these communities respond to an SVP placement? Would they, out of necessity, engage in political or legal mobilization, or would they sit back and allow the placement to proceed, knowing that they had little chance of affecting the placement decision? The next chapter answers these questions by analyzing the case of community opposition to an SVP placement in East City, a place in which community members were deeply suspicious of both political and legal authorities.

4

Politics, Litigation, and Disorganization in an Urban City

The more the people tried to explain [their concerns] to the
police, to the city council . . . nobody listened.
—East City mother, more than twenty years in the
community

The previous two chapters explained responses to SVP placements in
two predominantly white, lower- to middle-class communities with
some faith in formal institutions. Despite these communities' marginalization from political and legal systems, their positive perceptions of
political and legal authority stemmed in part from privileged racial and
class statuses, which allowed them to take advantage of formal institutions built by and for white middle- and upper-class individuals.
Communities whose experiences have taught them not to rely on political or legal institutions for help must find other ways to protest unfair
decisions and defend themselves against perceived threats. This chapter
examines one such community's response to an SVP placement.

The predominantly lower-class, African American and Hispanic/
Latino(a) community in East City had been alienated from formal political institutions and saturated in formal legal controls. Community
members' skepticism of both institutions manifested as ambivalence
toward political mobilization and exclusion from legal mobilization,
which contributed to the failure of either strategy to gain traction in
local efforts to oppose an SVP placement. By examining "choice points"[1]
at which political and legal mobilization might have become central
strategies for opposition in East City, this chapter shows how political
and legal institutions shaped local opposition efforts in a community
that had constantly experienced the oppressive sides of institutional
power.

In 2009, a police-issued flyer announced a proposed SVP placement
in East City, a Northern California city with a widespread reputation

as a dangerous, crime-ridden place. At the time, the city of less than three square miles housed almost thirty thousand people. Despite its geographically small size, East City had all the bureaucratic structures of a larger city, including a police department, city council, and mayor. The population of racially diverse, poor and working-class individuals lived in neighborhoods ranging from blocks of tattered apartment complexes to nondescript homes guarded by chain-link fences to larger homes hidden behind wrought iron gates. In the neighborhood of the proposed SVP placement, many residents owned their small homes. They kept their lawns well tended, and some had lived in the area their entire lives. Neighbors generally knew each other and believed they could rely on each other in times of need.

Despite the city's negative reputation, community members often remarked on its potential for improvement, as illustrated by a local school principal who described East City as a "great community, and with great people living in it. [. . .] [T]here's so much potential here to create a really positive vibe." The proposed SVP placement contradicted this shared optimism about the future of East City. Some residents feared that the notoriety of the placement would reinforce outsiders' negative perceptions of East City, and they began protesting what they believed was yet another attempt to keep their community down. These residents packed city hall for a community meeting, added their names to lists of potential activists, picketed outside the SVP's home, delivered a petition to the homeowners, and began discussing the possibility of a lawsuit. This flurry of activity lasted for about a week. Then, as quickly as they had started, the protests died, the idea of a lawsuit faded, and people returned to their daily routines.

Unlike the opposition efforts in Ranchito and Deserton, no one strategy gained prominence in the opposition to the SVP placement in East City. Despite community members' skepticism regarding formal political and legal institutions, there is some reason to believe that an oppressed community may not reject political and/or legal mobilization as viable strategies for achieving collective goals. Individuals tend to separate their beliefs about the essential natures of legal and political power from the unjust application of those powers. For example, Americans perceive the law as essentially unbiased and fair even when they believe it has been applied unfairly in particular cases or against particular groups.[2] In other words, the public believes that flawed human beings implement nearly flawless laws.

Formal political authority also stands relatively unscathed in public opinion as political injustices are seen as the result of politicians' unfair exercise of their political power. Even the strongest critics of specific politicians tend to advocate for voting "ordinary Americans" into office rather than eliminating political power altogether.[3] This separation of beliefs about the essential nature of formal power from perceptions of the actors who exercise that power means that communities such as the one in East City may not automatically reject political or legal mobilization even when they have been subject to the negative effects of those authorities. Furthermore, the community in East City had a history of somewhat successful large-scale collective action efforts involving both political and legal mobilization, indicating that either strategy may have been useful in opposing the SVP placement.

Despite these pathways for potential mobilization, the community in East City ultimately rejected political and legal strategies for opposition. This chapter explains how local contexts constrained the extent to which these types of mobilization gained traction in the community's response to the proposed SVP placement. The community's contemporary and historical relationships with politicians, political structures, law enforcement, and the courts contributed to dominant orientations toward political and legal authority that facilitated indifference toward and exclusion from political and legal mobilization. Skepticism of political and legal institutions did not translate into an outright rejection of their legitimacy, but the community's demographic makeup shaped its relationships with formal institutional actors in ways that kept political and legal mobilization at the margins of local opposition efforts. Overall, the East City case suggests that skepticism of formal institutions did not preclude the emergence of political and legal mobilization, but the community's interactions with formal institutions shaped the salience of these strategies in its response to the SVP placement.

Opposing an SVP in East City

One Monday in late August 2009, the East City Police Department distributed a flyer announcing a "special community meeting" to discuss the release of an SVP in the city. The flyer stated that a judge had ordered the placement "despite objections from the City and County Supervisor" and that the mayor, police chief, and county supervisor would be at the meeting "to discuss the steps the city and county will take to ensure the safety of our residents, including [the SVP]." The flyer also mentioned that the SVP's "prior offenses include violent sexual offenses, although these offenses do not include children." Residents would learn later that his victims had been elderly women.

As with local reactions to SVP placements throughout California, learning about the proposed placement incited fear in many community members. As an activist in a local interfaith alliance explained, "My initial response was fear. And the fear wasn't for the community or anything like that. I was truly thinking about my daughter. After the initial fear for my child, my mind expanded and opened up to senior citizens in this community. And, and as it opened up even more, it got to be just a concern for this community." One man, a longtime black resident in his midfifties who had served on local boards and had been generally active in local politics, noted, "In our community, you see a lot of kids, see a lot of elderly people living there. And they're living independently. So, you know, the fear factor went up very high among senior citizens." While both of those individuals referenced fear for the older population of East City, some also wondered how, given California's residence restriction laws, the placement could be allowed less than half a mile from a school.

One afternoon I stopped by a house a few doors down from the SVP placement. I had mailed a letter to let residents know I would be in the neighborhood but had found that most people did not answer their doors when I knocked. Feeling defeated, I decided to knock on one last door. To my surprise, a man answered and said he would like to do the interview right then. He invited me to sit with him and his wife in their kitchen. The interview with this Hispanic couple in their forties turned out to be one of the longer interviews I conducted, as the husband answered my questions thoughtfully and had very strong opinions.

Throughout the interview, the husband repeatedly expressed his adamant opposition to becoming involved in local politics despite his work as a contractor for a nearby city government. As we talked about how he had heard about the SVP placement and his initial reactions to it, he commented, "I heard the people that commit the crime like him cannot be living by the school. And I guess it's a policy or it's a law that's been in place. And it's funny [because] two blocks away is the school." Considering California's residence restriction laws, these concerns had some merit; however, some involved in the case argued that residence restriction laws did not apply to SVPs still under the DMH's supervision. The ambiguity of the law, along with the SVP's offense history and a lack of other housing options, had compelled the judge to approve the location in East City.

In line with signals from California's residence restriction laws, but contrary to a vast body of research on the issue, community members assumed that keeping an SVP away from children would reduce the likelihood of their children becoming his next victims. Ironically, while many in the community feared for their children, the judge had ordered the SVP to move into a home next door to an elderly woman with Alzheimer's disease. According to her family members, many of the windows and the back door of the SVP's new home faced the woman's bedroom window. As one of her granddaughters, a black woman in her late thirties who took care of her grandmother, explained, "When he goes to take his trash out, he looks directly into my grandmother's room. When he goes to his backyard, he looks directly into my grandmother's room. His kitchen is facing my grandmother's room. His bathroom, all his windows, except for his living room, is facing my grandmother's room." Thus, while many feared for the safety of their children, the family next door feared for their eldest family member, who more closely fit the SVP's previous victim type.

East City's Community Notification Meeting

The community notification meeting occurred two days after the flyer had been distributed. The flyer had increased awareness of the meeting, but many people heard about it through alternate methods such as media reports and word of mouth. A neighbor who had moved next door to the proposed placement location three years earlier explained, "I got bombarded with text messages, phone calls. [. . .] And everybody was telling me about it, like my friends and family were calling me, telling me that I should attend [the meeting], so we did." This Hispanic woman in her late twenties was joined by a racially and generationally diverse group of approximately seventy individuals who packed the city council chambers to learn about the SVP placement. During the meeting, which I attended with them, I wrote down as much as I could in a notebook that I kept on my lap. The following account of the meeting reflects my written notes, which included word-for-word transcriptions of key comments and phrases.

At the meeting, political officials, the police chief, and a representative of Health Corp sat behind long folding tables facing the audience. As community members filtered in, the police chief provided handouts that gave the legal definition of an SVP along with the SVP's photograph. To my surprise, at the designated start time, a police chaplain began the meeting with a prayer in which he called for, according to my notes, a "great and peaceful result" to the meeting and the placement itself. As far as I knew, this had never happened in notification meetings in other communities. The chaplain's participation seemed to signal the police department's efforts to connect with community members as they worked through the volatile issue of the SVP placement.

After the chaplain prayed, those on the panel at the front of the room began to speak. The police chief opened by saying that everyone there had the same question: "Why East City?" Many in the audience murmured their agreement. The chief assured the community that the police would maintain public safety, and he also noted that no one should commit illegal acts against the SVP. East City's mayor spoke next, noting his opposition to the placement and encouraging residents to "register your complaints with the judge." The county supervisor concurred but added that the SVP was going to be released, and they would all have to work together to provide services for him to ensure a better chance of successful reintegration. After brief comments from the police chief and the Health Corp representative, the chief opened the meeting to public comments and questions.

The meeting oscillated between residents voicing their concerns, asking for more information, and calling for action. The police chief fielded most questions, with the Health Corp representative and political officials filling in when necessary. Although the audience had been informed of the SVP's previous crimes, one of the first people to speak said that the placement location was the "worst place" to put him because of its proximity to day cares and schools. When those on the panel tried to reassure community members that the SVP had never targeted children, one woman asked, "How do you know his tastes haven't changed?" With this question, she revealed that part of the audience's fears lay in the unknown threat to the community. If the SVP's "tastes" changed after he moved into East City, then everyone could potentially be in danger.

While concern for children's safety arose early in the meeting, most comments focused on the specifics of the placement and how the community could organize against it. One woman asked how often the SVP's picture would be updated on the sex offender registry, in case he "changes his appearance." Others asked about the type of surveillance Health Corp would use, what the SVP's "objective" would be once in the community, the nature of his treatment program, and what other cities had been considered for a placement. Those on the panel explained the security guards and GPS ankle monitors, the goals of reintegration, how the treatment program worked, and the other potential locations that had been ruled out.

Other questions were more difficult to answer, as illustrated by one exchange in which a man in the audience asked the Health Corp representative, "Have you worked with him? Do you know him?" She responded, "I have had interactions with him. He is remorseful." Her response elicited a wave of murmurs throughout the crowd. The audience member went on to ask, "Would you feel comfortable living next to him?" Not knowing exactly how to answer that question, the Health Corp representative stated, "That is a hard question." This appeared to prove the man's point.

Calls for action against the placement erupted periodically during the meeting. One local resident encouraged action by saying, "Who owns that house is public information. We should get that information." Another man tried to focus attention on political mobilization by declaring, "The mayor is our voice," to which many in the audience mumbled their disagreement. Perhaps most surprising, the police chief made a concerted effort to incite community action throughout the meeting. At one point, a woman asked the chief, "What about communities that refuse to accept this?" The police chief told her, "Turn and ask the community. Direct that to the community." She complied, turning to the audience and saying, "We need to do that here." The chief also provided more specific strategies for action, as was the case when one man asked, "What responsible landlord would rent to someone like this?" The police chief responded by noting that the landlord had the authority to end the rental agreement and that the "community may want to focus here." The chief reiterated that the police department would work with the community to deal with this issue. When one man declared, "Tomorrow, you're going to see some serious protests. Especially you, lady [the Health Corp representative]," the police chief attempted to diffuse the tension by saying that Health Corp "will be our partner in this," which was characteristic of his repeated attempts to portray everyone at the head of the room as working together, and with the community, to ensure public safety.

Tensions rose as the meeting progressed. Toward the end, a retiree who lived a few houses down from the proposed placement site, whom I will call Marc, stood and said, "The people at the table, their hands are tied. They have to do everything legally. This is *our* problem. Tomorrow at 8:00 a.m. I'm going to the county assessor's office to find out who owns this property. The problem is this greedy landlord. From there, we form a committee to deal with the root cause." A few minutes later, a woman asked audience members to target their protests toward the judge, saying, "The judge made the ruling. We need write-in protests, picket protests against the judge and the courts." Both calls for action elicited general agreement from the audience.

At the end of the meeting, as the crowd began to disperse, a small group formed around Marc. He circulated a piece of notebook paper on which people wrote their contact information. I hung around the outskirts of a second group that formed near a man whom I will call Miguel. As the group began to disperse, I introduced myself to Miguel, and he offered to show me around the neighborhood where the SVP was to be placed. I took him up on the offer and followed him in my car to the placement location. In the neighborhood, television news vans shone bright lights on the modest ranch-style home that was to house the SVP. A line of traffic crept past a handful of pedestrians who milled about the street and sidewalks. Drivers leaned out of their windows exchanging information with other residents to discuss organizing protests. The community seemed poised for action.

Originally, the SVP was to arrive in East City five days after the community meeting. To residents' surprise, he arrived the day after the meeting. The man who lived across the intersection from the SVP's home expressed his discontent; as he described it, "The [police] chief did it real slick. [. . .] I just think the way they did it . . . he was here. And when they said he was going to be here, you know, a week and a half, he was actually there that Friday or something. He came early." For him and others I spoke with, the early arrival symbolized the covert nature of the entire placement process.

As in some other communities, some people made threats against the SVP. The woman who took care of her grandmother next door recalled hearing passersby threatening to "set his house on fire, shoot him, all kinds of stuff." However, she explained that she "don't want to have nothing to do with that." If someone tried to kill the SVP, she said, "that is on them. And their conscience. I don't agree with him being there, but I ain't gonna try and kill him." Similarly, Marc, the retiree who had taken names at the end of the meeting, told me in an interview that he "was hoping somebody would do a drive-by there." He went on to explain, "You know, I'm not gonna break the law, but you know I hear some of these brothers, these crack dealers, that's where they oughta do a drive-by up on that corner there as far as I'm concerned. [. . .] And shoot him up a couple times. I bet they'll move him then. But the state has a responsibility for his life and stuff." Both of these individuals recognized that while they might not have been upset if the SVP had been harmed, they also had to abide by the law and their own moral compasses in deciding how to oppose the SVP's presence in the neighborhood.

While none of the threats of violence or harassment came to fruition, Marc's comments about drive-by shootings implied that it would not have been out of the realm of possibility for someone to have engaged in violence against the SVP in East City. A couple of people I interviewed shed some light on why this might not have happened. The man who lived across the intersection from the SVP's home explained, "If he didn't have that protection that he has, they would have done something." For him, the SVP's round-the-clock guards were the only thing that had kept the violence at bay. The Hispanic man who adamantly opposed any involvement in local politics made similar comments when he explained that he had heard that "as soon as they leave the guy alone, they gonna kill him. [. . .] They waiting for the opportunity." When asked if he was still hearing those types of comments at the time of our interview a year later, he said, "Yeah. I mean, they is waiting. I mean, right now is guards twenty-four hours a day. And there is some people, I mean, I mean they, they do kill people." While he said that talk of killing the SVP may have been "just a rumor," he rooted his comments in the context of the city's history of violence when people would "just drive by and start shooting." Both community members believed that those who had contributed to East City's historically high rates of violent crime would have had no problem shooting the SVP; however, the protection provided to the SVP by the state had dissuaded them from doing so. These two people, as well as Marc and one of the neighbor's granddaughters, all stressed that they personally would not have engaged in violence, but that such an outcome might have been expected and perhaps condoned by some in the community.

Ultimately, instead of the violence that some may have expected, community members protested the injustice of the placement by engaging in a variety of nonviolent opposition strategies. As one woman who had been active in regular neighborhood meetings with the police explained, "We had to make sure we kept it low-key. We didn't want to get arrested for bothering him. Or God forbid somebody be stupid enough and try and do something to the property that he's living at." These "low-key" strategies included grassroots protests, political action, and talk of litigation. According to the longtime resident who had been active on local boards and in other local political issues, some even set up an informal surveillance network. He explained, "A group had taken initiative to, to monitor the house, you know for a while there. I think for like two or three months there were like people that would, you know, just watch the house." When asked to elaborate, he continued, "Well, you know, it was a group of people that was taking turns and, and just, you know, looking at the house and monitoring the house and seeing if he was coming and going and so forth." This kind of strategy may have kept community members informed of the SVP's whereabouts, but it did little to call broader attention to the community's concerns. Instead, more visible nonviolent strategies of resistance included protests and talk of litigation.

Grassroots and Political Protests

Two kinds of protests emerged after the SVP's arrival: grassroots protests, including picketing and petitions, and a more formal protest organized by the mayor. Grassroots protests began immediately. For about a week, neighbors stood on the sidewalk in front of the SVP's home, handing out flyers to passing motorists and holding signs. Protesters participated as their schedules allowed, and at any given time the group fluctuated from two to a dozen people. The protesters mainly wanted to disseminate information about the SVP's presence. For instance, late one morning, I found four of them standing on the sidewalk in front of the SVP's house. One man, the son-in-law of the elderly woman who lived next door, hailed passing motorists to hand out copies of the police-issued notification flyer. As cars passed, he yelled, "Sexual predator in our neighborhood!" His two teenage nieces followed his lead, shouting "Sexual predator!" at the passing cars. Cardboard signs reinforced the information-dissemination goal, with two signs reading, "The man who lives here likes to rape elderly women."

In addition to getting the word out, community members wanted to change the placement decision. After word began to spread that the landlord worked for a state agency and lived in a nearby wealthy neighborhood, some residents began to target him in their opposition efforts. One afternoon, I stood with Miguel at the neighborhood school during afternoon pickup while he tried to garner support for a petition to the landlord. The petition noted residents' dissatisfaction with the placement and asked the landlord to reconsider the rental agreement. He approached cars, explained the petition, and then asked parents to sign. Most readily added their names. When traffic died down, I accompanied Miguel and the school principal as they delivered a copy of the petition with more than four hundred signatures to the landlord's home.

The landlord's neighborhood represented a stark contrast to East City: million-dollar homes sat on large lots with neatly manicured lawns. A ring of the bell at the gate produced no answer, so Miguel left the petition in the mailbox. As we drove back to East City, Miguel and the school principal discussed their next steps, including a lawsuit and possible protests in front of the landlord's home. The principal asked Miguel on what grounds he could bring a lawsuit. "I'll find something," he replied. He went on to explain that even the threat of a lawsuit would probably be enough to get the landlord to agree to residents' demands. While Miguel had some doubt that the placement could be challenged on legal merit, he also believed that litigation could serve as a tool for opposition regardless of the outcome. Miguel may have been right; research on litigation as a strategy for collective action has shown that lawsuits can garner support for a cause and serve as a bargaining chip for future collective action against opponents.[4] Litigation may have been an effective strategy for opposing the SVP placement, but Miguel remarked that community members would never act without an "instigator."

Miguel seemed poised to become the "instigator" of further action. Yet, after our trip, I never heard of him organizing or being involved in any other opposition efforts. This reflected a general trend in the initial grassroots efforts in which disparate groups of residents engaged in sporadic, informally organized protest activities that never coalesced into broad community opposition. The principal's involvement in the opposition efforts might have helped provide institutional support for community members' actions against the placement, but he never acted upon his power to help mobilize more organized or sustained collective action against the placement.

Five days after the SVP arrived, the mayor's office announced a press conference and community protest. On the same day, East City's city council passed a resolution "expressing strong opposition to the placement" on the basis that the city was a small, "densely-populated and family-friendly" community with a high crime rate that could not "afford the risk of depositing such a violent career criminal" into its midst. According to a newspaper report, the mayor implored community members to "write letters, send e-mails, let the judge know that we're definitely not going to stand for this." The mayor's protest drew hundreds of attendees. They packed the streets, chanting slogans in opposition to the placement while the mayor stood in the crowd with a bullhorn. A list circulated among the crowd, and people added their names to show their opposition. The protest had the potential to spark a more lasting community response, but many attendees I interviewed did not participate in any other opposition efforts. For instance, one self-described African American woman in her midfifties had found out about the protest through her church. She explained, "That rally was one day and I don't think it ever came up again. Nothing ever came through the church again, so there was no follow-up." Her experience was typical of many of the community members I interviewed.

Some community activists attended the mayor's protest in hopes of organizing a more sustained response. One such person, a black man in his late fifties who had lived in East City for more than thirty years, had been involved in grassroots efforts to solve a variety of local problems, including mounting an organized campaign to stop drug dealing in his neighborhood in the 1990s. At that time, he explained in a telephone interview, "We were taking the license plates of the people coming to buy drugs. You stood out in the drug-dealing areas and really just ruined their business. Chased them out of many parts of town. [. . .] And, you know, people like us, we didn't do any publicity, but we were more effective than anything else. To clean up the neighborhoods of the drug users." He believed that this history of effective local activism contributed to people inviting him to the mayor's protest against the SVP placement. As he put it, "People knew I was very effective out on the street."

Aside from invitations to protest, he also believed that the SVP placement represented a disturbing trend of people profiting off of housing criminals in East City. He coined this the "criminal housing business" and explained, "We call them 'poverty pimps,' people that make a living off their nonprofits. This is their new cash cow." Although the state did not rent the SVP's home from a nonprofit organization, the landlord resided in a wealthy town just outside of East City, and he received above-market rent for the SVP's home. This activist recognized the exploitation of more marginalized areas, and he tried to fight against that in multiple ways. Yet, while he was very passionate about the "criminal housing" issue, he did not feel an immediate obligation to go to the mayor's protest. When asked why not, he explained, "It's not necessarily my fight." He did not see the issue as his "fight" because he did not live in the immediate vicinity of the placement location. Instead, he told me that he "went down to try to help the community deal with the problem." He wanted to help neighbors organize their own opposition but had little interest in leading their efforts.

Unfortunately, according to him, the protesters were not "trained" in how to effectively protest. "I did the chants, tried to lead some chants and stuff, but you know, people they haven't been trained," he said. "They don't know what to do." With previous groups, "We were effective because we trained the people before we took them out there, and then they knew what to do. And we organized them and organized the groups so they knew how to stand, and stand, and be there and have the longevity." This did not happen with the protests against the SVP placement. Instead, he said, "I talked with some people about [organizing] and none of the lights came on." Based on this experience, he believed that community members were not serious enough to bring about change. Rather than waste his time, he decided not to engage in subsequent opposition against the placement.

While it is impossible to know the extent to which this account accurately describes events during this time, this activist's experience reflects a different motivation for attending the protests. He was not particularly incensed about the placement itself, but because it symbolized the continuation of a problem that he had spent at least a decade working on in East City, he felt compelled to try to help organize the community. Instead, for him, the mayor's protest led not to further involvement in the issue but to increased skepticism about the ultimate goals and strategies of the community's opposition to the placement.

While the protest drew a large crowd, some people I spoke with did not participate in any of the opposition efforts. They cited having few concerns about the placement, a lack of time to participate, and skepticism that the community's response would change the placement decision. One self-described African American man and longtime resident on the SVP's block had worked as a social worker for the county. He called me one afternoon after I had left a note at his house explaining my research and desire to speak with him. As we talked, he answered my questions with a slow, deliberate pace that indicated his thoughtfulness. He was surprised by the community's response to the SVP placement, and, in our interview, he explained why. "This community's always been very accepting of people who may have issues," he said. "We've always been more accepting of people that probably would not have been accepted in other communities." He said that while parolees moved anonymously into East City every day, "at least we know about this one," and he is "being monitored." For him, the notification meeting represented a more transparent placement process than was usually the case with formerly incarcerated individuals returning to the city.

A city council member I interviewed took these ideas a step further. He believed that "as a community, we needed to figure out how we could accommodate him. [. . .] It's important for us to understand that as humans we need to understand that we can't throw away people as a society." Even this person in a position with access to political power recognized that neither law enforcement nor judges would or could successfully integrate the SVP into society. Instead, as he noted, the community had to take responsibility. This was a sharp contrast to traditional reentry processes in which probation and/or parole officers worked in conjunction with the courts to regulate those returning to the city after incarceration. The SVP was still highly regulated by the courts, but from the perspective of this city council member and a few sympathetic residents, attempts to inform community members and bring them into discussions about how to "accommodate" the SVP represented a departure from normal reentry processes.

Surprisingly, a disabled black woman in her early seventies who lived a few blocks from the SVP's house was also unconcerned about the placement. She very rarely left her house, but she had received a letter I had mailed to people in the neighborhood and wanted to discuss her thoughts on the placement. In our interview, she said that she was unconcerned about the placement. When asked why, she responded, "Well, like I said, the authorities that put him in there, they were supposed to watch him and as far as I was concerned, they were watching him." Although her gender and age fit the SVP's previous victim type, she trusted the "authorities" to do their job and keep tabs on the SVP. Yet, she attributed her lack of concern about the placement only partly to trust in these authorities. When she called me to schedule her interview, one of the first comments she made was about her ability to protect herself in any way necessary if the SVP ever came to her house. While she did not repeat these statements in the interview, she did state that he would have to go "a long ways" to get to her house. "If he came to my house," she said, "he's the one who'd suffer. Not me." For her, the conditions of the SVP's release and a bit of physical distance between her home and his decreased the chances that she would become his next victim. Even if the SVP sought her out, she believed she could defend herself.

Others expressed concern about the placement but did not become involved in the protests because they lacked time and motivation, or because they believed protesting would not change the situation. Just over a year after the SVP placement, I met some of these individuals one evening at a neighborhood meeting held in a community center inside a mobile home park a few miles away from the SVP's neighborhood. The police department organized these regular meetings, called "beat meetings," which were run by a local resident (the "beat captain"), with a couple of officers there to answer questions and inform the conversation. These meetings occurred in each of four zones, or "beats," throughout East City, and they served as a forum for neighbors to voice their concerns, learn more about police operations, and obtain information about addressing local problems. I did not expect the SVP placement issue to arise during this particular meeting, but I attended in search of people who might be interested in participating in interviews for my study. Sure enough, a few of the dozen residents who attended, including the beat captain and a couple other individuals, agreed to be interviewed.

These residents tended to be less involved in the SVP placement because they lived farther from the placement location. A white woman in her late fifties and an active member of the local beat told me that she perceived the SVP placement as something outside the realm of her everyday life. As she put it, "But you see, it wasn't something where I was going to be going by all the time, so out of sight, out of mind." Even though her distance from the placement location contributed to her ability to ignore the situation, later in the interview she did express concern about the SVP placement and her lack of involvement. She said, "And I really kind of slap my hand for not being more active in maybe a little protest, grabbing a lawn chair and sitting with [neighbors], whatever." She did not do so in part, she said, because of other pressing personal issues and a lack of time. While some of those who participated in the protests did not live in the immediate neighborhood, those closer to the placement location had stronger motivation to become involved because they believed it more directly affected their everyday lives.

A final group of nonparticipants believed that the protests would not force the SVP out. For them, the political nature of the decision meant that those involved in the placement process did not care about residents' opinions. As one of the beat meeting attendees, a white woman in her late seventies, put it, "[Protesting] is not my thing. It's not gonna do any good." Yet even some who attended the protests agreed that protesting probably would not influence the decision to place the SVP in East City. Despite the low probability of success, they believed in the importance of having a voice. When asked if she thought the protest had any sort of impact, the woman who had attended with her church group responded, "I don't know if it did or not, but at least, if nothing else, we as citizens of East City, we have a voice. And whether we were taken seriously or not, I don't know, but at least we tried something." These comments imply that even some who were skeptical about the power of community opposition still harbored some hope that their efforts would pay off.

Litigation

Picketing and protests brought public attention to the SVP placement, but some residents pursued other strategies that had the potential to bring attention to the community's cause. One group, spearheaded by Marc, the retiree who had said at the meeting that he would find the name of the landlord, began discussing a potential lawsuit. According to a news report, three hundred residents joined Marc in searching for an attorney to take the case as pro bono work; however, in an interview, Marc said the group consisted of approximately five or six core members who met a few times to discuss "every legal way we knew how." Whatever the size of the group, they discussed the potentially illegal aspects of the placement, including potential violations of city zoning laws and California's sex offender residence restrictions.

Soon after they began meeting, Jack (from Deserton) read about East City's SVP placement in a regional newspaper and contacted Marc.[5] Up to that point, the newspaper had publicized the litigation efforts, but residents had taken no concrete steps to pursue the lawsuit. Jack consulted with Marc on the merits of litigation, and they began discussing the possibility of either appealing the placement decision or pursuing a lawsuit against the county. During this time, I attended a meeting at the elementary school near the SVP's home in East City. At the meeting,

Jack explained to the principal how he had approached the lawsuit in Deserton and offered suggestions for next steps in East City. Jack believed the community could make a strong case for the illegality of the placement based on California's residence restrictions, and he explained to the principal that "protests won't get you anywhere" because no community wants an SVP in their neighborhood. Jack encouraged the principal to move forward with legal challenges at least in part because he wanted more communities to resist SVP placements to pressure the state into changing its placement process. Nonetheless, the principal seemed more interested in stopping the local placement than in bringing about state-level change.

The appearance of an outsider who was willing to help with the lawsuit could have spurred both the principal and Marc's informal group of community members to continue their efforts. Instead, I wrote the following observation in my field notes after the meeting with Jack and the principal: "When I talked to [the principal] after the meeting, he said that really, it's just himself and Marc working on this now. People haven't really been talking about it. He said there's a general feeling that nothing can be done, so they might as well move on." Indeed, talk of a lawsuit died soon after the meeting with Jack.

Unlike the community in Deserton, the community in East City had neither legal expertise nor resources to pay a lawyer. While residents might have relied more on Jack for legal expertise, he indicated they would have to do much of the work themselves. As Marc put it, "We would have to get an attorney and go from a legal angle, and we had no money, so [the idea died]." Ultimately, the small group of community members involved in discussions about litigation believed the law could have helped them achieve their goal of removing the SVP from the neighborhood, but they could not garner enough support (economic or otherwise) from the broader community to achieve their goals.

As the preceding story demonstrates, the community's response to an SVP placement in East City consisted of a variety of informal groups pursuing their own strategies to try to stop the placement. The mayor's protest was formally organized, but it never became the centerpiece of the community's response because, as I discuss in the following sections, community members dismissed it as political maneuvering rather than a true attempt to represent the community. Community members' discussions about litigation could also have become a key part of the response, especially when an outsider offered to help, but a lack of legal expertise and economic resources hindered litigation efforts.

Community Orientations to Authority in East City

In East City, the community's relationships with politicians, political structures, law enforcement, and the courts constrained the emergence of political and legal mobilization as central opposition strategies. The community had often been alienated from formal political power and controlled by those in positions to exercise legal authority. While community members in East City did not reject the legitimacy of these sources of power, their dominant orientations toward political and legal authority emphasized the oppressive sides of institutional power, which in turn made it more difficult for them to believe that these institutions would help them stop the SVP placement.

Political Authority as Alienation

Community members in East City perceived political authority as a source of alienation in which the power to govern seemed firmly embedded in and aligned with political institutions rather than the community. Historically, county politicians had treated East City residents as a problem community requiring outside governance. Community members also perceived local politicians as valuing their careers more than interests of the community, a perception further facilitated by the city council's position within the formal political structure.

RELATIONSHIP WITH POLITICIANS

East City's history as a problem area within the county strongly contributed to the community's identity and image within the region. The community members and local officials I spoke with repeatedly compared East City's crime rates, racial composition, and socioeconomic status with those of surrounding cities. In 2011, for example, East City experienced more than four times as many violent crimes as its two neighboring cities, despite having a smaller population.[6] East City also had a more racially diverse population than the two closest cities: nearly two-thirds of the population was of Hispanic or Latino origin, and non-Hispanic whites constituted the next largest racial group, followed by African Americans, Hawaiian/Pacific Islanders, Asians, and others. By contrast, the two neighboring cities were more than 60 percent non-Hispanic white, with Asians representing the next largest racial group.[7] Compared with neighboring cities, East City had half the median annual household income ($49,000); a much higher proportion of adults (14 percent) and children (21 percent) who lived in poverty; a drastically lower proportion of residents who had a high school diploma (65 percent) or a bachelor's degree (16 percent); and approximately four times more of its adult population employed in service jobs (40.5 percent) and four times fewer in management or business jobs (18.7 percent).[8] As a town surrounded by other cities with lower crime rates, higher proportions of white residents, and higher socioeconomic statuses, East City often bore the brunt of policies intended to maintain the quality of life of people living in nearby cities.

In the 1960s, East City activists mobilized to create equal education opportunities for their children. Over residents' objections, the county had closed their only high school because desegregation activities had bused black students out without bringing in enough white students to replace them.[9] When local residents pushed for incorporation in the late 1970s and early 1980s, divisions within the town and between the town and the county (which stood to lose revenue if East City incorporated) further intensified already contentious political relationships.[10] As the county supervisor described, "It actually was a big battle for it to become incorporated, and the reason the people were fighting so hard is because they wanted to be self-sufficient. They believed that they could be better served being a city as opposed to being a part of an unincorporated area." For activists during this time, the fight for incorporation reflected a fight for the power to govern themselves.

After protracted court battles, the town finally incorporated in the early 1980s. Incorporation brought increased opportunities for accessing political power through a city council and various city departments and commissions. Unfortunately, a decade after incorporation, crime rates skyrocketed, undermining activists' assertions that they could govern themselves. Some residents believed that local government did not do enough to stop the murders and overt drug selling that took over the town. The social worker I spoke with recalled that, during this time, there were "a lot of people on the streets dealing, a lot of time, you know the drug wars, all that going on. I kinda wondered about what commitment the county itself had to making sure these things were alleviated." While county politicians had little formal power to solve the city's crime problems, this resident implied that the county might have stepped back to prove that East City officials could not control their population.

Thus, East City began its cityhood as a problem community: residents of the unincorporated town had fought the county over desegregation, won the right to incorporate, and then experienced a crime wave, which, as I describe in more detail later, required the city's new police department to call in county reinforcements. This regional identity contributed to residents' continued sense that they lacked the political clout afforded to wealthier areas. As the woman from the church group explained, "I think people think that if you want to get rid of something, just bring it to East City and we'll just accept it." Similarly, the local board member and activist said that the SVP would not have been placed in neighboring areas because those areas, unlike East City, had "political juice." Even local political leaders felt the effects of their city's reputation as a problem community. A city council member said that East City's relative lack of resources made the city council's "job a lot harder, especially if you're being compared to another area maybe that has all the resources they need [. . .]. You're working at a deficit over here." The "deficit" came in the form of economic resources but also in the form of the clout required to procure necessary resources.

Although residents gained access to a city council when the town incorporated, some community members I spoke with were frustrated at infighting among city council members and the council's tendency to address issues only if and when it wanted to. The white woman who was active in the neighborhood beat meetings explained that she avoided city council meetings because "the city council ends up fighting [. . .] and it's ridiculous." She went on to explain, "I think it takes an act of Congress for anybody in this city to get anything done because they have to go in front of the city council. [. . .] [T]here is such animosity among the ones that sit up there that they can't even get through a session without having words right in front [of the public]." Miguel, the man who organized the petition against the SVP, said that when he attended a city council meeting on a different issue, he had had to wait until after midnight to comment. Because of this experience, he believed that the city council manipulated meetings so that most people would leave before they had a chance to comment on contentious issues.

A few residents countered these views. The social worker explained, "I think that people, when they're campaigning, they certainly present themselves as that they're doing, that they would do the best they can to meet the needs of the community. But there's so much more that goes into that in terms of, are they really able to do that? You know, and I think there's a lot of factors involved in that that would probably stifle them, you know." His comments suggest that although city council members may have been handling issues "the best they can," structural and systemic factors may have impeded their ability to "meet the needs of the community." Another local resident, a woman in her late fifties who worked at a nearby law clinic, also expressed a more positive view of city council members. She described local political leaders by saying, "There's a lot of people here who have created change." These comments indicate that not everyone viewed the city council negatively; however, despite these residents' favorable assessments, most perceived the city council as inaccessible.

Unlike the people in Ranchito who perceived their local leaders as empowered community members, many in East City described their city council members as politically motivated. For example, the Hispanic man who had stated his overall opposition to involvement in any kind of politics equated city council members with all other politicians. "All the politicians, they get hired to serve the people," he said. "They're for the people. And all that I see that they do, once they get into position, [. . .] they use the position as the first step and they campaign [. . .] for the next position." The activist who had been involved in antidrug efforts in the 1990s summed it up by saying, "They're totally insensitive unless it's something that can bring them money or political power; they ignore everything else." These two comments illustrate a broader trend in which community members perceived city council members as aligned more with political interests than with those of the community; far from being perceived as community members, local leaders were politicians first and foremost.

Not every individual I spoke with shared this perspective. The SVP's immediate neighbor explained, "They live here, so they want things to be done because that's their community. The current mayor of the city, I mean, his kids go to my girls' school, so we know that he wants things to be done because those are his children." While her comments more closely align the mayor's motives with the community, she still situated his concern for the community in terms of his personal investment in his children. As her statements suggest, perceptions of local political leaders as self-interested politicians did not always come across as negative.

The East City community's contentious relationship with county politicians and their perceptions of local politicians as self-interested contributed to a sense that political authority did not work in the interests of the community. When community members tried to access formal political authority through the city council and, before incorporation, county officials, they often found themselves fighting for resources and a voice in local decision making, which ultimately alienated them from the process. While interactions with politicians helped shape this orientation to political authority, the city council's position within broader political structures also contributed to the community's sense of alienation from political power.

POSITION WITHIN BROADER POLITICAL STRUCTURES

The city council's ability to exercise political power through a formal political structure may have made it more difficult for city council members to present themselves as community-oriented. The community's history of oppression by those in positions of political power contributed to a perceived separation between the community and political institutions. For instance, while the battle over incorporation represented a fight for control over local affairs, it also symbolized a perception that political institutions did not work in the community's interests. Local government structures may have been more community-oriented than those at the county level, but an inherent skepticism about political institutions persisted. For community members, those who could exercise formal political power either became more aligned with political institutions than the community or had their options limited by the constraints of political institutions. As the man who did not want anything to do with local politics put it, "Pretty much, the government runs the system. They make it and they manipulate it, and that's pretty much it."

At least one local politician, the city council member I interviewed, acknowledged the divide between the city council and the community. In our interview, he described some of the times they had tried to work with residents to solve local problems. When I asked him whether these were generally positive or negative experiences, he began by saying, "Well, the process . . . if one deliberately creates a process that allows for public and community participation, I think that the outcomes clearly are more reflective of community interests and people leave those forums, or leave those processes feeling that they have been heard." He then went on to say, "In those areas where we created a process that was as open and collaborative as possible, I think it's been good." While these comments suggest a collaborative relationship between residents and the city council on some issues, he ended by explaining, "We have a long way to go, like most communities, before we can really figure out how collaboration with community residents gets us to . . . is hardwired into everything we do." This qualification of his earlier statements demonstrates that despite efforts to be more "inclusive" and "collaborative," city council members exercised their power within a formal institution "hardwired" against community collaboration. While local politicians may have tried to blur the line between themselves and the community, their affiliation with a formal political institution overshadowed their local roots.

Some residents indirectly referenced the split between the community and those within formal political structures in their discussions of community activism. In our conversations, those who referred to local activism tended to focus more on volunteering and involvement in nonprofit organizations than on activity within formal political institutions such as voting, protesting, or otherwise pressuring local or county officials. While some community members had interacted with the city council by either attending meetings or bringing specific issues to their attention, others, such as the woman active in the local interfaith alliance, described joint efforts between local organizations and the police department. She explained that a few years prior to the SVP placement, "There was a lot of stuff going on crime-wise, and a lot of stuff gang-related and there was a lot of stuff going on drug-related. And it became quite clear that it was getting out of hand, so interested members of the community, nonprofit groups in the community alongside the city council and the police department, we all got together and we orchestrated a pride, a community pride day." Her description illustrates that local organizations sometimes partnered with formal institutions to address local problems.

Yet, earlier in our interview, when I asked how sensitive city leaders were to the needs and problems of the community, her response suggested an ongoing separation between informal and formal groups in East City. She explained, "I believe in their hearts, they're truly concerned about the community and its members. Now, the avenues it takes to get these things done [. . .] there's no leadership, there's no clear path." This lack of leadership resulted in regular meetings between her organization and city leaders "to discuss concerns of the community" because, as she put it, "a lot of things go through the cracks" unless community members actively brought issues to their attention. This perspective suggests that while some may have seen value in engaging with local politicians and other city leaders on community issues, their affiliations with formal political institutions made it more likely that community issues would fall "through the cracks."

The city council member and the county supervisor I interviewed both affirmed residents' civic engagement. According to the city council member, "We have a lot of nonprofits that are locally based. So, there is a lot of initiative within the community to create programs and internally address issues." The county supervisor echoed these statements when she told me, "So it continues to be a very strongly active—as a community they still have a lot of strong activism in the community that I think serves us well." In short, as the city council member put it, East City had, "a civil society that wants to participate, not just in city government, but in kind of the civic sector [. . .]. So I think that speaks well of the community that it doesn't feel like it is powerless to address the myriad of issues we have in East City [. . .]." This kind of involvement in the "civic sector" may have reflected and reinforced a sense of control over local issues that community members might not otherwise have had within formal political institutions.

East City's position as a problem community in the county, as well as activated residents' perceptions of local leaders as self-interested, and council members' ability to exercise formal political power, all contributed to a sense of political authority as embedded in and aligned with formal political institutions rather than the community. Like those in

other poor neighborhoods composed predominantly of racial and ethnic minorities, East City residents and political leaders found themselves
and their interests downplayed in the region's political landscape. When
local political leaders gained formal recognition through incorporation, their affiliation with the formal institution that had once failed to
protect the community's interests increasingly separated them from the
community.

While community members continued to be active in trying to solve
local problems, they remained skeptical of political authority. As the
man who had been active in local politics and served on local boards
put it, "The establishment is always doing what they choose to do, and
you know as people of color, we're always on the short end of that stick."
Thus, even though community members' activism sometimes aligned
them with city leaders, they continued to feel alienated from political
authority in part because formal political institutions had routinely facilitated the deployment of political power against their collective interests.

Orientation to Political Authority during the SVP Placement

When East City residents learned of the SVP placement, many perceived
it as yet another instance of political power being used against the community's interests. This interpretation often emerged in comparisons
between the SVP placement and other instances in which politicians
funneled unwanted people into East City, as well as community members' appraisals of the perceived political nature of the site selection
process.

For example, the woman who worked at a local law clinic wondered,
"Why did they have to choose East City if this is already a problem city?
[. . .] They always have to come to East City and bring them here. It's
not the first time that they bring a person like him. They've brought
other people. They always choose East City." The social worker implied
a similar perspective. After he said he believed the community in East
City was "misunderstood," I asked if he thought that might have played
a role in how the SVP ended up there. He quickly responded in the af-
firmative, explaining, "You know, the county's been up there fighting to
get him, dump him on us here. I'm saying if they had to live next door
to them, they would be singing a different tune." For both individuals,

the SVP placement reflected the county's desire to "dump" undesirable people in their neighborhoods.

The effects of this perceived dumping were reflected clearly in a statement made by the woman who had joined the protests after hearing about the issue through her church group. She described the people in East City as "a community that's trying to improve itself, and making some changes and some strides, trying to improve it to be better. And every time we think that we're going and working to change it and to improve it, things like [the SVP placement] happen." Thus, she perceived the SVP placement as a clear example of an exercise of political power that served to keep what the legal clinic worker had called a "problem city" from improving itself.

Sentiments from other community members who recognized the political nature of the site selection process provided more context for analogies between the SVP placement and the political establishment's ongoing trend toward funneling undesirable people into East City. Marc described the placement process as "crooked." "It was city and county in cahoots," he explained. "These things, they're not, they're orchestrated; it's an agenda to move these people in." The interfaith activist described the placement decision as "cruel and fully disengaged from the needs of the community." Together with the idea that the placement was "orchestrated," these comments suggest a broader belief not only that the SVP placement was political but that local and regional politicians had deliberately exercised their political power against the community.

This belief sometimes emerged in community members' concerns about a lack of input into the placement decision. As mentioned in chapter 1, the man who lived across the intersection from the placement location described feeling "like we been raped" by the placement decision because of the lack of local input. The man who avoided local politics explained that by the time the community found out about the placement, "the decision [had] already been made by government." The politically active former member of local boards implicated state officials when he explained that they had not extended the "common courtesy" of calling local political leaders to organize a "sit-down with them and explain the situation."

For these community members, politicians had purposely left local political leaders out of the decision-making process. While the residents

I spoke with differed in where they assigned blame for being left out, the overarching understanding of the placement became that of an outcome generated by a political decision-making system completely removed from the local context. Furthermore, their separation from the process represented alienation in which those in positions of political power deliberately kept community members, and sometimes even local politicians, from accessing the power necessary to stop the placement.

Legal Authority as Control

In East City, the community that opposed the SVP placement related to legal authority as a source of control of community members. East City residents were saturated in formal social controls in their everyday lives, and their interactions with courts tended toward defending themselves, family members, or other acquaintances. In short, the community's interactions with law enforcement and the courts emphasized the controlling aspects of the law.

RELATIONSHIP WITH LAW ENFORCEMENT

Before incorporating in the early 1980s, East City relied on the sheriff's department for local law enforcement. Unlike in Deserton, sheriff's deputies were very visible in East City. In fact, heavy-handed law enforcement tactics may have contributed to the movement to incorporate. As the local political activist and former board member explained, "The sheriff's department would come in and beat people down and arrest people and do what they wanted to do in the community. And the community used to demonstrate against that on a regular basis. And finally, you know, the movement was created to incorporate." Through incorporation, the community would be able to form its own police department, which residents hoped would react differently to local problems. According to the city council member:

> There was a lot of discontent over the way the sheriff treated the residents. [. . .] [The sheriff] didn't have a real understanding of East City. Residents felt that they weren't getting the services they needed. Rather than having [the sheriff] crack heads, they wanted [the sheriff's department] to look at people speeding through the city. Or they wanted [them]

to look at other issues related to community policing. And [the sheriff's department] wouldn't do that, so that was an imposition of county policing standards on a community that, unless you were on the board of supervisors, you could not have an impact on that. That's no longer the case because we now have police.

Thus, the East City Police Department was formed with high expectations: it would focus on problems that community members specified and would implement more acceptable solutions than the sheriff's department had.

Unfortunately, a few years after incorporation, East City earned the dubious distinction of having one of the highest murder rates per capita in the country. During this time, rampant homicides and blatant drug selling solidified the city's reputation as a place best avoided if possible. The antidrug activist recalled that the city had had "drug dealers on every corner," and the woman who had found out about the SVP placement through her church group described the neighborhood during that time as having streets "full of young people selling drugs." The mother who had lived in the neighborhood for more than twenty years summed it up by saying, "There was a lot of drug dealers and a lot of killings. [. . .] It was a terrible time then."

Residents wanted their local police department to curb crime, but the relatively new department was also contending with a lack of experience and resources.[11] A sheriff's detective whom I interviewed explained that the "fledgling" East City Police Department "didn't have the money or resources to combat the crime that was going on there." He went on to say that the police department and other "city leaders asked for assistance from outside agencies. And the sheriff's office, being the [. . .] agency that they came to, assist[ed] [. . .] in patrol and in investigations." Residents' perception of an ineffective local police force deepened the rift between community members and formal law enforcement agencies.

The persistent presence of law enforcement officers in East City contributed to an orientation to legal authority as a source of control of community members. Some spoke of law enforcement as a source of protection, but more often their comments and experiences framed law enforcement purposes and activities in terms of control. For instance, the heavy-handed tactics the community had experienced before incorporation did not disappear. A black woman in her midseventies whom I met at the neighborhood beat meeting explained that some officers would "try to bend the law to make it fit them. However that may go. I've seen them right out here on the corner of [an intersection]. They'll put their foot on somebody and smash it down. You know that they're doing damage on the other side, but they don't understand it, or they don't consider it." In addition to mentioning ongoing physical control tactics, some spoke more broadly about law enforcement as a source of control. The neighbor who had recently moved next door to the SVP placement site very explicitly linked control and law enforcement. She told me, "If you can't control a thing, then you call the police." Similarly, the antidrug activist I spoke with characterized the role of the police by saying, "They're here to arrest criminals." In a particularly revealing discussion, the woman who worked at a legal clinic said that she "would like to see that the police department is more attentive to everything that happens so that there's more control." These comments suggest that while residents wanted to protect their community from threats, they related to legal authority primarily as a source of power to control those who broke the law.

A decade after the crime wave, East City's violent crime rate fell to pre-1990s levels, mirroring crime trends across the country.[12] Some residents attributed at least some of the decline in crime to police department efforts. The woman from the interfaith alliance explained, "This [new] police chief has really made an impact in the city for a positive change, and part of that I have to accredit to his ability to put, put groups of people together that don't always necessarily agree with one another." The newcomer neighbor said that the police were "pretty good" at dealing with problems in the area, in part because "you always see a police officer at least once or twice a day, even if you're in the street for like five minutes, or ten, you're gonna see one or two police cars." A woman I met at the beat meeting echoed these statements when she told me that the police were "more tuned in to protecting the public" than they used to be. While these comments suggest a more positive relationship between residents and the police than in the past, a focus on control still dominated law enforcement activity in the area.

In the early 2000s, the East City Police Department implemented a modified version of community policing by dividing the city into beats and holding the aforementioned beat meetings. Local input and problem solving was the ostensible goal of beat meetings, but by involving community members in creating and maintaining public safety, the police department shifted some of the responsibility for crime control from the police to the community. During the meeting I attended, most of the conversation focused on responding to drug activity in the area. Police officers urged attendees to call an anonymous tip line, but residents questioned the effectiveness of these calls and the potentially dangerous consequences of becoming involved. One exchange in particular demonstrates how residents and police officers negotiated their roles in solving the local drug problem. As I wrote in my field notes after the meeting:

> A petite elderly black woman in a jumpsuit and feather boa around her neck sat next to me. She related a story of how she'd dealt with the drug dealers next door to her. She'd been calling the police for sixteen years before they could finally get the dealers out. Another woman said she'd been calling for a year about drug activity in her neighborhood, which she felt was too long to wait. The police officer at the meeting said that drug busts were tricky. The police couldn't just go onto private property and arrest a drug dealer, and the dealers knew that. The dealers also have scanners, so when they hear that police are coming, they just close up shop and wait until the police are gone. They also will step onto someone's front lawn, thus making it impossible for the police to arrest them.

These types of negotiations highlighted the contradictions of deploying formal legal authority: the police said they would protect residents, but such protection was not always legally possible. While police officers acknowledged that legal constraints sometimes prolonged the process of shutting down illegal drug operations, they continued to insist that they needed local residents' help, implying that the community bore some responsibility for solving the problem in East City. Yet, invoking such protection would tighten formal controls on local drug dealers who may then resent the interference and ultimately retaliate against those who report, even anonymously, to the police. Considering these constraints, residents at the meeting remained skeptical of the police department's power to protect them, but they also retained some belief in the idea that formal controls could help solve local crime problems.

The police department's attempts to involve the community in reducing crime were part of a larger trend toward improving East City's overall image. After the crime wave, residents began trying to combat their negative reputation in the region. When asked to describe their community, many residents and local officials I spoke with used the crime wave as a reference point against which to assess recent improvements and future potential. East City "has its problems," said the woman who worked at the legal clinic, "but it's a good community. It has good people in it too. It's not just bad people. [I]n the past, there's been a lot of stuff in the news about the crime and how [. . .] the city is the capital of crime, or whatever they call it. You know, there's a lot of bad things, [but also] a lot of good things." Others echoed these sentiments, noting that the city had improved because, as the man uninvolved in local politics put it, "I see less people selling drugs." When I asked the antidrug activist how he had seen the neighborhood change over the years, he responded, "A lot of old gangsters are gone. They're old too; they're worn out, and so they ain't doing anything." These comments suggest that in East City, improving the community's image required decreasing the prevalence and visibility of the "bad things," in part by reducing the visible presence of people engaging in criminal activities.

Yet, deploying legal authority to control residents complicated the relationship between the police department and community members. As in similar neighborhoods,[13] many in East City knew people who were or had been on parole or probation or had had contact with the criminal justice system as defendants. In this context, major law enforcement operations had the potential to alienate the community from the police. In a telephone interview, an East City police captain explained:

> Quite often, when we do major operations, joint operations with the state, local, and federal agents like FBI or DEA, quite often following those operations or those sweeps, we will have a town meeting or a meeting at city council with the residents and some of them—over a hundred and fifty people came to one of our last ones—so that we could explain about this big takedown that we did. [. . .] In that small community, people are gonna ask questions, they're gonna want to know about it. So what we do is we actually have a meeting following those type of sweeps to explain what was going on and get their feedback. Let them express what they

feel—and you'd be amazed to hear some of the comments that we get. But this is what we do just to try to stay ahead of it so, we . . . In our words, we kind of legitimize our department. You know, we're not afraid to take on the questions in the meetings. We would love to do that so that it doesn't fester and grow into something that it's not.

The captain's comments indicate that the police department recognized and tried to mitigate the potential negative impacts of its operations on police-community relations; yet, while community meetings kept residents informed, they also facilitated a relationship with law enforcement that revolved around controlling community members rather than protecting them.

Thus, for East City residents, creating and maintaining a community had been closely linked to law enforcement agencies exercising legal authority to control the population. Incorporation localized police power, but a crime wave in the 1990s fostered calls for increased police presence and more effective policing. More recently, community policing had improved police-community relations, but it still emphasized the controlling aspects of law enforcement. While residents wished for more control of certain lawbreakers, they also knew many of the individuals being targeted by the police. This position left residents wanting to invoke the protective aspects of legal authority to combat crime problems but also not wanting members of their community to become targets of the law enforcement activities that had in the past negatively affected residents of East City.

RELATIONSHIP WITH COURTS

Perhaps unsurprisingly, East City residents' relationships with the courts were heavily informed by their knowledge of or interaction with those who were or had been defendants in the criminal justice system. As in other neighborhoods with racially mixed populations and lower socioeconomic statuses,[14] East City had a high parolee population relative to surrounding areas. In part, higher proportions of those who have had contact with the criminal justice system within communities like East City stem from disproportionately high chances of incarceration among black men,[15] who then return to their communities after incarceration.[16] In East City, the legacies created by this relationship with the courts shaped the community's dominant orientation to legal authority as a source of control.

Many of those I spoke with in East City mentioned the portion of the community's population that had had contact with the criminal justice system. Their comments suggest three ways in which community members perceived the courts in relation to the community. Some implied that the courts tried to work with the community through reentry programs, others noted a lack of concern with helping the community, and at least one believed that judges conspired with other officials and entrepreneurs to make money off those returning to society after prison. While differing in their assessments of the motivations of actors within the criminal justice system, each of these perspectives assumed that the courts operated to regulate community members more often than to protect the community.

Those who articulated the first perspective noted the abundance of reentry programs in East City. The former board member explained that he viewed the SVP as one of many sex offenders in the community, and he tried to tell other residents to keep the issue in perspective because, as he explained, "the bigger issue is that, you know, the large numbers of people in the community that's going through rehab. And reentering the community and so from that standpoint you know they, they do seminars, they do workshops. And try to get them interacting in the community." The city council member also referred to the city's efforts to reintegrate formerly incarcerated individuals into the community, saying:

We have a parole reentry program, by the way. It's the only one in the state. I think there are now two. It is a model for the state, and the state is actually looking at it as a way to reduce recidivism. I mentioned to you that we have problems with the folks who are incarcerated. But, you know, most communities, you tell them you're going to have a parole reentry program, they would say, 'Go f yourself, not in my community.' East City said no way, we're gonna do that, right. If we can help two hundred of our folks, or people who are similar to our folks to reenter society and not reoffend, we're gonna, you know, we're for that. Now, we don't want a lot of our people to be in that program, but we think it's important to do that.

His comments, combined with those of the former board member, demonstrate that reentry programs were a pervasive and tolerated, if not welcomed, presence in East City. The courts' ties to the overall process of convicting and sentencing individuals meant that a focus on reentry was at least implicitly linked to the courts' ability to regulate those trying to reintegrate into the community.

The second perspective, that the courts did little to help the community, emerged as concerns about offenders cycling in and out of the system and, when not incarcerated, victimizing community members. According to the social worker, "A lot of people getting out of jail, they may get out for a couple of days and then they're back in again." The black woman I met at the neighborhood beat meeting described her frustration with the system's focus on light sentences for minor drug dealers. She said that when they get a "little" dealer, "and put [him] in jail for six months or a year, then he's back out. But if you get the [big] dealer, then you get the ones that are dealing it into the neighborhoods." For these community members, the courts had little concern for offenders cycling in and out of the system and the community.

This perspective closely aligns with more direct references to the impacts of such cycling on the community. The social worker who had explained that people who get out of jail end up back in again also said, "People feel like in general that this community has been kind of neglected when it comes to that, you know. That, you know, a lot of people have been victimized by people coming out of the penal system." The woman who worked at the legal clinic described an incident in which she felt victimized by a man whom she believed had recently returned from a term of incarceration:

> I had this other incident where I had a man who, I knew he was clearly placed in this community and he had one of those bracelets on his ankle and he really looked mean. And he was harassing me because I was dropping my child off at the babysitter and I was sort of parking at the driveway, sort of blocking the sidewalk a little bit to drop off my child and then come back to the car right away. He would come every morning at the same time I would drop off my son. And he spit on my car one time. And I was like, this is ridiculous not to feel safe in your community. And

if you don't feel safe, what are our officials doing? Why do these people get placed in East City?

Her description highlights the safety concerns associated with living in a community with a higher population of people returning from prison than in surrounding areas. Moreover, while the legal clinic worker never directly named the courts, the questions she posed suggest her discontent with how the courts handled the release of formerly incarcerated individuals into the community. This concern, along with those related to people with criminal records cycling through the system, suggests a pervasive sense that the courts did little to protect the community.

While some asserted a relatively passive role of the courts in not protecting the community, the antidrug activist advanced a more nefarious theory. He believed that the courts worked in conjunction with local officials and entrepreneurs to engage in the "criminal housing business." He explained that those in power "treat East City like a jail annex" in which individuals involved in a "criminal housing business [...] make a living off their non-profits" by "find[ing] the houses and load[ing] them up with criminals." While he was the only person I spoke with who made such extreme allegations, his comments suggest another way in which the courts may have been perceived as failing to protect the community.

Taken together, these perspectives on the role of the courts in the community demonstrate that for East City residents, the courts operated more as an institution of control—by regulating the reentry of formerly incarcerated individuals into the community and by cycling identified offenders through the system—than as one of protection. These everyday, indirect experiences with the courts shaped how community members perceived the courts in relation to the community. This, in turn, shaped the community's dominant orientation to legal authority as a source of control.

Orientation to Legal Authority during the SVP Placement

In many ways, the SVP placement in East City reinforced the community's dominant orientation toward legal authority as a source of control. Many community members linked the placement to the city's experiences with other formerly incarcerated individuals attempting to reenter society, but their discussions of how this placement was different revealed how their orientation to legal authority played out during the SVP placement. East City's history as a place with a relatively high proportion of individuals reentering society after incarceration might have engendered some compassion for the SVP, particularly because communities composed predominantly of racial and ethnic minorities tend to house more registered sex offenders than other communities.[17] Indeed, some of those I spoke with mentioned a disproportionate concentration of registered sex offenders in East City. As the man who lived across the intersection from the SVP explained, "I had gone online. I had seen all these pedophiles. You know, like there's pedophiles around. I was like, man, we just got a neighborhood full." With a "neighborhood full" of sex offenders, community members had likely interacted with these individuals throughout their daily lives, but this did not automatically translate into acceptance of sex offenders. The former board member and political activist described how he had previously tried to bring the issue of sex offender reentry to the community's attention:

> And when I attend those [reintegration seminars and workshops] I always bring up the fact that, you know, this large number of sex offenders are in the community. And, and how are we addressing that? And they aren't willing to address it. They want these individuals to be absorbed in the community and be accepted, but from my perspective there's not atonement that's being made to the community or to the people that they have wronged. So, you know, they just want to come back and be a part, but they don't want to make any atonement, so . . . I have problems with that.

His story demonstrates that knowing about and interacting with sex offenders in East City before the SVP placement did not always mean residents had more compassion for the SVP or other sex offenders. While the latter individuals may have been perceived as part of the larger problem of rehabilitation and reentry of formerly incarcerated people into East City, at least some people I spoke with saw sex offenders as a different kind of population of whom community members had different expectations for "atonement" for their previous crimes.

Instead of compassion for a formerly incarcerated person trying to reenter society, community members' comments about the SVP placement more often focused on how the exercise of legal authority had either allowed for or orchestrated the placement, demonstrating once again that those in positions to exercise legal power cared little about protecting the community. These residents attributed at least some of the blame for the SVP placement to law enforcement and the courts. The handful of community members I spoke with who either blamed law enforcement or expressed skepticism about their role in the SVP placement tended to believe that the police had withheld information about the placement from the community. Another granddaughter of the elderly woman next door to the placement location said that part of her goal in protesting and distributing information in front of his house was "letting people know that the police said they put out flyers, which they didn't because so many people that came to the little rally didn't know nothing about the dude being there, didn't know nothing about no flyers being put on the door." When I asked the black woman from the beat meeting how the placement had affected her perceptions of the police, she answered, "If they'll pull this off on you, they'll pull other things off on you too." She too believed that the police had withheld information to slip the SVP into East City with little say from the community. While both community members questioned law enforcement's attempts to control information about the placement, neither directly accused police officials of bringing the SVP to East City.

Two community members believed that the police had arranged for the placement in East City. When I asked one of the granddaughters of the woman next door what she thought might have been more effective in protesting the SVP placement, she answered, "Just keep on the police chief. It was, you know, his idea to move him here." She went on to say that more communication between the police and residents would have helped ease the controversy over the SVP placement. The woman who had recently moved next door to the SVP's house also blamed the police. She explained, "It was all the police. They knew about it. They attended the meetings. They did everything. They were supposed to let know their officials, they didn't. They never did." From her perspective, the police not only knew about the placement but also hid it from local officials and the community.

One event in particular informed this perspective. At the notification meeting, the chief of police told residents that there had been a court hearing in which members of the community could have voiced their concerns to the judge. Unfortunately, he said, law enforcement officials had mistakenly believed that the hearing was closed to the public, so they had not informed the community about it. The neighbor I spoke with later explained, "And the truth was that everybody was allowed in the meeting, it was an open court meeting, and nobody attended because nobody was told." She went on to question the police chief's role in the placement: "And the chief of police was saying that they didn't know anything about it? And the chief of police was saying that only he was allowed in that meeting? In the court meeting on the release? How convenient that he was the only one and the court meeting was open." This, combined with allegations from her and other community members that they had never received the informational flyers, strengthened her belief that the police had withheld information and that the placement process consisted of "a whole bunch of lies" by the police department.

Together, these community members' statements suggest that at least some people in East City believed that those in positions to exercise legal authority had withheld crucial information to exclude the community from the placement process. This perspective helps shed some light on the police chief's actions during the notification meeting. As described earlier, in a series of exchanges, the chief attempted to encourage collective action at the meeting by redirecting audience members' comments about what could be done to stop the placement back to the audience. In doing so, he was indirectly attempting to reshape the community's orientation toward law enforcement as a controlling institution. At one point, he told the group to think of the SVP placement as a "'we' and 'us'" problem rather than a problem of the community against law enforcement. This strategy suggests that the relationship between the police department and the community usually consisted of an "us versus them" dynamic in which community members either blamed the police for local crime-related problems or opposed law enforcement's attempts to impose formal social control. When the SVP placement occurred within this context, community members had a hard time believing that law enforcement's main goal was to protect the community.

A larger number of the residents I spoke with placed most of the blame on the courts, and specifically the judge, for the SVP placement. As with law enforcement, these people tended to believe that the judge cared little about the community. For instance, the antidrug activist described the placement as "illegal" because the landlord was affiliated with the county and was making money off the placement. He explained, "The judge never reviewed that, did he? I mean, how could he have allowed [the SVP] to go there if he never had proper review?" By his estimation, the judge had failed to consider all relevant information, and that had resulted in an injustice for the community. While the judge almost certainly did consider the legality of the placement, the activist's statement demonstrates skepticism that the courts operated fairly. In subsequent statements, he elaborated on his frustration, saying, "We're not rehabilitating him or nothing; somebody's making good money on a decent property." This comment suggests the beliefs that the judge failed to appropriately exercise legal authority and that the court had failed to provide the framework necessary for the SVP's rehabilitation. This activist's perceptions of the courts contributed to the belief that those exercising legal authority were, at best, indifferent to the community's concerns, and, at worst, deliberately disregarding the potential dangers posed by the SVP placement.

For others, the judge's decision to place the SVP in East City appeared to thwart local efforts to improve the city. The white woman who regularly attended beat meetings attributed the decision to the city's negative reputation, explaining, "I kind of feel that whoever made the decision, I guess it was the judge, [...] they chose East City because we're kind of like a throwback. Well, you know what, we're kind of coming around. We really are. Even though we still have our little gang wannabes and those that are going around shooting people and stabbing people and doing robberies and so on, we're not a throwback. And I'm kind of insulted by that." From her perspective, the judge had assumed that the city was a lost cause and thus cared little about implanting a dangerous threat in the community.

Her comment also implied that she believed the city had much potential to shed its negative reputation. Yet, as the woman affiliated with the church group explained, doing so required managing and controlling certain members of the city's population. She said that the community "just didn't want any more negative publicity in East City. We have enough to deal with and we didn't need another person that we had to watch or be concerned about." This statement illustrates a broader sense among community members that the placement decision represented an exercise of legal authority that added another challenge to the already difficult task of controlling crime in the community. In other words, by allowing for the placement in East City, the judge had exercised legal authority in a way that pushed the community further from achieving its goals.

The idea that legal authority had been exercised to hinder the city's progress also emerged in statements that those in positions of power had used their authority to control rather than protect the community. In one particularly revealing statement, the social worker I interviewed noted, "They were paying a lot of money for security that was not to . . . it was really to protect him against the community. Not to protect the community against him." This sentiment demonstrates that much of the frustration with the placement stemmed from community members' sense that legal authority—in the form of security as well as the placement decision itself—had not been exercised in the name of protecting the community. Instead, community members perceived the placement as another instance in which those in positions of power had exercised their authority not to protect the community but to undermine local attempts to control crime and maintain public safety.

Community Orientations to Authority and Political and Legal Mobilization

The community in East City took a skeptical stance toward the exercise of political and legal authority. The former had historically alienated the community, and the latter had been deployed to control community members. Yet the residents I spoke with did not wholly reject the legitimacy of political and legal authority. This section explains how the community's dominant orientations toward political and legal authority contributed to ambivalence and indifference toward political and legal mobilization, even when those strategies had the chance to become key components of the community's opposition to the SVP placement.

Ambivalence toward Political Mobilization

Political action did occur in response to the SVP placement: the city council passed a resolution opposing the placement, and the mayor organized a protest. As demonstrated by the case in Ranchito, either or both of these actions could have become a rallying point for opposition efforts. Instead, alienation from political institutions contributed to a sense that political mobilization neither constituted community action nor represented community interests. As the man who avoided local politics explained, "It's all just politics. [. . .] [Politicians] being on the street, to me, means nothing." For him and many other community members, the mayor and the city council were simply maneuvering to gain political support rather than exercising political authority for the greater good of the community. This perspective contributed to ambivalence toward political mobilization as a strategy to oppose the SVP placement.

Community members' interpretations of political reactions to the placement demonstrate how the community's orientation to political authority contributed to the lack of support for political mobilization as the centerpiece of its response to the placement. For instance, some people believed that neither the city council nor the mayor had stopped the SVP placement because they cared more about protecting their positions within the formal political institution than about advancing community interests. In one of my informal conversations with Marc, he described city and county officials as "part of the problem because they had to sign off on [the placement] in the first place." He then explained that the city and county would stick together on the placement issue. Later, in our interview, he described the notification meeting as proceeding in "the typical way. Everybody up there in front of the city council protesting and the city council not responding." For him and others I spoke with, the city council's actions during the SVP placement were little more than a bureaucratic mandate to hear public comment.

The city council member I interviewed hinted at this same notion when he described the notification meeting as providing a "forum in which the community would feel that the city was responding." Rather than refer to the meeting as the community's response to the issue, this council member's description suggests a separation between the community and political action in which politicians reserved the power to respond to local issues if and when they chose to do so. The city council member's perspective and community members' skepticism of political reactions to the placement suggest that while in other local contexts political mobilization might have become a rallying point for the community response, the East City community's orientation to political authority constrained the extent to which this happened.

Furthermore, considering the community's historical relationships with politicians, the city council's position within the formal political structure likely contributed to residents' ambivalence toward political mobilization during the SVP placement. As a formally recognized political body, the city council could exercise political authority to make legally binding decisions. Yet its status as a city council rather than a county- or state-level entity meant that it could not always achieve results that would be most favorable to the city. Although the city council had little say in the judge's order to place the SVP in East City, community members still believed it could have stopped the placement had it had the motivation to do so. By contrast, these same people may not have believed that an informal political or community group could have stopped the placement because of its lack of political power. This created a situation in which the city council, a formal entity within a formal political structure, had the nominal ability to exercise political authority, but when it could not use that power to stop the placement, its position within the political structure undermined its legitimacy with the community.

Community members' reactions to the mayor's protest illustrate how the city council's position within a formal political structure dampened support for political mobilization. By relying on a protest, an informal strategy more akin to grassroots opposition than formal political action, the mayor might have signaled his status as a community member. Yet, his ability to exercise formal political authority (successfully or not) undermined his attempt to align himself with the community.[18] The woman who worked at the legal clinic attended the protest but found it difficult to do so. She said, "I felt like we were harassing this poor man [the SVP]." She went on to explain, "City officials [were not] there listening to what people had to say [. . .]. Instead, I saw just a big number of people telling this poor person [the SVP] to get out of the city." Rather than the leadership she had expected given the mayor's formal position, she found that the protest resembled a grassroots opposition effort with little power to change the situation.

Her perspective on the protest reflected some residents' expectations that the mayor and other elected officials would make better use of their formal authority to address the SVP placement. As the man who actively avoided local politics described his reaction to the protest, "[The mayor] shows support to the community, so he's done. 'I support it, I was there,' and that's it. [. . .] And I mean if he had decided to do the right thing, he may not even show up right then. Because he knew he would not accomplish nothing by [protesting]." For these community members, the mayor occupied a position of power and should have used that power to stop the placement; instead, he chose what community members perceived to be a symbolic response to the issue.

A local reporter reinforced this perspective when he asked the mayor on television if it was "appropriate for a mayor to support something that [might turn violent]." By questioning the mayor's tactics, the reporter highlighted the irony of an official with the power to exercise formal political authority resorting to a protest, a means of opposition more commonly employed by people with relatively little power. The reporter's question and residents' reflections on the protest suggest that the mayor's reliance on an informal strategy for opposition contributed to a perception of a lack of formal political leadership. This perception fit well within a local context in which the community related to political authority as a source of power that often advanced political institutional interests over those of the community.

Some community members did recognize the institutional constraints on the city council. Marc told me in our interview that the city council "don't have that kind of clout" to stop the SVP placement. As the white woman from the neighborhood beat meeting explained, "They did *not* want him released here. They did everything in their power. But like I said, I think it fell in the hands of that judge." The woman from the church group echoed these sentiments when she said, "I think a lot of our city council, their hands were tied in a lot of ways to do a lot of things." All three of these individuals believed that the city council did what little it could, but ultimately it could not stop the placement because of institutional limits on its power. While these residents gave some benefit of the doubt to the city council, one city official I spoke with expressed frustration with community members' lack of recognition of the limits of the city council's power. He said, "There was a misunderstanding of the power of the city to do anything about it. [. . .] [The community] wanted the city council to do something to prevent him being placed in the community. The city doesn't have the power to do that." For him, community members wanted the council to do something that political and legal institutions had made impossible.

Rallying around politicians' actions would have contradicted the community's dominant orientation to political authority as a source of alienation. Community members' perceptions of their local politicians as separate from the community and aligned with political institutional interests constrained the extent to which political actions could become a key part of the community's response to the SVP placement. Regardless of whether community members distrusted their local politicians or had faith in them but distrusted larger political institutions, they were skeptical of political strategies as viable options for stopping the placement decision.

A grassroots effort to leverage political authority may have drawn more community support, but even a community-based group would have had to overcome residents' skepticism that political authority could have worked in the community's interests. A few residents lamented the community's political inaction. When I asked the antidrug activist what he thought the community should have done differently in protesting the placement, he answered, "Well, you have to lay siege to it. And come up with people who are used to standing out there and laying siege. You know, instead, excited crowds for an hour and then go home. And then the few people that sort of hung around doing a vigil were like doing a vigil. And that's no pressure on him, basically. It's no pressure on the cops and it's no pressure on the public leaders." For him, more organized, sustained protests would have applied more pressure to those with the power to change the placement decision.

The local activist and former board member shed some light on why some community members may not have put more pressure on their local politicians: "Well, I think it's a combination of two things. One, you don't know. And if you do know, sometimes you're so darn busy it's hard to . . . I mean you got families, you got kids, it's hard to go out and do what you need to do. [. . .] Reality kicks in sometimes." For both men, political authority may have provided leverage to stop or reverse the SVP placement, but the "reality" of structural constraints on the everyday lives of the working poor precluded them from applying the political pressure necessary to achieve their goals. Thus, ambivalence toward political mobilization did not necessarily reflect an outright rejection of political authority as a potentially useful tool for opposition. It more likely indicated a combination of skepticism of how politicians exercised their authority and the reality of structural constraints that made it harder for community members to access political arenas.

Exclusion from Litigation

Many community members believed that either litigation or an appeal in court had a better chance of stopping the placement in East City than in-person protests or other political action. When I asked the man who avoided local politics to explain his skepticism of the protests, he answered, "I heard that there is a law violation, so you have to use the system. [. . .] And that's how you approach it. I mean, you're not gonna accomplish nothing [protesting] in the street right there." Later, when I asked what he thought local residents should have done, he answered, "Well, I mean, I guess, the way I, if everybody, I mean to do something about this, I mean, the community, I guess they can unify and hire a lawyer and go after him directly. And the local authorities . . . In my suspicion is authorities cannot go against authorities." For him, a "law violation" required working within the legal system rather than trying to fight using political tactics. The antidrug activist concurred. He told me that the best way to fight the placement would have been to "lawyer up" and "get it in front of a judge." He characterized this strategy as a "nuisance lawsuit." Even outsiders such as Jack from Deserton and a retired deputy police chief told community members that they could only stop the placement by going through the legal system.

When Marc began talking with other residents about the potential for a lawsuit, the small group utilized a similar tactic as the people in Deserton by trying to get the word out that other strategies were a "dead end" and that there was "nothing else we could do other than hire an attorney." When Jack consulted with Marc and the principal of the neighborhood school, community members could have leveraged his legal expertise to guide them through the process of either litigation or appeals. The school principal's connections to local parents, the police chief's attempts to connect with the community, and Marc's connections to a broad base of residents through his longtime residence and activism in the community could have helped mobilize local residents around legal strategies. Despite these opportunities, neither the idea of a lawsuit nor other legal action drew community members together to oppose the SVP placement.

According to Marc, the small group that considered litigation went as far as it could, but ultimately a lawsuit seemed infeasible without legal expertise, money, or a lawyer willing to take the case pro bono. This interpretation of the failure of litigation to take hold as a key strategy in the opposition efforts fits with the ground-level realities of going to court; however, the failure of litigation to galvanize a base of activists to oppose the SVP placement also suggests that the idea of a lawsuit did not appeal to people in East City as much as it did to those in other places such as Deserton. Some people in East City clearly hoped that legal authority might be able to help them, but the community's dominant orientation to legal authority as a source of control undermined the appeal of leveraging legal authority, even when a person with some legal expertise offered to help.

The belief that without a lawyer the community could not successfully navigate the court system to oppose the SVP placement suggests that community members did not feel entitled to access the law and have it work in their favor. Litigation would have invoked different aspects of the legal system than law enforcement, but the community's historical and contemporary relationships with the police had downplayed the protective aspects of the law and highlighted the need for community members to go through formal structures and processes to access the legal system. Even in the SVP placement process itself, the police chief's central role in organizing and moderating the notification meeting underscored the necessity of working with law enforcement agencies to maintain public safety. Against this backdrop, those pursuing litigation believed they needed someone to provide an "in" to the court system. As Marc put it, the county was "a rich county with people who carry a lot of weight," so they had to mount their opposition in the "right" way, meaning that they needed a lawyer to proceed.

Interactions with the courts that tended toward criminal defense may also have constrained the appeal of litigation as a central tactic for opposition. While the courts had granted the community the right to incorporate, subsequent efforts to reverse the crime wave focused on identifying and controlling local residents who had committed crimes or knew others who had. These efforts highlighted the role of the courts in controlling crime, especially as they brought many East City residents into court as defendants. Even after crime rates decreased, many residents became intimately familiar with criminal courts as they or their family members or acquaintances went through criminal proceedings. These experiences contributed to an environment in which the courts were generally perceived as inaccessible without the aid of a lawyer.

In short, from community members' perspectives, someone with legal capital would have had to facilitate their encounter with the court. While Jack agreed to provide guidance, he made it very clear that he would not fight the legal battle for them. They would have to do it themselves. When no one stepped forward to speak for the community in court, the idea of litigation died. The community's dominant orientation toward legal authority as a source of control had facilitated its exclusion from the legal system.

The Aftermath

When I visited East City two weeks after the SVP had arrived and one week after the mayor's protest, all signs of protest outside the SVP's home had disappeared. Jack met with the school principal two months later, and when I spoke to Marc two months after that, he characterized the opposition efforts as being at a "dead standstill." The lack of options for opposing the placement and the approaching holidays had pulled people's attention toward their families, so there were no plans for future action. As one of the neighbor's granddaughters put it, "It's not that we didn't care anymore. . . . It's a lot of work [to protest]." Others echoed her sentiment, with the school principal explaining, "You can spend all your days protesting outside somebody's house . . . or you can get on with your life." The mother of six who had lived in the neighborhood for decades said that "the person" who made the placement decision "was not doing anything, so why keep protesting?" In short, the opposition efforts died when community members in East City realized the SVP was there to stay.

A city official I spoke with believed that the protests failed to achieve their goals because they were "not carefully researched" or "carefully calculated." Some community members had a different perspective on the result of the protests. The Hispanic man who avoided local politics told me, "Other communities where they do this, I heard that the same violations [unclear] nearby to the community, and I guess they last longer, but with the same outcome. Nothing changes." This assessment more closely represents the realities of protesting SVP placements; in most cases in California, local opposition did not change placement decisions.

When asked about changes in the community after the placement issue, many residents told me that essentially "nothing changed," but others noted subtle changes in everyday life. For instance, some noticed more parents walking with their children to school. Others stopped to look at the SVP's house when they passed it in their daily routines. "I think about him every time I walk by that house," said the interfaith activist. "I think about him every time I drive down that street, I'll think about him. He has not left the back premises of my mind since he moved here." The white woman from the beat meeting described similar curiosity after the protests. "Trust me, I've been curious," she said. "We've driven by. But there's been nothing. I mean it's just like a normal house and there's not much to it and you don't really see any activity or anything."

Others had a bit more interaction with the SVP after he moved in. When I asked the man who lived across the intersection if he had seen the SVP around, he answered, "Yeah, he comes around. I wave at him, 'Hi.' He's outside, and sometimes he prunes the yard, rakes up the leaves, but there's always [a security guard] close by." A few other people also mentioned that they had seen the SVP engaging in the mundane tasks of yard work. As the mother of six described, "But now, he's very comfortable. Now he come, Mr. [SVP], he come outside and cut the plants around the garden in front of his house. So now it seems like everything is normal now." These brief interactions directly contradict the stereotypical pitchforks and torches responses that tend to dominate popular portrayals of local reactions to sex offenders. Neighbors were by no means overly friendly to the man who had moved into their neighborhood, but they did try to engage with him as a person at least some of the time.

At the same time, others were more cautious. For example, the neighbor who had recently moved to the neighborhood portrayed the SVP's yard work in a more sinister light. She explained, "He goes outside and takes care of his roses. He can just go and cut the roses. He has a knife and he's just chopping them with hate and breaking them to pieces. And it's like, you see such violence, the way he is as a person." She too said that she greeted him whenever she saw him, but she remained skeptical about his potential for violence. One of the granddaughters of the elderly woman next door took a similar position. She told me that when she saw him in his backyard, "I just say, 'Hi. [. . .] How you doing.' Yeah, I don't strike up too much conversation with him. I don't want to be too friendly and then he think he can come over into my grandmother's yard and get hurt. That's what's going to happen to him." These comments indicate that while some people felt compelled to interact with their new neighbor, the label of "sexually violent predator" shaped how they perceived his intentions in their brief social interactions. As a result, at least some remained cautious about getting too close for fear that he might victimize them or someone they knew.

A handful of community members described some positive effects of the opposition efforts on the community itself. These tended to be discussed in terms of deeper connections with neighbors who participated in the opposition efforts. "I think any time something like that happens, you connect with people where you might not have at the same level as before," said the school principal. The mother of six mentioned that she felt closer to her neighbors after the opposition efforts because "if somebody calls for help or something, I think we gonna help each other." Even the police chief picked up on these changes in the community. He characterized the entire situation as a "negative" that "turned into a positive because I think it brought a lot of community members together who live within a block or two of one another, who'd never really spoken or had anything to talk about, but now they had this one problem in common. They came together and said we're gonna all make sure nothing happens." That sense of connection may not have transformed into collective action on other issues, but the neighbor of the SVP's home explained that "being scared [of the SVP] forced everybody to look after each other, and the community, at least on this side, became a lot closer to each other."

Despite these occasionally noted effects on the community, neither community members nor local politicians believed that issue had changed the local or regional political landscape. While community members had made their discontent known, by all accounts, the local political scene remained unchanged. When asked how the placement affected their perceptions of local political leaders, residents typically answered that neither the placement nor the opposition efforts had altered their views. Those who were skeptical of politicians before the placement remained so after it; those who tended to believe politicians tried to address local concerns maintained their optimism.

From the criminal justice perspective, the placement was successful. As of February 2017, the SVP still resided in the same house in East City. He had not been readmitted to the state hospital for a violation, and no serious threats had been carried out against him. In addition, the city had not experienced another SVP placement as of that time.

Conclusion

The community in East City had experienced the dual forces of political and legal authority trying to keep their community at the bottom of social, political, and legal hierarchies. The community's lack of support for political and legal mobilization makes sense within a local context that highlighted the oppressive elements of institutional power. Yet community members continued to believe in the legitimacy of political and legal authority as they separated the promises of legal and political power from the ways they had been exercised against the community. While community members experienced ambivalence toward political mobilization and exclusion from legal mobilization, they did not denounce the potential utility of these strategies given proper implementation. Indeed, some believed that in the right circumstances, politicians and litigants could leverage institutional power to work in the community's interests.

The community's dominant orientations toward political and legal authority shaped how its members responded to opportunities to mobilize these sources of authority. Politicians' resolution to oppose the placement and the organization of a protest did not galvanize a community response, in part because the community's orientation toward political authority involved a sense of that power as embedded in and aligned with the interests of formal political institutions. Political mobilization in this context represented a display of institutional power to advance political interests. Similarly, community members' pursuit of litigation failed to gain momentum in part because the community's dominant orientation toward legal authority involved a sense of the law as a source of control. In this context, when a handful of community members could not find a lawyer to take on their case, they essentially gave up on the opposition efforts instead of trying to gain more local support for their cause or navigate the legal route themselves. This practical choice makes sense in the context of the time and resource constraints of working poor families and their lack of connections to lawyers, but it also suggests that an underlying orientation toward legal authority contributed to a sense of exclusion from the very possibility of litigation.

The outcomes of political and legal mobilization in East City sharply contrast those in Ranchito and Deserton. The latter two communities enjoyed the privileges associated with their racial and class makeup, and they both put some faith in political and legal institutions. By contrast, the community in East City occupied positions of racial and class disadvantage, which manifested in skepticism toward formal institutions. Given the very different experiences that communities in various positions of privilege and disadvantage have with formal institutions, the next chapter compares the orientations to authority and mobilization strategies across all three cases to draw out how communities' configurations of race, class, and geographic locations impact their relationships with legal and political authorities and, in turn, their mobilization strategies.

5

The Local Context of Community Opposition
to SVP Placements

The preceding three chapters have demonstrated the extent to which the community responses to SVP placements in Ranchito, Deserton, and East City involved attempts to leverage formal institutional authority to achieve collective goals. As I have discussed, differences in communities' relationships with the public faces of formal institutions facilitated and constrained political and legal mobilization. The Ranchito community's sense of political authority as entitlement contributed to the centrality of political mobilization in its response. The community in Deserton rallied around litigation in the context of a sense of political authority as a source of invisibility and legal authority as a source of community protection. In East City, the community's orientation to political authority as a source of alienation and legal authority as a source of control constrained the extent to which political and legal mobilization gained traction. Despite different orientations toward authority, none of these communities completely rejected the legitimacy of the power exercised by those in formal political and legal institutions. Instead, these institutions played important roles in shaping each community's response to an SVP placement.

In light of similar interpretations of SVP placements across communities, divergent strategies for opposition call for greater attention to how local social, political, and legal factors facilitate and constrain mobilization strategies. This chapter compares community orientations to authority and mobilization strategies in Ranchito, Deserton, and East City to explain how these communities' unique configurations of race, class, and geography shaped their opposition strategies. In doing so, the chapter provides a foundation for discussing how to solve the problem of where to house sex offenders while also empowering communities to maintain local control over public safety, a discussion to which I turn in the next chapter. Furthermore, by shedding light on the factors that facilitate and constrain local opposition to SVP placements, the discussions in this chapter expand upon existing sociolegal theories to show how race and class intersect with geography to shape community members' perceptions of and interactions with authority, which in turn impact strategies for political and legal mobilization.

Community Opposition in Light of Unique Local Landscapes

A combination of structural and cultural factors intertwined to shape opposition strategies in Ranchito, Deserton, and East City. Each community's position relative to regional and local political and legal structures, and its contemporary and historical relationships with politicians and law enforcement contributed to prevailing orientations toward political and legal authority that enabled and precluded various courses of action. For the community in "countrified suburban" Ranchito, the SVP placement was a political problem that required a political solution. This community had the most social, economic, and political capital to mobilize political authority. Community members were predominantly white and middle-class, they lived relatively close to regional centers of power, and they had an informal political entity to represent them. The planning group's meeting and resolution against the placement became the centerpiece of the community's response.

Residents in rural Deserton, the other predominantly white community in my study, also perceived the SVP placement as a political issue, but they had less capital to draw upon for political mobilization. They were lower-class and geographically isolated, and they had no local political body representing their interests. Having little access to political power, community members mobilized the law to make themselves heard in the regional political landscape. While they were also isolated from legal institutions, one local resident's legal skills enabled them to take their fight to court.

Community members in urban East City saw the SVP placement there as a political problem first and foremost but also as linked to the city's high crime rates. While East City was closer geographically to regional centers of power and, unlike Ranchito and Deserton, had a formalized local political body, the community's predominantly black and Hispanic/Latino(a) population and low socioeconomic status meant that it was socially and economically distant from those centers of power. The mayor organized a protest, and community members discussed litigation, but neither strategy ultimately gained traction. Instead, their activism resembled the "informal and loosely organized groups" that characterize mobilization in other poor urban communities.[1]

This brief comparison suggests that dominant orientations to authority emerge from and interact with communities' unique racial, class, and geographic features to shape mobilization strategies. A closer look at these orientations and their localized features can help illuminate how local landscapes facilitate and constrain communities' choices of opposition strategies.

Community Orientations to Political Authority

The dominant community orientations to authority in Ranchito, Deserton, and East City can be broadly described as involving community members' perceptions of the role of formal institutional authority in local life (as indicated by relationships with politicians and law enforcement) and in solving local problems (as indicated by relationships with formal structures such as political and legal systems). Table 5.1 details the orientations to political authority that emerged in each place. An orientation of entitlement emerged in Ranchito, the most privileged community in terms of race, class, and geography. In this orientation, community members felt entitled to political power as a way to govern themselves. The formation of the planning group after a protracted fight with the county's board of supervisors symbolized community members' perceived right to govern themselves. The planning group exercised what little power it had to serve the interests of the community, and regional politicians treated the community as an autonomous entity, especially after the planning group learned to play the political game by adhering to county rules and regulations. These local dynamics translated into community members' sense of an entitlement to access and deploy political authority.

TABLE 5.1. Community Orientations to Political Authority

	Political authority is a source of . . .		
	Entitlement (Ranchito—semi-urban, mostly white)	Invisibility (Deserton—rural, mostly white)	Alienation (East City—urban, racially mixed)
Relationship with Politicians			
Outside politicians treat the community as . . .	Autonomous entity	Irrelevant	Problem community
Local politicians act in the interests of . . .	Community	N/A	Their careers
Relationship with Political Structures			
Ability of local entities to exercise formal authority	Low	None	High

Rather than characterize the SVP placement as a failure of local political power, residents blamed the state and the landlord for proposing
it. In this version of what Miller has termed the "politics of the local,"[2]
community members perceived political authority as empowering them
to hold state and regional authorities accountable for trying to encroach
upon local control over a local issue. When the planning group organized the community meeting about the placement, community members had faith in their authority to exercise local control over the issue.
They described the planning group's actions as "working with" and
"responding to" the community in ways that demonstrated that these
local politicians were part of the community rather than an external
governing body. Thus, the planning group's actions became indistin-
guishable from the community's response, which in turn reinforced the
idea that the community had a right to exercise political authority for
self-governance.

Community members in Deserton had a more neutral orientation
toward political authority. In this case, political authority had essentially
"rendered largely invisible" the community in Deserton, just as it has in
more urban, racially mixed communities.[3] Miller has extensively documented how the American federalist system silences the voices of poor,
urban communities in state and national politics, leaving the largest
potential for political visibility at the local level.[4] The case in Deserton
suggests that similar processes apply to rural areas, albeit for different

reasons. While community members in Deserton had the most potential for political action at the local level, their lower socioeconomic status, small population, and geographic isolation constrained political influence and action, allowing politicians to exercise political authority in ways that kept the community invisible in the regional political landscape.

For these reasons, politicians treated the community in Deserton as irrelevant rather than a potential threat. Neither local politicians nor political entities existed to increase the community's political visibility. Community members appreciated their invisibility, and they rarely mentioned local or regional politics. In short, the community in Deserton related to the political arena as essentially a nonentity that local residents would not and could not access to assert their opposition to the SVP placement. At the same time, community members blamed county politicians for choosing their town to host an SVP because the placement would have been "off the radar" for the county. Despite the perceived political nature of the placement decision, political leaders neither organized nor attended the community meeting in Deserton.

While community members' blame of county politicians for the placement suggests a negative orientation toward political authority, most of them perceived this authority as neither enabling nor constraining local control over local issues. This neutral stance reflected and reinforced the community's privileges based on their predominantly white racial composition. Rather than experience political authority as an oppressive force, the community's exclusion from political arenas contributed to a perception that regional politics largely did not apply to them. Some political decisions clearly had negative effects on the community, but community members generally felt free to do as they wished with few political ramifications.

By contrast, the community in East City experienced the multiple disadvantages associated with being predominantly African American and Hispanic/Latino(a), lower-class, and urban. Compared with Ranchito and Deserton, East City residents may have been privileged in one respect: they had a formal municipal political system that could have translated into greater local political power. Their community meeting included greater representation of local and regional political officials than those in Deserton, and, as in Ranchito, residents tended to blame the state for the SVP placement. Yet, unlike the community in Ranchito, East City residents did not perceive their local political leaders' actions as part of their community's response to the SVP placement. When the mayor organized the protest in front of the SVP's house, some dismissed his actions as political gaming to gain favor with constituents. If he had really wanted to change the placement decision, they reasoned, he would have worked through official channels to exercise his political power. These sentiments reflected a broader mistrust of political authority. As a result, none in the community pushed for sustained political action against the SVP placement.

The community's dominant orientation toward political authority as a source of alienation facilitated a lack of support for political mobilization. In the local political landscape, regional politicians treated people in East City as part of a problem community that needed constant intervention to suppress, for example, desegregation efforts, plans for incorporation, and the city's relatively high crime rates. While local political arenas may provide the most promise for poor, urban minorities to have their voices heard,[5] community members in East City perceived city council members as acting more in the interests of their own political careers than on behalf of the community. This perception further alienated them formal political institutions and precluded engagement in these institutions. Community members' "collective memory" of political success during historical fights for incorporation might have increased the chances of political mobilization in response to the SVP placement,[6] but more recent experiences with local politicians contributed to disillusionment with political strategies. These findings suggest that in East City, greater access to formal political structures may have alienated community members from political arenas as they recognized the structural constraints associated with trying to bring about change within formal political institutions.

Together, the local political landscapes in Ranchito, Deserton, and East City reflect these communities' racial, class, and geographic positions within their respective regions. Local residents in all three places were skeptical of the implementation of political authority, but those in the most privileged community still believed they were entitled to exercise political power, and they actively sought to deploy that power to fight the SVP placement. This finding extends other research on the role of race and class in political interactions. Formal political institutions at state and national levels routinely privilege the life experiences of white middle- and upper-class citizens,[7] and some of the most notorious crime policies such as California's three-strikes law and Megan's Law have been enacted in response to white, middle- and working-class victims.[8]

Comparing the cases in Ranchito, Deserton, and East City suggests that privileged communities' interactions with local leaders and political structures can create and reinforce community members' perceived rights to access and exercise political authority, which in turn emphasizes the potentially positive effects of political mobilization. At the same time, poor, urban minorities who find themselves and their interests organized out of political structures fight to have their voices heard,[9] which can, in turn, increase skepticism about the benefits of political mobilization because such actions rarely work in their favor. Accordingly, while political leaders in both Ranchito and East City acted against the SVP placements in their towns, only in Ranchito did political mobilization constitute the main feature of the community's opposition to the placement.

These communities' orientations toward political authority facilitated and constrained the centrality of political mobilization to collective action, in part by shaping the extent to which political responses appeared to be community-based or politically based. In Ranchito, a place in which political authority seemed embedded in and aligned with collective interests, community members perceived political mobilization as a community-based response in which politicians served as activists within and for the community. In East City, neither the city council's resolution against the SVP placement nor the mayor's protest galvanized a collective response in part because community members saw political authority as embedded in and aligned with the interests of formal political institutions. East City's dominant community orientation to political authority highlighted that authority as a force external to and imposed upon the community, which contributed to community members' perceptions of local politicians as more rooted in political institutions than in the local community. While some in East City tried to engage politically to stop the SVP placement, their skepticism of local politicians combined with the structural constraints of living in a predominantly poor to working-class, racially mixed community to further alienate them from political arenas.

While the comparison between Ranchito and East City suggests a strong racialized component to orientations toward political authority and subsequent mobilization efforts, accounting for the case in Deserton suggests that racial dynamics interact with the geographic features of a place to shape mobilization strategies. Community members in both Deserton and East City felt marginalized by local and regional politics, but this perspective resulted in opposing orientations to political authority. The geographic isolation of the more racially privileged community in rural Deserton contributed to a sense of political invisibility in which political authority worked neither for nor against the community. Community members' interpretation of political authority aligned more closely with that in East City because this authority appeared more as an external force, but it also differed in that community members in East City had a more malevolent view of political power as actively oppressing them through alienation from formalized political structures. They had fought for a formal political system in their battle to incorporate as a city, believing that this structure would increase their power to control local issues. While the formalized structure did facilitate more political mobilization in East City than in Deserton, in neither place did community members believe that the exercise of political power would stop the SVP placements in their towns.

Despite their skepticism of the implementation of political authority, residents in all three places acknowledged the legitimacy of political authority. They all affirmed the need for a system of governance, but they differed in their experiences and perceptions of how formal institutions interact with communities. These differences contributed to different mobilization strategies as people in each place acted upon their particular interpretations of the community's relationship with formal political institutions.

Community Orientations to Legal Authority

Table 5.2 summarizes the dominant community orientations to legal authority in each place. These orientations capture the order maintenance, protective, and controlling functions of the law. In semi-suburban Ranchito, community members perceived the law as a source of order maintenance. The low crime rate and the presence of a sheriff's substation in town contributed to a welcomed law enforcement presence in which community members relied on them to deal with public order crimes. While not everyone believed that all officers did a good job, community members tended to write off negative experiences as failings of individual officers rather than the sheriff's department as a whole. When sheriff's deputies attended the community meeting about the SVP placement at the request of the planning group chair, the audience members I spoke with welcomed the deputies' "professional" presence as a way to maintain order at the meeting if necessary.

TABLE 5.2. Community Orientations to Legal Authority

	Law is a source of . . .		
	Order (Ranchito—semi-urban, mostly white)	Protection (Deserton—rural, mostly white)	Control (East City—urban, racially mixed)
Relationship with Law Enforcement			
Degree of police presence	Medium	Low	High
Responsibility for crime control	Formal controls	Informal controls	Formal + informal
Relationship with Courts			
Why go to court?	Unclear	Assert collective rights	Defend individual selves

The people I spoke with in Ranchito had little to say about the courts. They may not have accessed the courts for public order issues, but their relationship with the courts was unclear because only one person mentioned the role of local courts in everyday life. While they did not see the SVP placement as a law enforcement problem, their generally positive orientation toward legal authority suggests that they might have mobilized the law if the landlord had not backed out of the placement agreement after the planning group's meeting.

Community members in Deserton had a similarly positive perception of legal authorities, but their orientation to the law emphasized protection. The town's defunct prison, the employment of some residents at the state prison, and previous lawsuits facilitated a perception that legal authority could be leveraged to protect the community when necessary.

There, the police very rarely came to town before the SVP placement, and the community relied primarily on informal controls to maintain order. Community members' response to a heavy law enforcement presence at the meeting about the SVP placement illustrated and reinforced their dominant orientation to legal authority. Unlike in Ranchito, community members in Deserton criticized law enforcement's presence at the meeting. To them, law enforcement appeared to be trying to usurp local informal controls, and audience members became frustrated at the apparent overreach of legal authority into their everyday lives. In short, the unexpected law enforcement presence challenged residents' perceptions of the police as protecting them from harm only when called to do so.

While the community's dominant orientation toward political authority precluded political mobilization in response to the SVP placement, community members in Deserton turned to the law to gain a foothold in the political controversy over the SVP placement. They believed they could litigate to protect their collective rights, in part because they had witnessed the effects of grassroots litigation against a proposed landfill in Deserton. Their history of successful litigation to exercise local control over a political issue demonstrated the potential power of that strategy to oppose the SVP placement. For these community members, legal authority appeared to enable self-governance in a similar way as political authority did in Ranchito.

In both places, the communities' predominantly white racial makeup and geographic locations outside of major urban areas facilitated positive perceptions of legal authority. Neither community experienced the heavy-handed formal control tactics present in East City and other urban, predominantly African American and Hispanic/Latino(a) communities.[10] They also had more choice over when and how they interacted with legal institutions. For people in Deserton, this meant turning to the law to help them solve the political problem posed by the SVP placement, a solution that never gained support from those in East City.

The community in relatively poor, urban East City experienced the controlling aspects of the law. Their orientation to legal authority as a source of control reflected their experiences with a constant, everyday police presence. The city's historically high rates of murder and drug crimes, the partnership model of policing that provided high levels of contact between residents and police officers, and interactions with criminal courts encouraged a sense of legal authority as power leveraged by formal legal entities to control community members. Residents relied on a mixture of formal and informal controls to address local crime problems, and their relationship with the courts emphasized defending themselves against criminal charges.

While the police chief led the notification meeting in East City to emphasize the police department's commitment to working with the community, his visibility there may have increased the extent to which some community members blamed law enforcement for the SVP placement. Whether they believed that the police department had orchestrated the placement or that it had deliberately withheld information about it, some residents were skeptical that local law enforcement's main goal was to protect the community. Community members were also skeptical of the role of the courts in bringing the SVP to the city, which reflected their previous interactions with the courts as defendants rather than plaintiffs. Once again, their interactions with legal actors had suggested to them that they could not trust the courts to protect the community. The SVP placement seemed to confirm their beliefs.

Community members in East City believed in the power of litigation, but unlike in Deserton, they could not mobilize the resources necessary to take their claims to court. They discussed litigation and searched for a pro bono lawyer, but a lack of economic and social capital posed insurmountable obstacles. Skepticism about the power of the law to help them also dampened support for litigation, as did the belief that they could only access the courts through a lawyer. This latter belief was facilitated by community members' direct and indirect experiences with the courts as defendants.

The differences in legal mobilization efforts in Deserton and East City reflect broader racial differences in trust in and mobilization of the law to solve local problems. Marginalized communities experience the more controlling aspects of the law, in which the exercise of legal authority tends to disempower local residents to govern themselves. This facilitates the emergence of "legal cynicism," or a perception of "the police and the courts [. . .] as illegitimate, unresponsive, and ill equipped to ensure public safety."[11] Legal cynicism can decrease engagement in the types of informal social controls that help control crime, which can, in turn, increase the perception that law enforcement and the courts cannot create public safety.[12] Perhaps because of this cynicism, African American individuals are more likely to "do nothing" when they believe their rights have been violated.[13] Although community members in East City expressed some elements of legal cynicism, they still engaged in a variety of actions to try to stop the SVP placement. They protested, met in small groups, signed petitions, and considered litigation. While these actions were not as organized as those in Ranchito and Deserton, they still amounted to "doing something" about the problem.

As these cases suggest, belief in the legitimacy of the law does not always translate into invoking legal authority to solve local problems.[14] Those who have more direct experiences with crime and law enforcement may recognize the limits of legal approaches to solving local problems. In East City, community members' discussions of litigation over the SVP placement indicated that they believed in the fundamental power of the law to help them achieve their goals, but they realized the difficulties inherent in accessing the courts to make their claims. Thus, the orientation toward legal authority as a source of control in East City amounted to a skepticism of the implementation of legal power rather than a critique of the inherent nature of the law itself.

The law purports to protect people from crime and injustice but at the same time exerts social control to provide this protection. The orientations to legal authority in Ranchito, Deserton, and East City demonstrate how these multiple facets of the law translate into varying community orientations toward legal authority, which are shaped by communities' unique configurations of race, class, and geography.

Unique Local Landscapes and Mobilization Strategies

Thus far, I have separated political and legal contexts. Yet the local landscapes from which mobilization emerges consist of overlapping orientations toward various sources of formal authority. Examining these communities' orientations to political and legal authority together provides a more comprehensive picture of the local contexts that facilitate and constrain mobilization strategies. For instance, the communities in Ranchito and Deserton had more positive orientations toward political and legal authority than the community in East City. The orientations of entitlement and order in Ranchito and invisibility and protection in

Deserton emphasized the ways in which political and legal institutions empowered these communities to govern themselves.

In the predominantly white communities in Ranchito and Deserton, residents felt they had more local control over local problems, which manifested institutionally as a hands-off approach in which institutional actors tended to let these communities choose when and how to access political and legal authority. This was a unique privilege of whiteness in that community members did not fit broader societal stereotypes about dangerous criminals as either poor African American men who live in urban ghettos or Hispanic immigrants who have entered the country illegally.[15] It was also a privilege of living in relatively low-crime areas in which the public's expectations of police focused on order maintenance and protection rather than the more difficult task of solving entrenched crime problems. While residents in Deserton and Ranchito had more choice about when and how to deploy political and legal power, their local geographic contexts constrained their access to political and legal institutions. Being unincorporated meant that they relied on county institutions for formal governance, and these institutions could not always attend to local interests as well as community members may have liked. In both cases, formalized authority allowed a leeway not usually granted to groups designated as problem communities.

East City residents ostensibly had greater access to formalized political and legal power through their city council and police department, but they also experienced the more oppressive aspects of formal authority. Of the three communities, East City had the most entrenched crime problems. Community members constantly referred to the town's historical experiences with increasing crime rates shortly after it incorporated. The local police department was supposed to address these crime problems better than the county sheriff's department had before incorporation, but residents found that this did not happen. This collective memory, along with their constant, everyday experiences, suggested that law enforcement and legal solutions more generally would not necessarily fix crime-related issues and might in fact increase the intervention of institutional actors into their daily lives.

In contrast to the community response to the SVP placement in Deserton, when those in East City tried to mobilize the law, their local context translated into little institutional or community support for their efforts. The East City community's orientations to political and legal authority reflect the ways in which institutional agents have exercised both types of power to alienate and control racial minorities who live in predominantly poor, urban areas. For example, housing policies can concentrate minorities in poorer neighborhoods, facilitating political alienation and increasing the chances of being subject to surveillance and incarceration.[16] Accordingly, community members in East City interpreted institutional power as more often exercised upon them rather than left as an option for grassroots mobilization. The presence of local formalized political and legal structures facilitated more negative perceptions of authorities because community members perceived the exercise of power within these institutions as counter to their collective interests.

When problems such as SVP placements arose, these features of local contexts facilitated and constrained the extent to which community opposition strategies engaged with formal political and legal systems. In Deserton and Ranchito, communities' social and geographic distance from formal institutional structures constrained their access to these institutions, but their dominant orientations to authority emphasized that political and legal power could work in their interests. Accordingly, they attempted to leverage political and legal authority to oppose SVP placements. For community members in East City, where local political entities could make legally binding decisions and residents mostly went to court as defendants, political and legal institutions seemed ubiquitous and imposed upon the community. This in turn contributed to a belief among residents that they could not leverage political and legal authority to help them solve local problems. Consequently, despite some movement toward political and legal mobilization during the opposition to the SVP placement, neither strategy garnered widespread support in the community.

The Importance of Local Contexts

The analyses presented in this chapter highlight the importance of examining how the structural and cultural features of local contexts shape community opposition efforts. As previous scholars have pointed out, much of the work of crime control occurs at local and regional levels, and attending to the dynamics at these levels can help solve seemingly intractable crime problems.[17] One of the key findings emphasized in this chapter is that local landscapes, consisting of interactions between communities and formal institutions, shape community responses to public safety issues. Although the communities in Deserton, Ranchito, and East City differed in their configurations of race, class, and geography, they typically did not question the legitimacy of political or legal authority. Instead, they developed multiple and sometimes contradictory orientations to these sources of authority, which further reinforced the power of law and formalized systems of governance.

As the case studies have shown, political and legal institutions shape local opposition efforts in ways unique to the local contexts of communities' relationships with these institutions. These institutions not only draw community members into conflicts over issues such as SVP placements by siting undesirable individuals in their midst, but they do so in ways that reinforce the power and perceived legitimacy of political and/or legal authority to help solve local problems. This is true even when political and legal actions systematically marginalize and disempower the very communities that tend to turn to political and legal authority for help.

Examining how communities interpret and mobilize the sources of power offered by political and legal institutions has provided a more nuanced explanation of societal reactions to sex offenders than can be found in previous studies. The possibility of stereotypical vigilantism driven by hysterical moral panic arose in all three places. In Ranchito, at least one community member condemned talk of physical violence against the SVP, but others unapologetically stated potential violence as a fact of life in the semi-suburban town. With many people owning guns and a strong sense of self-preservation permeating the local culture, some said they expected the SVP would have been shot had he moved in. Those in Deserton also noted that community members owned guns and would use them for self-protection, but community members saw violence as not worth the potential cost of going to jail. In addition, the emergence of litigation as a concrete action to protest the placement helped dampen support for vigilante violence.

Discussions of vigilantism in East City most closely mirrored those in Ranchito. East City residents also talked about gun violence as a fact of life in their neighborhoods, and many did not explicitly condone or condemn talk of violence against the SVP. Their matter-of-fact perspective on the issue recognized the realities of living in a place where some individuals had engaged in violence on a regular basis and may have done so against the SVP had the guards not been there to protect him. In each of these places, the potential for stereotypical vigilantism against the SVPs arose but never occurred. While it is difficult to pinpoint the causes of events that did not happen, my interviews with community members suggest that a combination of formal and informal social controls kept the violence at bay.

The occasional accounts of potential violence against SVPs that arose in my research seem to reinforce the stereotype of hysterical, moral panic–driven vigilantism against sex offenders. Yet, the bulk of reactions to the SVP placements in Deserton, Ranchito, and East City looked more like the everyday politics of communities struggling to exercise local control over local issues. While moral concerns and misinformation played into opposition to SVPs in local neighborhoods, broader issues of trust in government institutions and interference of government in local lives played a central role in communities' responses to SVP placements. These findings suggest that research on the factors that predict public support for sex offender policies and treatment would benefit from more focus on how the dynamics of local political and legal arenas shape public reactions to sex offenders.

The same may be true of public support for other punitive policies such as mandatory sentences and the death penalty, which appears to be driven at least in part by racial bias.[18] Individual perceptions and prejudices may matter in explaining reactions to sex offenders,[19] but the results from the current study have shown that local political and legal contexts shape these reactions. Exploring this finding in relation to a broader range of "criminals" could provide new insight into why the public supports punitive policies, how and why that support varies across places, and, ultimately, how to begin dismantling systems of punishment that contribute to mass incarceration and its associated problems.

As the three case studies demonstrate, unique configurations of race, class, and geography influence local relationships between communities and political and legal institutions, which in turn guide local interpretations of and solutions to the problem. These findings suggest that community opposition to sex offenders stems from place-specific relationships between communities and formal institutions. In other words, local controversies over sex offenders can be better understood as institutionally informed local political battles. As I discuss in the concluding chapter, this new perspective on societal reactions to sex offenders furthers scholarly understanding of the role of institutions in creating the seemingly intractable problems that prompt collective action and then constraining local efforts to solve those problems. More practically, reconceptualizing local opposition to sex offenders in this way illuminates some key issues that must be addressed in order to solve the problem of where to house these stigmatized social pariahs.

6

Solving the Sex Offender Housing Dilemma

The scope of laws devoted to defining new sex crimes, ratcheting up sentences, and monitoring sex offenders upon their release has reached epic proportions over the past decade.[1] More than 750,000 individuals are registered as sex offenders in the United States,[2] and California's sex offender registry alone includes more than 120,000 individuals.[3] We have spent countless dollars protecting our society from these known sex offenders with little evidence that our policies and practices reduce the risk of new sex crimes. More concerning is that current policies such as registration and community notification exacerbate the problems that many offenders experience after incarceration, which may in turn increase the odds of reoffending.[4] Without the social supports necessary to help these offenders reintegrate into society, they are more likely to pose the public safety threat that community activists fear.

Communities, politicians, and criminal justice officials often work at cross-purposes as they try to achieve a shared goal of public safety. Nationally, politicians have served as middle-level actors who shape moral panic over sex offenders while also gaining legitimacy by playing off emotional reactions to the threat of sex offenders.[5] At the same time, all three branches of government have begun to "govern through crime." In this reorganized system, citizens are perceived as potential victims of an array of serious offenses, which enables political leadership to subvert individual rights ostensibly to protect American citizens.[6] Within this national context, politicians gain legitimacy by opposing sex offenders in their communities. In effect, the sex offender housing dilemma has become a zero-sum game in which any advocate for effective housing solutions is perceived as threatening "good" citizens. To remain in office, politicians have little choice but to speak out against policies that would encourage sex offenders to live in their districts. Underlying this current state of affairs is a portrait of community members as panicked, vigilante crusaders trying to keep dangerous individuals out of their towns and cities.

Against this backdrop of public condemnation and restrictive, punitive policies, identified sex offenders must find a place to live. Successful reintegration of these hundreds of thousands of individuals requires stable housing and prosocial networks, but community members generally recoil at the idea of a registered sex offender trying to integrate into their communities. How can we solve this problem? Should we focus our efforts on mitigating local opposition? What about changing the political and legal institutions that label these offenders as dangerous and then require their release? Can housing decision-making processes be improved to smooth reintegration processes? The main findings from throughout this book help answer these questions. They point to the importance of including communities in decision-making processes and holding institutions accountable for perpetuating inequalities and disempowering communities that are actively trying to control their own public safety.

Holding Institutions Accountable

When it comes to SVP placements, legal and political institutions facilitate and constrain local opposition efforts, with SVP statutes categorizing some individuals as dangerous and then requiring their release with very little guidance on where they should live or how decision makers should find housing for them. Site selection processes result in a disproportionate share of proposed placements occurring in marginalized communities, which fuels local outrage. In these ways, SVP laws that have tried to address national and statewide political problems related to moral panic and fear have brought about a host of new local and regional political problems that contribute to communities' negative responses to SVP placements. These dynamics played out clearly in Ranchito, Deserton, and East City. While people in these places expressed the same kinds of concerns as those found in national public opinion surveys about punitive sex offender policies,[7] their community responses focused on broader concerns about government officials and other decision makers usurping local control over public safety issues. This finding suggests that at least some responsibility for negative community reactions lies within the formal institutions that socially construct undesirable people, funnel them into specific types of communities, and then ask those communities to bear the burden of reintegration.

When community members refuse, they do so within the context of their contemporary and historical relationships with political and legal actors. Communities' racial, socioeconomic, and geographic characteristics inform these relationships, which in turn shape opposition strategies. In Ranchito, political authority had been deployed in ways that allowed the community to govern itself, so political mobilization drew community support. In Deserton, where community members perceived political authority as essentially having no influence on everyday life, they turned to legal mobilization because legal authority had protected them in the past. In East City, where orientations to both types of authority had contributed to the community's oppression and disenfranchisement, neither political nor legal mobilization took hold as a central strategy for opposition. Despite their different mobilization strategies, community members in all three places perceived proposed SVP placements as political problems that they had to resolve not through violence but through legitimate engagement with political and legal institutions.

This portrayal of community responses to SVP placements as legitimate engagement with local institutions challenges that of weapons-yielding vigilantes lying in wait to lash out against the latest threat. Moral outrage and NIMBY concerns play a part in strong negative reactions to sex offenders,[8] but when sex offenders come to the more marginalized towns and cities in a state or region, community members' experiences with their local institutions inform how they react. They recognize that some neighborhoods house more registered sex offenders than others[9] and that state and regional authorities have the power to funnel these offenders away from some areas and toward others. They also see that they have little say in who comes to their neighborhoods. As the cases in Ranchito, Deserton, and East City demonstrate, community members fight this sense of powerlessness in ways that make sense within their local contexts. Thus, the "perpetual panic" over sex offenders that some scholars have identified[10] may instead amount to a perpetual failing of formal institutions to equally empower all communities to maintain local control over local issues.

In short, the story of community responses is not solely about moral outrage or the failures of formal institutions to keep the public safe. Instead, actors within formal institutions facilitate and constrain specific types of community responses by burdening more marginalized communities with reintegration efforts, interacting with those communities in different ways based on their sociodemographic characteristics, and empowering some to mobilize political and legal authority while alienating others from those sources of power.

In this new interpretation of local opposition to sex offenders, political and legal authorities take center stage for their role in shaping how communities respond to attempts at sex offender reintegration. In Ranchito, Deserton, and East City, community members' sense of injustice stemmed not only from the specific issue of SVP placements but also from historical patterns of disempowerment perpetrated by those in positions to exercise power. Residents felt excluded from and belittled by political and legal institutions. They also found that community notification meetings did not always provide them the opportunities they needed to have their interests represented in placement decisions. These dynamics mirror those in other studies of marginalized communities' involvement in national, state, and local politics. Communities with few resources to organize sustained mobilization efforts and claims that transcend the single-issue politics of state and national arenas find that they cannot access these arenas to prompt reform.[11] When they turn to local political institutions, their concerns may be more likely to be addressed,[12] but the case in East City showed that even local political relationships can result in restricted access to local political institutions, which can in turn fuel community members' discontent and exacerbate the problem of sex offender reentry.

When community members turn to legal institutions, they find that a lack of resources and the framing of their concerns can hinder efforts to influence state-level decisions through legal mobilization. Successfully mobilizing the law in service of collective goals requires open legal opportunity structures, including not only access to the courts but also the availability of justiciable rights and judicial receptivity to rights claims.[13] Although members of marginalized communities may articulate their claims in terms of justiciable rights and judges may be responsive to their claims, they often lack the resources available to more privileged communities and larger social movement organizations. While the community in Deserton had few economic resources, the legal skills provided by a community member served as the human capital necessary to access the legal system. When he did so, the community's previous positive experiences with law enforcement and the courts contributed to community support for litigation.

By contrast, when community members in East City tried to litigate, they found themselves unable to access the courts. They had few economic resources and no social or human capital to facilitate their entry into the legal system. Their previous negative experiences with actors within the legal system indicated that legal authority likely would not work in their interests, so they found little local support for sustained efforts to fight the SVP placement through court appeals or litigation. Other activist groups may litigate even in the face of closed legal opportunity structures,[14] but marginalized communities cannot do so, especially when they cannot access the courts in the first place.

These political and legal realities undermine a common assumption that the problem of sex offender housing stems solely from panicky, misinformed community members with knee-jerk opposition to any mention of housing a sex offender in their neighborhoods.[15] While the community members in my study sometimes reacted based on misinformation and an initial feeling of panic, they all acted in different ways based on their local contexts. By revealing the institutional roots of this variation in local opposition to SVP placements, this book has shown that solving the problem of where to house sex offenders requires serious consideration of how local political and legal institutions create and perpetuate inequalities between communities. While communities do react to sex offenders out of fear, their opposition also involves deep-seated, ongoing concerns about how political and legal institutions have differentially empowered some communities to maintain local control over local issues while marginalizing others from the very political and legal power necessary to keep themselves safe. From this perspective, the solution requires more than simply educating the public about the realities of sexual violence.

Including Communities in Sex Offender Housing Decisions

Moral panic and traditional NIMBY explanations for local opposition to sex offenders constrain innovative and effective solutions to the dilemma of where sex offenders should live. If communities truly are hysterically trying to banish dangerous individuals from their midst at all costs, then two solutions would make sense. One would be to incarcerate or otherwise segregate identified sex offenders from society forever. This solution would be made possible by the social construction of sex offenders as abnormal others who have no place in mainstream society.

Given the portrait that the legal label of "sexually violent predator" implies, it is not surprising that when I asked community members what they thought should happen to sex offenders, separation from society came up most often. Many cited their beliefs that these individuals cannot be rehabilitated and therefore should not be allowed to reenter society. Some advocated for life in prison, while others posed more unique forms of isolation. "If it were up to me," said the café waitress in Deserton, "I would find a little island in the middle of nowhere and just put them all on that little island and let them do whatever to themselves." The general store clerk agreed, saying, "Let's make a community out in the middle of the desert for them where only they could be and there's nobody else for two hundred miles in either direction. [. . .] It's like lepers on an island." While these types of solutions appear to reinforce the idea that community members just want sex offenders out of their cities and towns, they rely on a false assumption that these offenders are fundamentally different from "normal" people. Most sex offenders know their victims and could be described as community members themselves.[16] Relying on incarceration and other methods of segregation allows society to continue to deny the reality that sex offenders already live in everyone's proverbial backyard. As more and more cases of sexual abuse perpetrated by well-known figures such as legislators, Catholic priests, national celebrities, and sports players and coaches come to light, it becomes clearer and clearer that societal norms about gender, sexuality, and power create the problem of sexual abuse. Segregating sex offenders from society as we identify them will not stop new sex crimes from occurring. Instead, we need more systemic changes.

If the moral panic explanation for local opposition to sex offenders is true, then the second potential solution would be to exclude communities from housing decisions altogether. By this logic, community members are so emotional and hysterical that they cannot rationally participate in decisions about where sex offenders should live. This solution mirrors those advocated by punishment scholars who argue that the erosion of insulated experts in criminal justice policy making has contributed to the rise of populist punitive policies such as three-strikes laws and mandatory sentencing, which in turn create new problems such as mass incarceration.[17] From this perspective, insulated experts can help mediate the impacts of public demands on the criminal justice system because they can act more rationally and objectively than the general public.

The cases in Ranchito, Deserton, and East City highlight the flaws in the insulated expert perspective. In these places, removing communities from decisions about housing SVPs inflamed ongoing tensions between communities and local authorities, which in turn exacerbated the problems associated with SVP placements. These findings mirror those in Barker's study of criminal justice policies and politics in California, which found that excluding citizens from decisions contributed to a sense that decision makers neither cared about nor accounted for public concerns.[18] Her study also revealed that consistent public inclusion in punishment policy decisions in Washington State facilitated an open and collaborative decision-making process that served the interests of those involved. The experiences in both states, along with the findings from my study, lend support to calls for solving criminal justice problems not by removing the public from decisions but by embracing the diverse political, emotional, and cultural perspectives that they can bring to solving complex problems such as the sex offender housing dilemma.[19]

In addition to these critiques of the insulated expert perspective, excluding communities from sex offender housing decisions also has the potential to reinforce inequalities between communities. As I have demonstrated throughout this book, unequal access to and contradictions within formal institutions create the very problems that spur local opposition to sex offenders in the first place. As Barnett has explained, experts rely on institutional authority to "use their expert judgment and autonomy to make decisions that benefit the public."[20] Autonomy from public pressure may insulate experts from public pressures, but their positions within formal institutions shape how they deploy their authority. When those institutions are structured in ways that disproportionately empower some communities over others, decisions made within them will have disparate impacts on different communities. Furthermore, communities' varying orientations to formal political and legal authority will shape the extent to which experts' decisions are accepted within these communities. In the cases in this book, community members quickly recognized and resisted the state's attempts to reinforce regional inequalities between communities by monopolizing the power to control what happened in local cities and towns. Relying on experts within the very same institutions that usurped local control in the first place would exacerbate the problems they are attempting to solve.

The unequal structure of formal institutions and the clear agency of community members in trying to solve their own problems suggest that insulated experts will not solve the sex offender housing dilemma. Rather than buying into the paternalistic notion that experts must take over because members of the public cannot or do not know enough to act in their own best interests,[21] we must seriously consider the public's concerns and recognize community members as legitimate political actors trying to protect their communities. In short, we must include communities in SVP housing decisions.

My proposal to include communities in housing decisions is fundamentally rooted in a new interpretation of local opposition to sex offenders as civic engagement. As I have shown throughout this book, gut reactions to sex offenders belie deeper concerns about relationships between communities and their governments. The formation of a chamber of commerce in Deserton after the community's opposition to the SVP placement provides an excellent case in point. The general store clerk explained that the chamber brought "a lot more people out that sat in the back row before, that didn't really get involved. And it's got a lot of people doing different things in the community. How can we make this community better, how can we make it safer, how can we spend the county's money." In this case, local debate over the SVP placement encouraged civic activism, even among those who had never been previously involved in local political issues. For these residents, involvement in local opposition to an SVP placement led to a stronger community finding new ways to assert its political voice.

While local conflicts over SVP placements do not usually result in such dramatic changes in local political structures, the case in Deserton illustrates the connections between responses to SVP placements and civic activism. Community members want to be involved in decisions affecting their cities and towns. We should harness this motivation for civic engagement by involving community members in placement processes. Incorporating them into discussions about SVP placements from the start of housing searches sets up the process as a collaboration rather than a conflict in which communities must react with hostility because they have lost the power to control what happens in their neighborhoods.

Community inclusion may seem unrealistic when it comes to "siting" SVPs, but some evidence suggests that community members can and will collaborate in efforts to reintegrate sex offenders into society. Circles of Support and Accountability (COSAs) provide one model by which this can happen. In this model, community volunteers build a network of support for sex offenders reentering society after incarceration, and they hold these individuals accountable for their actions within the community.[22] COSAs have been implemented for high-risk offenders in a number of countries, including the United States, and they have contributed to successful reintegration efforts.[23] Employing a similar model with SVP placements would provide multiple benefits, including more social supports and accountability for those trying to reenter society, opportunities for community members to become actively involved in public safety, and increased accountability and transparency in government.

The current SVP placement process provides almost no opportunity for meaningful public engagement in placement decisions. Community members can give input during public comment periods, but the information they provide almost never changes siting decisions. Instead, these forums highlight marginalized communities' lack of control over placement decisions and exacerbate tensions between community members and decision makers. Some local residents I spoke with indicated that a more democratic process would have helped ease local tensions. As the retired ex-cop in Deserton explained, "The people who make the decisions need to get down with these people where they live and discuss what their problems are and what their options are and that kind of thing. Try to work through it instead of just 'Here you are. Good luck.'" By "getting down with" community members, decision makers have an opportunity to reframe the discussion in terms of problem solving. This would facilitate more support for placement decisions because, in his words, "any time you get people to be part of the decision-making process, then you're more likely to live with it [. . .] because then they become part of the decision." The man in East City who lived across the intersection from the SVP placement took the suggestion one step further when he told me, "We should be able to, whoever comes, we should know and be able to say no. Or yes. You know, and get a chance to meet with the guy, ask questions and you know make us comfortable." While his first response was to "say no," his qualification of that statement suggests that being involved in the process and meeting the individual coming to the community may have helped ameliorate some tensions over the SVP placement in East City.

As these comments indicate, including communities in placement processes before specific sites have been chosen can transform conflicts over where to house SVPs into collaborative dialogues about how to solve a local problem. Furthermore, with increased opportunities for true collaboration between marginalized communities and decision makers, relations between these two groups could begin to improve. Community members would gain more control over public safety, and they would be better situated to hold government officials accountable for their decisions when necessary. In short, community inclusion in SVP placement processes can contribute to stronger, more engaged communities.

Incorporating communities into siting decisions requires distinguishing between public participation and inclusion in decision-making processes.[24] Many community members I spoke with wanted decision makers to be more open with the public, but as I have shown throughout this book, simply providing forums for participation via public input is not enough to mitigate siting conflicts. Instead, communities must be fully included in placement decisions so that their ideas actively influence siting decisions and processes. For instance, a study of decision-making processes in one Michigan city documented community inclusion in creating the city's master plan. According to those who conducted the study, "Throughout the process, the community provided information, the planning staff and consultants would use the community's input to come up with a series of ideas, and then everyone would meet to evaluate whether they had gotten it right yet."[25] Instead of a series of public meetings requesting input, this inclusive process recognized community members as legitimate and important actors in local planning efforts. The ultimate success of the project had the additional side effects of contributing to community members' satisfaction with final decisions and increasing their civic motivation and skills for public engagement. Their subsequent work with local authorities on other issues further demonstrates that community inclusion in decision-making processes can create pathways for future collaborations between communities and government officials.

One of the benefits of full inclusion in local decision-making processes is the breakdown of rigid categories that pit the "government" against the "public."[26] When these two groups truly work together, the lines between government and public become blurred, facilitating mutual collaboration in solving local problems. Yet, before communities will even come to the table, policy makers must address the underlying issue of the SVP label. Categorizing individuals with the highest levels of risk as "sexually violent predators" serves little purpose other than to exacerbate local opposition to placement decisions and direct the public's attention away from the broad societal causes of sexual violence.[27] While other sex offender laws would continue to hinder reintegration efforts,[28] eliminating the SVP label would remove one hurdle in the already fraught process of reintegrating these "high-risk" sex offenders into society.

To eliminate the label, lawmakers should look to models that employ actuarial risk assessment tools to categorize sex offenders in terms of numbered tiers. California is one of only four states without a tiered system for sex offender registration, and the state's Sex Offender Management Board has consistently recommended the implementation of tiers in order to enhance public safety and decrease the cost of the state's registry.[29] While most states with tiered systems categorize sex offenders based on their offense at conviction,[30] offense-based tiers tend to overestimate risk levels and have little correlation to empirically derived estimates of recidivism risk.[31]

Instead, sensible policy would assess sex offenders' risks of recidivism and then calibrate risk scores to specific tiers. Empirically grounded, actuarial assessment tools that evaluate sex offenders' static and dynamic risk factors have been shown to be most useful in determining the public safety risks posed by different groups of offenders.[32] California already uses one risk assessment tool, the Static-99R, to aid in supervision plans for registered sex offenders on probation or parole, and the state could expand the use of this tool to provide the foundation for a tiered classification system. While some states with tiered systems continue to denote some offenders as SVPs, the highest tier number should replace the SVP label to facilitate reintegration when the individual is ready to begin the process of reentry. The highest numbered tier would still categorize some sex offenders as having higher risks of recidivism, but a number would remove some of the stigma invoked by the SVP label. This could in turn facilitate more productive conversations between states and communities about where to house these individuals upon release.

With the SVP label removed, community members may be more likely to become involved in housing decisions. Housing search groups in California already include a variety of stakeholders from throughout the designated counties. Once potential housing areas have been narrowed based on legal mandates, members of potentially affected communities should become part of search groups. After receiving an overview of the legal mandates for SVP releases and placement processes, community members should then be presented with the legally acceptable range of options for placement sites. They should be encouraged to engage in discussions about the specific features of local areas that make them more or less conducive to successful reintegration, and the range of options should then be adjusted based on this local input. These conversations would also serve a secondary purpose of helping to map inequalities in the region by highlighting the strengths, weaknesses, and resource needs of various communities in the area. Doing so could contribute to more equal siting outcomes as communities and decision makers work together to ensure fair site choices. Power dynamics would still play into siting decisions, as differentially situated community members would have more or less influence on final siting recommendations, but true inclusion of more marginalized communities in these decisions would increase the chances of more equal siting outcomes.

Fully integrating communities into decisions made within formal institutions is a difficult task. Community activists never represent all segments of a population, as demonstrated by the demographics of the activists I interviewed. They were more likely to be older women with higher socioeconomic statuses than the broader communities they purported to speak for. While individuals from other groups also engage in their communities, their voices may be quieted or completely silenced in local decision-making processes. To mitigate inequalities in siting outcomes, every effort must be made to ensure that the most marginalized groups within potentially affected communities are fully included in SVP placement processes. They too must have control over what happens in their cities and towns.

Attempts to implement community policing across the nation provide a clear example of the challenges inherent in trying to restructure formal institutions in ways that truly redistribute power from those in official positions of authority to communities. When community policing emerged in the 1980s as a central strategy for repairing a growing rift between the police and marginalized communities, the underlying philosophy was that community members should be empowered to collaborate with the police to prevent and control crime. In this new model, community members would become full partners in crime prevention and local problem solving as police departments restructured themselves to facilitate community partnerships. Despite the promise of blurred lines between communities and law enforcement, most police departments that purported to have adopted community policing failed to fully integrate community members into crime prevention and control efforts.[33] As one study of community policing in Seattle found, "Various internal dynamics limit the capacity of the police to engage in genuine partnerships with community organizations."[34] While changes such as increased foot patrols create more opportunities for the police to interact with the public, organizational structures continue to distance officers from the general public by, for example, failing to "civilianize" positions within police departments, relying on specialized units rather than more holistically trained officers, and implementing rigid sets of rules and policies that constrain officers' flexibility in helping to solve local problems.[35] Adherence to rigid hierarchies within some departments also means that community members' input matters less than that of sworn officers and administrators.[36]

The institutional barriers encountered by community policing advocates provide important lessons for those trying to involve communities in SVP placement decisions. A mandate for inclusion will not on its own result in equal collaborations between community members and decision makers. The mandate must be accompanied by institutional changes that empower community members to shape siting decisions. Housing search groups must reserve a set proportion of positions for more marginalized subsets of potentially affected communities. They must hold public meetings outside of business hours and in locations convenient to local residents. Officials and those in positions of authority in housing search groups must privilege ideas from the community by allowing community members to state their ideas before those of outside experts. Their thoughts and opinions about potential local sites must be given equal weight.

After each meeting, those in official positions must be required to return to subsequent meetings with plans that clearly demonstrate incorporation of at least some of community members' ideas. In-depth discussions about new plans should be expected and encouraged. While equal partnerships require compromises on all sides, officials should take great care to ensure that community members do not have to compromise more often than others. In these interactions, it will be important to remember that community members know their communities much more intimately than outsiders. They have the power to help solve the sex offender housing dilemma, and their inclusion in and support of placement processes will ultimately impact the outcomes of SVP placements.

The Myth of "No Good Place" for Sex Offenders

I began this book with the story of Tammy Gibson, the woman in Washington who beat a registered sex offender with a baseball bat after she was notified about his presence in her neighborhood. While neither her actions nor those of others who engage in violence against sex offenders should be condoned, we must take them as indications that something is amiss in how our society handles identified sex offenders. Looking deeper into the issue reveals that local reactions to these individuals more often take the form of nonviolent civic, political, and legal actions. Regardless of the strategies used for opposition, scholars and the media alike often dismiss community responses to sex offenders as hysterical, irrational panic. In the current system, no community wants a sex offender in its midst; however, disregarding the institutional roots of local reactions to sex offenders contributes to the assumption that finding housing for them is an intractable problem that can only be solved by keeping them segregated from society in isolated "colonies," prisons, or state hospitals.

Instead, one of the main goals of this book has been to demonstrate that solving the problem of where to house sex offenders means taking seriously community members' pleas for local control over public safety and their concerns about the state-level decisions that threaten their safety. Political and legal institutions create and perpetuate the problem of where to house identified sex offenders, and they send contradictory messages about the dangers related to sexual violence and community members' responsibilities in protecting themselves from those dangers. While many people recognize that perpetrators of sexual violence usually know their victims, laws such as SVP statutes heighten fears of strangers preying upon women and children. Community notification laws and residence restrictions fuel these anxieties and suggest that communities must insulate themselves to avoid new victims. Unfortunately, perpetrators of sexual violence already live in communities. They are neighbors, coaches, teachers, fathers, brothers, and other trusted individuals. When new victims inevitably come forward, political and legal institutions remain intact, and communities shoulder the blame.

Successfully reintegrating perpetrators into society has the potential to reduce sexual violence, but reintegration does not address the intrinsic causes of sexual crimes. To prevent sexual violence, we must change basic societal structures that perpetuate gender inequalities and empower men to use sex as a tool for dominance and oppression.[37] Until this happens, we will be reintegrating sex offenders into an inherently unequal society that encourages them and their as-yet-unidentified peers to continue their behaviors. The notion that there is no good place for sex offenders to live belies the underlying reality that we have created institutions within our society that provide very "good" places for continued patterns of sexual violence. Solving the sex offender housing dilemma will require empowering communities not only to collaborate in decisions about sex offender reintegration but also to hold politicians and legal actors accountable for perpetuating a system that supports continued sexual violence.

At some level, community members recognize the role of formal institutions in creating and perpetuating the public safety problems they experience in their communities. While they may not articulate their anger in these terms, their vehement negative reactions to identified sex offenders represent struggles to gain local control over the problem of sexual violence and other public safety issues. Those who assume that there is no good place for sex offenders because of hostile, irrational communities perpetuate the problem by letting political and legal institutions off the hook. These institutions unjustly exacerbate fears of perceived dangers and then impose those perceived dangers on the communities that have the least power to resist.

To ensure public safety, policy makers must consider the signals that state laws send to the public about the nature of sexual violence and potential solutions to the problem. Where these signals contradict decades of empirical research, laws must be changed. Those in positions to exercise political power must recognize the value in including communities in decision making about public safety issues. Community members must become equal partners in figuring out how to facilitate the successful reintegration of sex offenders and minimize the chances of sexual violence in the future.

As I have demonstrated throughout this book, the process by which community members become integrated in local formal institutions will look different across places. In some communities, the first step may be rebuilding local political and legal institutions to provide real opportunities for inclusion in decisions about important local issues. Other communities may leverage existing institutional structures to create new pathways for inclusion in decision making. In any of these cases, contemporary and historical relationships with legal and political authority will shape whether and how community members work with their local institutions to solve seemingly intractable problems.

Locking community members out of political and legal institutions may sound like the best option when it comes to housing socially undesirable people. Yet, doing so fuels local hostility and ultimately exacerbates the very problems that we work so hard to solve. Instead, including community members in solving tough problems such as sexual violence can increase civic engagement and improve public safety, especially in places where communities have little access to political and legal institutions. Inclusion can also create more vibrant, civically engaged communities that help reshape institutions to adequately empower those they purport to serve. In these ways, recognizing community members as legitimate partners in solving tough criminal justice problems has the potential to strengthen communities, ease reintegration efforts, and enhance government transparency and accountability. These effects provide ample reason to begin including communities in solving local problems as soon as possible.

ACKNOWLEDGMENTS

In many aspects of life, I am drawn to investigate the reality behind taken-for-granted truths. I find myself intrigued by works that illuminate ideas lying just out of sight, rendering the familiar unfamiliar. This curiosity led me to the fields of sociology and law and society, both of which inform the subject of this book. Early in my career, I became intrigued by the constant outrage over sex offenders, especially as reported in the news media. As I began studying the assumptions underlying this outrage, I questioned other scholars' dismissal of public concern as irrational, misinformed, and therefore unworthy of in-depth empirical attention. Wondering how we—both the public and scholars—had come to this point, I embarked on a study to understand the roots of public responses to sex offenders.

The ensuing eight years of research have culminated in this book. Along the way, I have been extremely grateful to the people and organizations that have encouraged and supported my research. First and foremost, the community members and local and state officials who took time out of their daily lives to speak with me about their communities and experiences made this book possible. They provided an incredible amount of in-depth information that enabled me to understand and vividly describe their experiences and perspectives.

A handful of educational and government institutions provided the financial support necessary to complete my research. A dissertation improvement grant from the National Science Foundation funded much of the data collection, including multiple trips to the communities I studied and the technology needed to complete a project of this scope. In addition, the Department of Sociology at the University of California Davis, UCD's Office of Graduate Studies and Institute for Governmental Affairs, and the Department of Criminal Justice at Weber State University all funded or otherwise supported various aspects of my research.

A handful of people provided invaluable assistance throughout the research and writing process. My adviser, Ryken Grattet, helped me muddle through the development, design, and implementation of my project. When I began writing up my findings, his feedback forced me to clarify and be more specific about my ideas. Bill McCarthy, Valerie Jenness, and Tom Beamish also supported me along the way. Bill's meticulous feedback, openness to frequent informal conversations, and constant reminders to celebrate accomplishments strengthened my initial ideas and my mental health in the early stages of the project. Val's consistent support included challenging me to answer the tough questions that always lingered in the back of my mind. Discussions with Tom helped push my research forward, especially when he told me from the very beginning to just start writing.

Mark Denniston, Chrysanthi Leon, Robin Pleau, Mary Rose, Aaron Roussell, Lori Sexton, and Elizabeth Sweet all read and commented on early drafts of the book chapters. Their feedback vastly improved each chapter, and I am extremely lucky to count them among my friends and colleagues. I am also grateful to Ilene Kalish, the NYU Press team, and the anonymous reviewers for their input and suggestions on the manuscript. While these individuals helped shape this book, any mistakes or omissions are solely my own.

Finally, I could not have completed this book without support from my close friends and family. Ruth Alminas provided immeasurable encouragement, talking me through countless research and writing puzzles and listening to my rants about everyday problems. Her consistent, unwavering support motivated me to continue researching and writing until the work was done. My mom, Jeanne Hoeft, helped me work through the challenges of being a researcher, graduate student, assistant professor, and mother. Her advice on balancing these roles kept me on track and intact. Countless other family members and friends, too many to mention, have made it possible for me to have a life while also pursuing my career. I am extremely grateful to them all.

The support of all these people would not have been enough without my husband, Matthew Scanlon, to whom I dedicate this book. I can always count on him to talk me through anxieties, remind me to practice self-care, and encourage me to persist despite any obstacles. In addition to these emotional and mental health supports, he literally made this book possible by staying at home to care for our son. I cannot begin to express my gratitude for his partnership in making my career possible.

APPENDIX

*Selecting Cases, Gaining Access, and Collecting Data
in Three Communities*

The research on which this book is based sought to uncover the dynamics and social processes that underlie community opposition to SVP placements. Qualitative data provide an excellent opportunity to study how people interpret their interactions and the contexts that shape those interpretations. Luker's in-depth discussion of the strengths of qualitative data for answering certain types of questions heavily informed the design of my study.[1] This appendix details how I selected the three cases, gained access to them, and went about studying them. The discussion demonstrates the quality of the data and the strength of the conclusions I have drawn from those data throughout the book. It also explains some of the common practices and pitfalls of qualitative research, which may be useful for those pursuing their own comparative ethnographic case studies.

Case Selection

To choose my cases, I began by collecting every media article and broadcast I could find online about every SVP placement in California to date. These data generated information on twenty-one SVP placements, which I then divided into two groups: those that involved only one community (N = 12) and those that involved placement attempts in multiple communities (N = 9). Those in the first group represented relatively easier placements because they did not require restarting a housing search after a failed initial attempt. Next, I focused on variation in local political circumstances, operationalized as the level of public resistance to and support from local officials for the placement. I measured public resistance in terms of the duration, organization, and intensity of the community response, and I measured support from officials as local

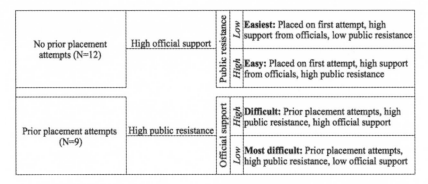

Figure A1. Case Selection Strategy

political leaders' and law enforcement's cooperation with Health Corp (the agency contracted to run the SVP conditional release program) during the placement and community notification processes. I labeled the four categories of SVP placements that emerged from my data as easiest, easy, difficult, and most difficult. Figure A1 illustrates the elements of each category.

After grouping the placements into these four categories, I focused on cases in the categories that involved high official support for the placement ("easiest," "easy," and "difficult") because the dynamics of local opposition would have been very different in cases in which officials were aligned with community members in their opposition to the placement. To maximize the chances that community members, decision makers, and other local and state officials would remember the details of specific SVP placements and local opposition to them, I chose the most recent cases within the target categories. These cases turned out to be those in the towns that I call Ranchito, Deserton, and East City. During my preliminary research, I had already attended the community notification meetings in Deserton and East City, which provided an additional advantage to choosing those two cases. The meeting in Ranchito had occurred earlier in the year, but I was confident that I could reconstruct it through archival documents, media coverage, and interviews with those who had organized and attended the meeting.

The four-category classification scheme simplified some of the complexities of the community responses in each of these places. During the course of my research, I did find some differences between the selected cases and the categories I had constructed, but none of these differences substantially changed the fit of each community's response within the assigned category. While variation in demographics did not factor into how I selected these cases, all three responses involved very different types of communities, which created a rich data set for exploring the role of local contexts in community responses to SVP placements. Table A1 summarizes the differences in the three SVP placements and the local contexts in which they occurred.

TABLE A1. Characteristics of SVP Siting Conflicts and Local Populations

	East City ("Easiest")	Deserton ("Easy")	Ranchito ("Difficult")
SVP Placement Characteristics			
Prior placement attempts?	No	No	Yes
Support from public officials	High	High	High
Level of public resistance	Low	High	High
Placement outcome	Placed in city	Placed in town	Placed in another town
Population Characteristics			
Population size	28,155	204	20,292
Race/ethnicity[a]			
White	28.8%	80.4%	78.3%
Hispanic or Latino	64.5%	18.6%	31.2%
Black or African American	16.7%	0.5%	0.7%
Education			
< HS graduate	32.9%	23.3%	24.6%
HS graduate	27.6%	19.0%	27.5%
Some college or associate's	23.2%	51.8%	32.5%
Bachelor's degree or higher	16.3%	5.8%	15.4%
Household income (median)	$50,142	$27,031	$64,882
Geographic location	Urban	Rural	Semi-suburban/rural

TABLE A1. (*continued*)

Political structure	Incorporated city	Unincorporated town	Unincorporated town, semiformal planning group
Law enforcement structure	City police department	Sheriff's department (50 miles away)	Local sheriff's department

Note: Population statistics for sex, race/ethnicity, and age are derived from 2010 U.S. Census estimates. Statistics for education and income are derived from the U.S. Census Bureau's *2009–2013 American Community Survey 5-Year Estimates.*
[a] Race/ethnicity statistics may total more than 100 percent because respondents could choose Hispanic or Latino ethnic origin in conjunction with any race.

In East City and Deserton, the "easiest" and "easy" cases, respectively, Health Corp placed the SVP on the first attempt and had a good working relationship with local officials. For example, the East City police department worked with Health Corp on the logistics of the placement there. The police chief demonstrated his cooperation during the community notification meeting by redirecting hostile comments away from the Health Corp representative. When I interviewed the representative, she remarked, "I came to respect the police chief very, very much. He and I worked closely together and seemed to develop a good working relationship under very, very difficult circumstances."

In Deserton, a variety of county officials were involved in the search for housing, but they regularly suggested potential placement sites. According to the Health Corp representative, the chief probation officer who chaired the housing committee "advocated for working collaboratively with [Health Corp]," which helped county officials buy into the process early on. While there were disagreements between county officials and Health Corp representatives, the overall relationship involved cooperation to ensure the best possible outcome.

Despite similar levels of support from local officials in Deserton and East City, the levels of public resistance varied between places. East City residents protested and signed petitions, but these activities died down a few days after the SVP moved in. By contrast, Deserton residents stalled the placement for a few months by bringing zoning issues to the judge's attention and ultimately suing the county. Their response was more organized and lasted longer than the one in East City, and Deserton's opposition to the placement gained an intensity that ultimately resulted in changes to the town's political structure.

Ranchito (the "difficult" case) involved high public resistance and high levels of support from county officials for the placement. While relatively short-lived, the community's response was similar in intensity to that in Deserton. The SVP in this case had previously violated one of the terms of his release after being placed in another town. His notoriety in the region undoubtedly contributed to the vehement opposition. The landlord felt such pressure during the planning group's town hall meeting that he tore up the rental contract in front of television cameras. Nonetheless, official support for the placement in Ranchito was very high, and Ranchito's county had a formalized procedure for handling SVP placements.

Gaining Access

Once I had chosen my cases, I needed to find a way into these communities. "Outsider" researchers have two primary avenues for gaining access: find an "existing social tie to the setting or group" or "identify key gatekeepers and develop ties with them."[2] At the outset of my study, I had no direct or indirect ties with any of the three communities; I assumed that I would have to rely on gatekeepers, or those I called key informants. When I attended notification meetings in Deserton, East City, and unincorporated Monterey County (a case that I ultimately did not select for this study), I did not yet know if I would choose any of them for my research; however, I treated each meeting as a potential entry point into the community. In each case, I talked with audience members and officials before and after the meetings, making sure to identify myself as a graduate student conducting research on community reactions to sex offenders. These informal conversations served both a substantive purpose of providing rich data about community members and their concerns about SVP placements, and a practical purpose of developing what I hoped were ties to people who might later serve as key informants. Ultimately, I gained access to the three communities using both key informants and newly developed social ties.

The meeting in Deserton was the first I attended. The day of the meeting, I flew in to the closest airport (about an hour from Deserton) and checked into my hotel before heading out to the meeting. I started on the road with what I thought was plenty of time, but extensive construction on the highway created stop-and-go traffic for nearly an hour. I arrived late and had to stand at the back of the room. After the meeting, I lingered to talk to those who milled about in the gravel parking lot outside the community center where the meeting had been held. I approached a pair of women who were talking about the placement and introduced myself as a graduate student interested in community reactions to sex offenders. Then I asked what they thought of the SVP placement. This simple question sparked an animated discussion of their frustrations and concerns. Rather than peppering them with questions, I listened, interjecting only a few noncommittal "uh-huhs" at the appropriate times and trying to remember their key points so I could write them down later. When the conversation waned, I handed each of them my business card and asked them to call me if they wanted to talk more about the placement.

Back in the car, I jotted down a few notes and then headed to the café, hoping to talk with more residents about their thoughts and experiences. I sat at the diner-style counter and ordered a cheeseburger, which had been recommended by one of the women I had spoken with after the meeting. While I ate, a man I had seen at the meeting came in. He briefly mentioned to me that he owned land next to the proposed placement site and was resigned to the fact that the placement was going to happen despite any objections from the community. He did not seem to want to elaborate further, so I finished my burger and left. On the way back to my hotel, I realized I had made a major mistake: I had no way of contacting any of the people I had spoken with. This proved especially problematic in Deserton because its remote location and tiny population meant less media coverage from which I could garner names of potential respondents. I had given the two women after the meeting my card, so I just had to hope they would contact me. They never did.

About a month and a half later, I attended the meeting in East City. As with the meeting in Deserton, all did not go according to plan. I had been following the case in the media, waiting for news of the notification meeting. To my surprise, one morning a local news station reported that the meeting would be held that evening. I scrambled to rearrange my day so I could make it to East City before the meeting. Luckily, I arrived at city hall a few minutes early, which gave me time to chat with a woman standing outside who was also waiting for the meeting. I introduced myself to her in the same way I had in Deserton and asked for her thoughts on the placement. She had moved into the area a few years earlier and, as it turned out, lived next door to the placement location. I got her name, made sure I knew which side of the placement home she lived on, and followed up later for an interview.

As in Deserton, I hung around after the meeting in East City to see who else I could connect with. On one side of the room, a man talked boisterously to a small group of people who had gathered around him. I made my way into the group and told him about my research. That I had chosen to talk to him seemed to make him feel important, and he offered to show me around the neighborhood where the SVP would live. Before we left city hall to drive to the neighborhood, I made sure to get his name and contact information. He turned out to be Miguel, the man who started and delivered the petition to the landlord's home.

We drove separately from city hall to the neighborhood and met in front of the proposed placement location. The street was packed with slow-moving cars in which passengers and drivers craned their necks for a glimpse of the home. People stood in their front yards exchanging thoughts about their potential new neighbor. Miguel spent about an hour showing me around the neighborhood and his son's school, which was a block away from the placement location. He mentioned a few times that maybe I could help them stop the placement. While I explained that I had no connections to those who could change the placement decision, he seemed committed to the idea that I could be a resource for the opposition efforts. When I left East City that night, I thought the visit had been a success. Unlike in Deserton, I had contact information for at least two people who seemed to be active in the placement issue. I thought for sure that Miguel would prove to be a key informant into the networks in the SVP's new neighborhood.

These experiences suggest that while public settings can be advantageous for covert researchers observing social life,[3] even overt researchers can benefit from being present in public spaces. I found that the public setting of notification meetings mitigated some of the problems with gaining access to community members I might want to interview later. People's willingness to talk with me before and after the meetings may have stemmed from some of the specific features of these meetings: emotions ran high, audience members came ready to voice their opinions, and they wanted someone to do something about what they perceived as a grave injustice. In this sometimes chaotic environment, I was there, ready to listen.

Unfortunately, despite some East City residents' willingness to talk at the meeting, none of those I met there turned out to be key informants. The neighbor I met did end up participating in an interview, but she provided no further connections to the community. Miguel proved less reliable. The day after the notification meeting, he and I checked in by phone. He told me that he planned to take a petition to the landlord's home the next day, so I booked a hotel for one night and headed out to East City the next afternoon. After delivering the petition to the landlord's home, Miguel seldom returned my calls, and then he stopped calling back altogether.

The day after delivering the petition, I drove over to the placement location to talk to a small group of protesters who had gathered there. When I introduced myself as a graduate student researching what communities are doing about sex offenders, one man launched into his thoughts about the SVP placement. I did not get a chance to write down what he said, but I did stand with the protesters for a while, reading their signs, watching them pass out flyers, and talking with them when no cars were passing by.

Still searching for a key informant, I began scouring news articles for names of potential respondents. One of these respondents turned out to be Marc, the retiree who had gathered signatures after the community meeting and later spearheaded the litigation efforts. I could not find his phone number, but I found his address online and visited his home one afternoon. His wife answered the door. When I explained that I was interested in talking with Marc about the local response to the SVP placement, she said he was out but should be back soon. She gave me his cell phone number, and I promised to return within the hour. Later, when he still had not returned, I promised to call him another day. Two days later, I left a message for Marc, and he called back a few minutes later. He filled me in on the community's litigation efforts and agreed to let me keep calling him for updates.

A month later, I returned to East City for one of at least four times that I visited to find people to interview about the SVP placement. Some days, I would canvass entire blocks of houses, knocking on doors and leaving letters that explained my research and gave my contact information. On the rare occasions when someone answered a door, I found the person agreeable to an interview either right then or on the phone at another time. I occasionally visited Marc on these visits, and we continued to keep in touch and eventually scheduled an interview.

During one of our telephone check-ins, Marc mentioned that someone from another town had offered to help strategize about how to overturn the SVP placement in East City. Intrigued, I asked who it was. He said it was a man from Deserton named Jack. I could not believe my extraordinary luck. With neither a key informant nor existing ties, I had been trying to figure out how to gain access to the community in Deserton. Suddenly, a key informant from a completely different community had turned out to be the existing social tie I needed to gain access to those in Deserton. This was even more surprising given that, to ensure confidentiality, I had never told anyone I spoke with the names or details of the other communities in my study. For these reasons, Marc could not have known the importance of the connection he had just provided for my research.

Thus, I gained access to the community in Deserton through a highly unlikely connection based on a common experience with an SVP placement. I had no reason to believe that Deserton and East City would ever be connected. The SVP placements were the only thing these two places had in common, and the communities were almost completely diametrically opposed in terms of demographics, region, and geography. With one telephone conversation, I had gone from no access to the community in Deserton to connecting with a person who turned out to be the quintessential key informant. While luck played a role in connecting the two men, staying in touch with my contacts in East City had paid off in an unexpected way.

Marc was hesitant to give me Jack's contact information, so I asked him to give my telephone number to Jack the next time they spoke. A few minutes later, Jack called me and filled me in on the community's litigation efforts. During our conversation, it became very clear that I had found my way into the community in Deserton. Jack wanted to bring more publicity to his community's fight against the SVP placement, and my interest in community responses to SVP placements fit well within his broader agenda of making potential placements more visible to the general public before they occurred. Toward the end of the conversation, he asked more specifically about my research. I explained that I was looking at the SVP placement process because every placement seemed to go the same way, with sites selected and communities opposing those decisions. I told him there must be a better way. He agreed and we promised to stay in touch via phone calls and e-mail.

Five months later, after monthly check-ins with Jack, I returned to Deserton for a three-day visit to learn more about the community and conduct interviews with residents. Jack helped plan my visit and shuttled me around town to meet with various residents. While I appreciated his enthusiasm for my study, I also recognized that I was seeing the Deserton that Jack knew and wanted me to see. For this reason, on subsequent visits, I actively sought out opportunities to connect with residents before or after meeting with Jack. The small population facilitated my entry into the community, as most people knew each other and could easily recommend others I should talk with about the SVP placement.

It turned out that I had the hardest time accessing the community in East City. Although I had more contacts there than in the other two places, I never established the same level of rapport with residents there as I did in the other two towns. I attribute this in part to East City's larger population size and more urban setting, which contributed to fewer connections between respondents. Community members' contentious relationships with those in power may also have increased their wariness of outsiders, especially when a middle-class white woman who clearly did not "belong" in the community started asking questions. To make matters worse, university affiliates from an adjacent town often studied East City residents, and one community member explained to me that people in the city may have been burned out on participating in yet another research project that probably would not directly benefit them or their community. In this respect, Miguel's lack of participation in my study may have reflected a realization that I had little to offer in the way of helping the community stop the placement, so it was not worth his time to continue talking with me.

Reciprocity has long been a concern of ethnographers who fear exploiting the people in their studies without much benefit to those under study.[4] During my interactions with community members, I did my best to position myself as a neutral sounding board willing to listen to concerns without necessarily acting upon them. When asked, I told respondents that I hoped that my research findings would contribute to changes in the SVP placement process, but I never promised any benefit for them or their community beyond the chance to have their voices heard. Even so, the skeptics in East City may have been correct: my research contributes to critical conversations about societal reactions to sex offenders and crime more generally, which may in turn change how politicians, criminal justice professionals, and community members approach the difficult problems of how to deal with ex-offenders returning to society. Yet, at the same time, I am pessimistic about the extent to which these changes will directly improve the lives of the community members in my study.

This is not to say that community members did not benefit from participating in interviews. As I have shown throughout this book, they often had few venues for voicing their concerns, and the interviews and conversations about SVP placements that I had with residents gave them opportunities to discuss a wide array of topics from governance and the legal system to sex offenders and public safety. By taking their words seriously and not writing them off as hysterical vigilantes, this book makes a small contribution to their goals of having a voice amid the politicians and criminal justice professionals who often purport to have all the answers about how communities should respond to perceived threats.

Ranchito was the last community I visited and the easiest to access. Although its town hall meeting occurred before the start of my research, the meeting itself served as a reference point through which I identified respondents and began conversations with them. Local newspaper accounts and the town's website helped me obtain the names of planning group members and other residents who had attended the community meeting. Having neither existing ties nor a key informant, I began by cold-calling planning group members. Luckily, the first one I reached agreed to participate in an interview. Through voice mails and returned calls, I began connecting with planning group members and other residents mentioned in the media. Once I got people on the phone and explained my research, they almost always agreed to be interviewed. Cliff, the landlord of the proposed placement home, was a bit warier. After a lengthy conversation about the placement and my research, he asked me to e-mail him a summary of my project. I sent him the summary, and he eventually agreed to the interview.

Soon, with a handful of interviews scheduled, I headed down to Ranchito. While there, I found those I interviewed eager to tell me about their town and to talk about the SVP placement. Many easily connected me with others who would participate in my study. By the end of the five-day visit, I had conducted more interviews than I had originally scheduled.

In addition to interviewing, I made sure to explore the town to get a feel for the place and help me develop rapport with those I later contacted for telephone interviews. During one such exploration, Cliff called to see if I could meet him at the proposed placement location. A few minutes later, I arrived at the vacant home. Awaiting Cliff's arrival, I walked around the exterior, taking pictures of the expansive views and marveling at the swimming pool and hot tub embedded in a slate patio. A few minutes later, Cliff arrived and led me through the inside of the home, which had a unique layout in which bedrooms and bathrooms were arranged around their own separate living spaces. He explained that he had been trying with little success to market it as a senior living home. As we toured the home and the grounds, he listed other ideas he had had for the property, including turning it into a winery or a bed-and-breakfast. Throughout the tour, Cliff also maintained a running commentary on his frustrations with the SVP placement process, including his belief that he had been "railroaded" by the state.

My spontaneous interaction with Cliff outside of the formal interview setting demonstrates the benefits of visiting Ranchito and the other two places in my study. Although my short visits to each place did not lead to complete understanding of local life, they did enhance my understanding of the local contexts in which community members responded to SVP placements, which in turn facilitated greater access to community members in each location. Whether conducting interviews or talking with activists during protest events, demonstrating a passing familiarity with their towns seemed to encourage potential respondents to talk more about their perspectives on their communities, their relationships with political and legal institutions, and SVP placements. These experiences suggest that visiting the towns under study and talking with people about their experiences in their communities helped me access the sites I had chosen.

Data Collection

The primary sources of data generated and analyzed in my study included media articles, field notes, and interviews. Media articles constituted the bulk of my preliminary research. To find them, I conducted comprehensive searches of all SVP placements in California using various library databases as well as simple Internet searches. I also set up e-mail news alerts to let me know whenever new information came up about SVP placements in California. I compiled these articles into case files on each SVP placement, which included notes about the timeline of each placement, the community's response, and contacts I could pursue if necessary.

In the process of attempting to gain access to the three communities, I also generated a substantial number of field notes. When interacting with community members, I used a "participating-to-write" style,[5] which looked different based on the setting. For instance, journalists often attended community meetings, so I felt comfortable taking notes during the meetings. In Deserton, when I had to stand at the back of the room, I jotted down key events and phrases in a small notebook I kept in my bag. In East City, I sat in a chair in the middle of the room, so I felt less conspicuous about writing down nearly all comments and events. By contrast, when I hung around before and after meetings, I made mental notes of key phrases and events, which I later jotted down in my notebook.

Regardless of the context, I ended each experience in the field with extensive writing sessions in which I focused on "getting it down" as soon as possible.[6] In my car, I outlined the events and phrases that would help me remember my experiences in the field. Then, as soon as I returned home or to my hotel room, I typed up as much of my experience as I could remember, using the notes I had written in my notebook to fill in every possible detail. I included both in-depth stories of key events and overviews of other, seemingly minor encounters. I also included my reactions to events in the field, as these provided important insights to explore in future research in each community. While my field notes surely missed some details of my encounters, my choice to focus on identifying significant features of each community's response to the SVP placements likely produced more detailed field notes than if I had focused on immersing myself in each community.[7]

The bulk of my data came from in-depth interviews. In early 2009, I informally interviewed a key informant at Health Corp as part of my preliminary research to understand placement processes across the state. I used the data from these interviews and the preliminary research I had conducted to develop interview guides. Unlike a traditional survey, interview guides give a list of topics to cover, with sample questions to spur conversation about the intended topic.[8] My interview guide included topics such as the respondent's perspectives on the community in general, the community's response to the SVP placement, personal involvement in the response, the purpose and goals of the response, and the future of the community in light of the response to the SVP placement.

Between June 2010 and May 2011, I conducted formal in-depth interviews with residents and officials in all three places. I conducted a handful of in-person interviews in each place, but contrary to my initial expectations, people seemed to prefer telephone interviews. For respondents, this was partly a matter of convenience. On the phone, I talked with people while they went about the mundane routines of their everyday lives, including commuting to and from work, picking up kids from day care, and cooking dinner. While the traditional conception of telephone interviews is that this method may stunt "natural" communication[9] and produce a "shallower connection" with respondents,[10] I found that respondents seemed more comfortable and provided more detailed, honest answers over the telephone. Other qualitative researchers have reported similar findings.[11] I attribute this in part to the increasing ubiquity of cell phones in everyday life. Now that cell phones mediate many of our social interactions, telephone conversations may feel more "natural" to some than in-person conversations. As a result, telephone interviews may seem less "unnatural" than they used to. In my research, spotty cell phone coverage posed problems from time to time, but overall, telephone interviews yielded richer data while also being more efficient and cost-effective to conduct.

At the outset of each interview, I explained the purpose of my research and the interview, and I obtained permission to audio record our conversations so that I could pay more attention to the conversation than to writing down everything respondents said. In the first few interviews with community members, I started by asking about the SVP placement. Unfortunately, in each of these early interviews, the transition from administrative background information to the substance of the interview seemed clunky. Respondents took a few minutes to warm up, and they often did not provide as much detail as I had hoped. As can be the case with inductive, qualitative interviewing,[12] I found that I needed to revise my interview guide based on these experiences.

A colleague suggested that it might help to start by having respondents describe the everyday life of the community. Taking her advice, I moved questions about overarching perspectives on the community to the start of the interview. Surprisingly, this simple reorganization of topics created a much better flow to the interviews and facilitated more detailed answers to my questions. This may have been because respondents had some level of expertise on their communities and thus felt comfortable teaching me, an "acceptably incompetent" outsider, about the everyday experiences that seemed so normal to them.[13]

Initially, I expected to conduct approximately ten interviews with residents in each community. However, this number increased because I continued interviewing until I reached "theoretical saturation," or the point at which each new interview seemed only to repeat old information.[14] In East City, I did not reach this point because of the lack of an organized opposition to the placement and a general distrust of outsiders. Both elements made it difficult for respondents to recommend others whom I should speak with, which in turn meant that I had to spend more time and effort finding respondents in East City. When I did find people who were willing to participate in an interview, they had few overlapping networks and thus little overlap in their experiences of the SVP placement.

Table A2 provides information about the characteristics of my samples. In conjunction with the population characteristics shown in table A1, table A2 shows that relative to overall populations, a higher proportion of those I interviewed in each place were female, and they were older and had higher levels of education and income. I also interviewed a higher proportion of white individuals in Deserton and Ranchito. In East City, my sample overrepresented those who identified as black or African American. These differences between population and sample statistics are not surprising given that older individuals with higher socioeconomic status are more likely to participate in civic life in California. Civic engagement is also patterned by race in that a larger proportion of whites reports civic engagement, followed by those who identify as black.[15]

TABLE A2. Sample Demographics

	Deserton ($n = 12$)	Ranchito ($n = 20$)	East City ($n = 18$)
Sex			
Male	33.3%	35.0%	38.9%
Female	66.7%	65.0%	61.1%
Race/Ethnicity			
White	91.7%	95.0%	11.1%
Hispanic or Latino	0.0%	5.0%	16.7%
Black or African American	0.0%	0.0%	55.6%
Not reported	8.3%	0.0%	16.7%
Education			
< HS graduate	0.0%	0.0%	16.7%
HS graduate	16.7%	0.0%	22.2%
Some college or associate's	25.0%	45.0%	16.7%
Bachelor's degree or higher	50.0%	55.0%	33.3%
Not reported	8.3%	0.0%	11.1%
Age (median)	53.0	52.0	54.0
Household income (median)	$61,000	$95,000	$65,000

Table A3 provides a list of the positions of the officials I interviewed in each town. The types of officials I interviewed were relatively consistent across places, with a few exceptions. For instance, the county supervisor for Deserton died before I began my research, so I spoke with the supervisor in a neighboring district about his recollections of the board of supervisors' discussions about the placement. Other variations between places reflect the difficulties inherent in gaining access to and rapport with prominent public figures such as politicians, those in county administration, and state-level officials. Often, these individuals either were too busy to speak with me or had no interest in participating in my research.

TABLE A3. Position Titles of Officials Interviewed

	Official Position
Deserton (n = 6)	Deputy district attorney Deputy public defender Chief deputy, division chief, sheriff's department Chief probation officer Communications director for county supervisor County supervisor, neighboring district
Ranchito (n = 6)	Deputy district attorney Deputy public defender County supervisor County sex offender task force commander County representative for California Department of Health and Human Services Representative for state senator
East City (n = 8)	Deputy district attorney Deputy district attorney City council member City attorney Captain, East City Police Department Detective Sergeant, sheriff's department County supervisor Deputy attorney general

The recorded interviews helped immensely when I began data analysis. I personally transcribed all interviews, which, as others have noted,[16] allowed me to identify, revisit, and expand my initial impressions of common themes. The transcription process also helped me identify themes and generate new ideas that I could then "test" against later interviews as I continued to transcribe. After completing all transcriptions, I imported them, along with all other documents related to each case, into qualitative coding software for inductive coding. In the end, these methods yielded a rich data set that allowed me to triangulate various sources of data to understand communities' responses to SVP placements within their local contexts. The case studies I developed based on these data provided comprehensive pictures of opposition efforts and local life in each community, as experienced and retold by the activated residents and decision makers who participated in siting conflicts over SVP placements.

Lessons for Future Qualitative Studies

From the outset, I explicitly chose to study activated residents' perspectives. As I have discussed in this appendix and in the introduction to the book, this choice served the goals of my study well. At the same time, it meant that the portraits of the communities that emerged from the data downplayed the perspectives and experiences of some marginalized groups in each place. To capture these groups' experiences, I would have had to extend the length and cost of the study. Doing so would have been necessary if I had aimed to develop in-depth understandings of all facets of life in each place to generalize the findings to other places.

Instead, the scope of my research questions and the limitations of time and money led me to choose the research design best suited to answering questions about community responses to sex offenders. That said, future researchers who study community dynamics must remain attentive to the benefits and drawbacks of defining "community" in terms of the perspectives of activated residents. Recognizing that multiple communities exist in any given place can help researchers design their studies in ways that have the best chances of answering the research questions they have developed. Where the goal is theory building, it makes sense to focus on the specific instances in question. Where the goal is generalizability, researchers must cast a broader net to ensure that they do not misrepresent the experiences of differentially situated groups in each place.

As I have indicated, the research process provided lessons on case selection, accessing communities, and collecting qualitative data. Preliminary research and interviews helped me categorize and choose cases based on variation in factors important to answering the research question. While convenience sampling may have been easier and more straightforward, choosing communities out of convenience would have left more to chance. Had I done so, I would have been less confident in finding the variation between communities that was necessary to parse out how local contexts shaped responses to SVP placements.

Once I had chosen the three communities, I learned that luck plays an important role in gaining access. No one can predict exactly when a researcher will successfully work her way into a community, and, as some have noted, gaining access is an ongoing negotiation that occurs throughout the research process.[17] I found that continuing to push ahead, learning from mistakes, and adopting new methods all helped create opportunities for access. In Deserton, showing up to the community meeting and dining in the café produced few leads. My connection there ultimately came through a source in East City, which demonstrates how key informants in one community can transform into social ties that can help gain access to other communities. In my case, staying in touch with my contacts in East City created an opportunity for access in Deserton.

In East City, I tried to create similar opportunities by employing multiple tactics to connect with community members. When telephone contacts failed to garner enough interviews, I tried letters and in-person visits. Some individuals responded to the letters I sent, but I had the most success with in-person visits. The same could not be said for Ranchito, where I had no ties or key informants. Despite advice to cultivate such connections to gain access,[18] I found that cold-calling people in Ranchito whom I knew had been somehow involved in the SVP placement issue produced the interviews I needed to complete my research.

My experiences in each of these three communities demonstrate that strategies that work in one community will not necessarily work in another. Variations in geography and demographics may contribute to these differences. Going into my study, I had anticipated an easier time collecting data in urban East City because of the larger, more dense population and the availability of more public places to recruit potential respondents; however, I encountered more difficulties there than anywhere else. In part, this may have been due to the nature of communities in poor, urban places, which can be more insular and skeptical of outsiders, particularly a young, white woman affiliated with a formal institution. Indeed, I constantly felt like an outsider, which for qualitative researchers has been described as feeling like "you are not getting sufficiently close to your informants and their activities to understand what they are up to from their vantage point."[19] Compared with the communities in Ranchito and Deserton, my skin tone and markers of social class (physical appearance, mannerisms, etc.) made me the least visibly similar to community members in East City. As I went door-to-door looking for potential respondents, and even when I talked to people on the phone, my social position clearly demarcated me as an outsider. In Ranchito and Deserton I could blend in to some degree because of my skin tone, but that was much more difficult in East City. These dynamics may have hindered my ability to connect with community members in East City.

Even when I did make contacts in East City, they did not always translate into connections to other community members. For example, I met both Marc and Miguel, but neither man knew of the other. Similarly, during the brief time that I had some rapport with Miguel, his connection to the school principal might have translated into access to the school's network of administrators and parents, but the principal was generally hesitant to talk at length with me about the community and the SVP placement. Finally, very few respondents in East City recommended other people I could speak with. This may have stemmed in part from skepticism toward and distrust of outsiders, but it may also have been a result of the lack of an organized opposition to the placement as compared with Deserton and Ranchito. Because of these dynamics, I constantly found myself looking for access to different communities in East City.

While I ultimately knocked on doors to find respondents in East City, rural communities such as Deserton and, to some degree, Ranchito are often spread so far apart that the door-to-door strategy can be inefficient and potentially unsafe. More rural areas also tend to have fewer public venues in which to get to know the place and connect with potential respondents. When I entered the café in Deserton for the first time, I mentioned my research to a few people as I ate my dinner. They were friendly but ultimately had little to say. It was not until Jack introduced me to people that they began to talk. These close-knit communities can make it harder to get potential respondents to agree to interviews, but once one person agrees, it can be much easier to connect with others in the community.

Once I had established some connections in each place, I found that data collection methods must also be fluid and adaptable. Although I had planned for in-person interviews, the circumstances of people's everyday lives, including my own, required more telephone interviews. I adapted to this situation and found that it generated richer data than I had anticipated. Furthermore, I found that familiarity with the places that people call home and an openness to hearing about those places at the beginning of interviews helped establish rapport with those I interviewed.

These experiences represent only a small slice of the challenges and rewards of conducting qualitative research in multiple communities. As

I have demonstrated throughout this book, in-depth community studies provide outstanding opportunities to understand how people's everyday lives intersect with formal institutions to shape local action, especially when these studies take up the task of comparing experiences with similar issues across disparate places. While comparative case studies require more time and resources than single case studies, they yield rich data sets that can be used to parse out how the unique features of local contexts shape community experiences.

NOTES

INTRODUCTION

1 ABC News, "Mother Who Beat Sex Offender.'"

2 Epstein, "Community Attacks Detroit Man Accused in Rape."

3 Action 4 News, "Harlingen Couple Jailed for Beating Convicted Sex Offender."

4 Kent, Vaughn, and Pereira, "Homicide Suspect Calls Victim 'Pedophile' and 'Demon.'"

5 Rocha, "Convicted Child Predator's Proposed Home Destroyed in 'Suspicious Fire' in Rural Fresno County."

6 Hudson, *Offending Identities*; Robbers, "Lifers on the Outside," 5–28.

7 Lovett, "Building Tiny Parks to Drive Sex Offenders Away."

8 Hudak, "Sex Offender Village in Sorrento."

9 Levenson, "Sex Offender Policies in an Era of Zero Tolerance," 229–233; Levenson and Tewksbury, "Collateral Damage," 54–68; Sample, Evans, and Anderson, "Sex Offender Community Notification Laws," 27–49; Tewksbury, "Policy Implications of Sex Offender Residence Restrictions Laws," 345–348.

10 Mancini, Barnes, and Mears, "It Varies from State to State," 166–198.

11 Barnes, "Place a Moratorium on the Passage of Sex Offender Residence Restriction Laws," 401–409; Socia, "Residence Restrictions Are Ineffective, Inefficient, and Inadequate," 179–188.

12 Huebner et al., "The Effect and Implications of Sex Offender Residence Restrictions," 139–168; Zandbergen, Levenson, and Hart, "Residential Proximity to Schools and Daycares," 482–502.

13 Mustaine, "Sex Offender Residency Restrictions," 169–177; Socia, "Residence Restrictions Are Ineffective, Inefficient, and Inadequate," 179–188.

14 Bandy, "Measuring the Impact of Sex Offender Notification on Community Adoption of Protective Behaviors," 237–263.

15 Zevitz, "Sex Offender Placement and Neighborhood Social Integration," 203–222; Zevitz, "Sex Offender Community Notification and Its Impact on Neighborhood Life," 41–61.

16 Zevitz, "Sex Offender Community Notification: Its Role in Recidivism and Offender Reintegration," 193–208.

17 Sample, "The Need to Debate the Fate of Sex Offender Community Notification Laws," 265–274.

18 Huebner et al., "The Effect and Implications of Sex Offender Residence Restrictions," 139–168; Socia, "Residence Restrictions Are Ineffective, Inefficient, and Inadequate," 179–188; Mustaine, "Sex Offender Residency Restrictions," 169–177.

19 ABC News, "Mother Who Beat Sex Offender."

20 Ibid.

21 KOMO-TV Staff, "Woman Gets Three Months for Attacking Sex Offender with Bat."

22 I am critical of the "SVP" label because it unnecessarily stigmatizes and dehumanizes the individuals who carry this legal label. At the same time, I aim to accurately portray the perspectives of community members who experience and respond to SVP placements. Because community members perceived and discussed these individuals largely in the context of the SVP label, I use "SVP" throughout the book to refer to those individuals legally designated as "sexually violent predators." This decision risks reinforcing the oppressive power of the label, but I hope that my explicit critiques of the label within the book highlight the need to eliminate it altogether to change societal perceptions of these individuals.

23 The Department of Mental Health has since been renamed the Department of State Hospitals. I use the former designation to reflect the department's name at the time I conducted my research.

24 I use pseudonyms to protect the identity of the places, their residents, and their political and legal officials.

25 Jackson and Covell, "Sex Offender Civil Commitment," 406–423.

26 Leon, *Sex Fiends, Perverts, and Pedophiles.*

27 D'Orazio et al., *The California Sexually Violent Predator Statute.*

28 Cal. Welf. & Inst. § 6600(a)(1). The state laws discussed in the book have remained substantively the same since 2011, when I conducted my research. The descriptions of SVP placement processes in this and subsequent chapters reflect data from interviews from 2009 through 2011. Since that time, media reports of SVP placements throughout California have provided no indication that placement processes have changed. There may be some differences between placement processes today compared with the time of my research, but minor changes in the internal workings of the process would not affect the overall theoretical argument advanced throughout the book.

29 Janus, *Failure to Protect*; Prentky, Barbaree, and Janus, *Sexual Predators.*

30 California Attorney General's Office, personal letter, February 3, 2014.

31 California Sex Offender Management Board, *End of Year Report.*

32 D'Orazio et al., *The California Sexually Violent Predator Statute.*

33 Cal. Welf. & Inst. § 6604.9(d).

34 The number of releases reported here reflects my estimate based on media reports and verbal confirmation from the former executive director of the conditional release program at Health Corp.

35 California Sex Offender Management Board, *End of Year Report.*

36 Cal. Welf. & Inst. § 6608(i).

37 Douard and Schultz, *Monstrous Crimes and the Failure of Forensic Psychiatry*; Goode and Ben-Yehuda, *Moral Panics*.

38 Goode and Ben-Yehuda, *Moral Panics*.

39 Jenkins, *Moral Panic*, 216.

40 Ibid.

41 Simon, "Megan's Law," 1111–1150.

42 Janus, *Failure to Protect*.

43 Barker, "The Politics of Pain," 619–664; Irvine, "Emotional Scripts of Sex Panics," 82–94; Lancaster, *Sex Panic and the Punitive State*.

44 Pickett, Mancini, and Mears, "Vulnerable Victims, Monstrous Offenders, and Unmanageable Risk," 729–759.

45 Leon, *Sex Fiends, Perverts, and Pedophiles*; Janus, *Failure to Protect*; Williams, "Constructing Hysteria."

46 Stojkovic and Farkas, "So You Want to Find a Transitional House for Sexually Violent Persons," 659–682.

47 Guillermo, "Treating Sexual Predators."

48 Gilmore, *Golden Gulag*; Bonds, "Economic Development, Racialization, and Privilege," 1389–1405; Pellow, *Garbage Wars*; Beamish, *Community at Risk*.

49 Gilmore, *Golden Gulag*; Bonds, "Economic Development, Racialization, and Privilege," 1389–1405.

50 Pellow, *Garbage Wars*.

51 Beamish, *Community at Risk*.

52 Ruming, "'It Wasn't about Public Housing, It Was about the Way It Was Done,'" 1–22.

53 Devine-Wright, *Renewable Energy and the Public*.

54 Young, "Necessary but Insufficient," 281–293.

55 Beamish, *Community at Risk*.

56 Tyler, *Why People Obey the Law*.

57 Goodyear and Hallissy, "Paroled Inmate Loses Lodging Offer."

58 Mohai, Pellow, and Roberts, "Environmental Justice," 405–430; Pastor, Sadd, and Hipp, "Which Came First?," 1–21; Pellow, *Garbage Wars*; Bullard, *Dumping in Dixie*; Saha and Mohai, "Historical Context and Hazardous Waste Facility Siting," 618–648; Williams, "Constructing Hysteria."

59 Clear, *Imprisoning Communities*.

60 Hoppe, "Punishing Sex," 573–594.

61 Mustaine, Tewksbury, and Stengel, "Social Disorganization and Residential Locations of Registered Sex Offenders," 329–350.

62 Aldrich, *Site Fights*; Aldrich, "Location, Location, Location," 145–172.

63 Gilmore, *Golden Gulag*; Pellow, *Garbage Wars*.

64 Putnam, *Bowling Alone*.

65 Wuthnow, *Loose Connections*.

66 Garland, *Culture of Control*; Simon, *Governing through Crime*.

67 Simon, *Governing through Crime*.

68 Garriott, *Policing Methamphetamine.*

69 Miller, *The Perils of Federalism.*

70 Miller, "The Invisible Black Victim," 805–842.

71 Zevitz and Farkas, "Sex Offender Community Notification," 393–408.

72 Anderson and Sample, "Public Awareness and Action Resulting from Sex Offender Community Notification Laws," 371–396; Bandy, "Measuring the Impact of Sex Offender Notification on Community Adoption of Protective Behaviors," 237–263.

73 Stein, *The Stranger Next Door.*

74 Devine-Wright, "Rethinking NIMBYism," 426–441.

75 Bridger, "Community Imagery and the Built Environment," 353–374; "Community Stories and Their Relevance to Planning," 67–80; Johnstone, *Stories, Community, and Place*; Driskell and Lyon, "Are Virtual Communities True Communities?," 373–390; Keller, *Community*; Kusenbach, "Patterns of Neighboring," 279–306.

76 Zevitz and Farkas, "Sex Offender Community Notification," 396.

77 Becker, *The Outsiders*; Lichterman, *Elusive Togetherness*; Stein, *The Stranger Next Door.*

78 Small, "'How Many Cases Do I Need?,'" 5–38.

79 Luker, *Salsa Dancing into the Social Sciences*, heavily influenced my case selection strategy. Luker argues that inductive, qualitative research designs should focus on finding instances in which the larger theoretical phenomenon of interest is likely to occur.

80 Stojkovic and Farkas, in "So You Want to Find a Transitional House for Sexually Violent Persons," reported on a case in which the goals of community members and political officials aligned in trying to oppose transitional housing for SVPs in Wisconsin. In that case, the housing committee failed to successfully find housing anywhere in the designated county, in part because political officials refused to publicly support the committee's work.

81 Eliasoph and Lichterman, "Culture in Interaction," 737.

82 Ellickson, *Order without Law.*

83 Greenhouse, Yngvesson, and Engel, *Law and Community in Three American Towns*; Merry, *Getting Justice and Getting Even*; Kirk and Papachristos, "Cultural Mechanisms and the Persistence of Neighborhood Violence," 1190–1233.

84 Bourdieu, "Rethinking the State," 1–18; Weber, *The Theory of Social and Economic Organization.*

85 Weber, *Basic Concepts in Sociology.*

86 Carr, Napolitano, and Keating, "We Never Call the Cops and Here Is Why," 445–480; Kirk and Matsuda, "Legal Cynicism, Collective Efficacy, and the Ecology of Arrest," 443–472.

CHAPTER 1. THE PRODUCTION OF SITING CONFLICTS OVER SVP PLACEMENTS

1 Allen, "Give Sex Offender Chance to Live."

2 Mohai, Pellow, and Roberts, "Environmental Justice," 405–430.

3 Pastor, Sadd, and Hipp, "Which Came First?," 1–21; Pellow, *Garbage Wars*; Mohai, Pellow, and Roberts, "Environmental Justice," 405–430.

4 Mohai, Pellow, and Roberts, "Environmental Justice," 405–430.

5 Bullard, *Dumping in Dixie*; Pellow, *Garbage Wars*; Saha and Mohai, "Historical Context and Hazardous Waste Facility Siting," 618–648.

6 McDowell, "'Becoming a Waste Land Where Nothing Can Survive,'" 394–411; Beamish, *Community at Risk*.

7 Beamish, *Community at Risk*.

8 McDowell, "'Becoming a Waste Land Where Nothing Can Survive,'" 394–411.

9 Purcell, "Ruling Los Angeles," 684–704; Harvey, "The Right to the City," 939–941; Marcuse, "From Critical Urban Theory to the Right to the City," 185–197.

10 Edelman, Leachman, and McAdam, "On Law, Organizations, and Social Movements," 653–685.

11 Ibid., 662.

12 Paris, *Framing Equal Opportunity*; Paris, "Legal Mobilization and the Politics of Reform," 631–681.

13 Abrego, "Legitimacy, Social Identity, and the Mobilization of Law," 709–734.

14 McCann, *Rights at Work*; Vanhala, "Legal Opportunity Structures and the Paradox of Legal Mobilization by the Environmental Movement in the UK," 523–556.

15 Ewick and Silbey, *The Common Place of Law*.

16 Blackstone, Uggen, and McLaughlin, "Legal Consciousness and Responses to Sexual Harassment," 631–668.

17 Bumiller, *The Civil Rights Society*.

18 Morrill et al., "Legal Mobilization in Schools," 651–694.

19 Within quoted passages of words spoken by individuals in interviews, at meetings, and so forth, ellipses that are not enclosed in brackets indicate long pauses in the speaker's speech; ellipses enclosed in brackets indicate places where I have altered the speaker's words for clarity.

20 Stojkovic and Farkas, "So You Want to Find a Transitional House for Sexually Violent Persons," 659–682.

21 Aldrich, "Location, Location, Location," 145–172; Bullard, *Dumping in Dixie*.

22 Pellow, *Garbage Wars*; Saha and Mohai, "Historical Context and Hazardous Waste Facility Siting," 618–648; Taylor, *Toxic Communities*.

23 Eason, "Mapping Prison Proliferation," 1015–1028.

24 Cal. Welf. & Inst. § 6608.5.

25 Cal. Welf. & Inst. § 6608.5(b)(1).

26 Ibid.

27 Cal. Pen. § 3003.5(b).

28 Cal. Welf. & Inst. § 6608.5(f).

29 See, for example, Aldrich, "Location, Location, Location," 145–172; Bullard, *Dumping in Dixie*.

30 Eason, "Mapping Prison Proliferation"; Pellow, *Garbage Wars*; Saha and Mohai, "Historical Context and Hazardous Waste Facility Siting," 618–648; Taylor, *Toxic Communities*.

31 The focus of the analysis here is on the communities themselves rather than their responses. For this reason, I exclude three regional or county-wide responses from the following discussion. I also treat communities that dealt with multiple potential SVP placements at different time points as single cases.

32 Littlefield, "Housing Proposal for Sex Predator Rescinded."

33 Wheeler, "Two Sexually Violent Predators Ordered Released to Home Near Jacumba."

34 Galvan, "Horn Placement Hits a Road Bump."

35 Dum, *Exiled in America*, 43.

36 Ibid.

37 Cal. Welf. & Inst. § 6609.1(a)(1).

38 Cal. Welf. & Inst. § 6609.2. In 2014, California lawmakers signed a bill that requires the state to notify county officials of an upcoming SVP release early in the placement process so that the officials can be heard in court and gain jurisdiction over these placements. While this attempt to involve local authorities sooner in the process represents a movement toward more transparency in decision making, the law still does not address broader public input.

39 Cal. Pen. § 290.46(a)(1).

40 Zevitz and Farkas, "Sex Offender Community Notification," 393–408.

41 Planty et al., *Female Victims of Sexual Violence, 1994–2010*.

42 Levenson, "Sex Offender Residence Restrictions," 267–290; Terry, "What Is Smart Sex Offender Policy?," 275–282.

43 Hanson and Morton-Bourgon, "The Characteristics of Persistent Sexual Offenders," 1154–1163.

44 Bandy, "Measuring the Impact of Sex Offender Notification on Community Adoption of Protective Behaviors," 237–263; Terry, "What Is Smart Sex Offender Policy?," 275–282.

45 Zevitz and Farkas, "Sex Offender Community Notification," 393–408.

46 Logan, *Knowledge as Power*.

47 Ruming, "'It Wasn't about Public Housing, It Was about the Way It Was Done,'" 1–22.

48 Krutli et al., "The Process Matters," 79–101; Leonard, Doran, and Fagan, "A Burning Issue?," 896–916; Wolsink and Devilee, "The Motives for Accepting or Rejecting Waste Infrastructure Facilities," 217–236.

49 Berton, "Oh, Give Me a Home."

50 Moran, "Offer to House 2 Sex Predators Rescinded."

51 Berrey, Hoffman, and Nielsen, "Situated Justice," 1–36.

52 Reed and Matthai, "Jittery Soledad Copes with Freed Molester."

53 Thomas, "Lompoc's Most Unwanted."

54 Nation, "Ghilotti Leads Isolated Life in Vacaville."

CHAPTER 2. POLITICAL MOBILIZATION IN COUNTRIFIED SUBURBIA

1 Beamish, *Community at Risk*; McDowell, "'Becoming a Waste Land Where Nothing Can Survive,'" 394–411.
2 Tilly and Tarrow, *Contentious Politics*.
3 Baldassare, *Improving California's Democracy*.
4 della Porta and Diani, *Social Movements*; Hunt and Benford, "Collective Identity, Solidarity, and Commitment," 433–457; Polletta and Jasper, "Collective Identity and Social Movements," 283–305.
5 Wozniak, "American Public Opinion about Prisons," 305–324.
6 Lenz, "'Luxuries' in Prison," 499–525.
7 Sexton, "Penal Subjectivities," 114–136.
8 Soule and Earl, "A Movement Society Evaluated," 345–364.
9 Tarr, "Turmoil in Turkey Town."
10 This finding mirrors those of Ellickson, *Order without Law*, who finds that strong informal social controls may take the place of the law in resolving disputes in some close-knit communities.
11 Miller, *The Perils of Federalism*.

CHAPTER 3. LITIGATING IN A RURAL OUTPOST

1 See, for example, Greenhouse, Yngvesson, and Engel, *Law and Community in Three American Towns*; Merry, *Getting Justice and Getting Even*; Paris, "Legal Mobilization and the Politics of Reform," 631–681.
2 Kirk and Papachristos, "Cultural Mechanisms and the Persistence of Neighborhood Violence," 1190–1233.
3 Kairys, *The Politics of Law*.
4 Soule and Earl, "A Movement Society Evaluated," 345–364.
5 Garriott, *Policing Methamphetamine*.
6 Zevitz and Farkas, "Sex Offender Community Notification," 393–408.
7 Ellickson, *Order without Law*.
8 Alexander, *The New Jim Crow*.
9 Beckett, Nyrop, and Pfingst, "Race, Drugs, and Policing," 105–137; Rios, *Punished*.
10 Herbert and Beckett, "Zoning Out Disorder," 1–25.
11 Sampson and Raudenbush, "Seeing Disorder," 319–342.
12 Gelman, Fagan, and Kiss, "An Analysis of the New York City Police Department's 'Stop-and-Frisk' Policy in the Context of Claims of Racial Bias," 813–823.
13 Kirk and Papachristos, "Cultural Mechanisms and the Persistence of Neighborhood Violence," 1190–1233; Carr, Napolitano, and Keating, "We Never Call the Cops and Here Is Why," 445–480.
14 Carr, Napolitano, and Keating, "We Never Call the Cops and Here Is Why," 445–480.
15 Parent and Snyder, *Police-Corrections Partnerships*.
16 Garriott, *Policing Methamphetamine*.

CHAPTER 4. POLITICS, LITIGATION, AND DISORGANIZATION IN AN URBAN CITY

1 Jasper, "A Strategic Approach to Collective Action," 11.
2 Carr, Napolitano, and Keating, "We Never Call the Cops and Here Is Why," 445–480; Silbey, "After Legal Consciousness," 323–368.
3 Hibbing and Theiss-Morse, *Stealth Democracy*.
4 McCann, *Rights at Work*.
5 I had chosen to study both Deserton and East City before Jack found out about the placement in East City. The appendix provides more details on how Marc and Jack became connected.
6 Federal Bureau of Investigation, *Uniform Crime Reports*.
7 U.S. Census Bureau, *2010 Census*.
8 U.S. Census Bureau, *2006–2010 American Community Survey 5-Year Estimates*.
9 Maliska, *Dreams of a City*.
10 Hale et al., "East City."
11 Maliska, *Dreams of a City*.
12 Snyder, *Arrest in the United States, 1990–2010*.
13 Venkatesh, *American Project*.
14 Clear, Rose, and Ryder, "Incarceration and the Community," 335–351.
15 Pettit and Western, "Mass Imprisonment and the Life Course," 151–169.
16 Petersilia, *When Prisoners Come Home*; Travis, *But They All Come Back*.
17 Hoppe, "Punishing Sex," 573–594.
18 The mayor did not respond to my requests for an interview.

CHAPTER 5. THE LOCAL CONTEXT OF COMMUNITY OPPOSITION TO SVP PLACEMENTS

1 Miller, *The Perils of Federalism*.
2 Miller, "The Local and the Legal," 725–732.
3 Miller, "The Invisible Black Victim," 806.
4 Miller, *The Perils of Federalism*; Miller, "The Invisible Black Victim," 805–842; Miller, "The Local and the Legal," 725–732.
5 Miller, "The Invisible Black Victim," 805–842; Miller, *The Perils of Federalism*.
6 Messer, Shriver, and Adams, "Collective Identity and Memory," 314–339.
7 Miller, *The Perils of Federalism*.
8 Simon, "Megan's Law," 1111–1150.
9 Miller, *The Perils of Federalism*.
10 Rios, *Punished*.
11 Kirk and Papachristos, "Cultural Mechanisms and the Persistence of Neighborhood Violence," 1191.
12 Kirk and Matsuda, "Legal Cynicism, Collective Efficacy, and the Ecology of Arrest," 443–472.
13 Morrill et al., "Legal Mobilization in Schools," 651–694.

14 Greenhouse, *Praying for Justice.*
15 Leverentz, "Narratives of Crime and Criminals," 348–371; Hagan and Palloni, "Sociological Criminology and the Mythology of Hispanic Immigration and Crime," 617–632.
16 Miller, *The Perils of Federalism*; Soss, Fording, and Schram, *Disciplining the Poor.*
17 Miller, *The Perils of Federalism*; Miller, "The Invisible Black Victim," 805–842; Miller, "The Local and the Legal," 725–732; Lynch, "Mass Incarceration, Legal Change, and Locale," 673–698; Lynch, *Sunbelt Justice.*
18 Williams, "Beyond the Retributive Public," 93–113; Unnever and Cullen, "The Social Sources of Americans' Punitiveness," 99–129.
19 Pickett, Mancini, and Mears, "Vulnerable Victims, Monstrous Offenders, and Unmanageable Risk," 729–759.

CHAPTER 6. SOLVING THE SEX OFFENDER HOUSING DILEMMA

1 Leon, *Sex Fiends, Perverts, and Pedophiles.*
2 Hoppe, "Punishing Sex," 573–594.
3 State of California Department of Justice, "California Sex Offender Registry."
4 Levenson and Cotter, "The Effect of Megan's Law on Sex Offender Reintegration," 49–66; Tewksbury, "Collateral Consequences of Sex Offender Registration," 67–81; Tewksbury and Lees, "Perceptions of Sex Offender Registration," 309–334.
5 Irvine, "Emotional Scripts of Sex Panics," 82–94.
6 Simon, *Governing through Crime.*
7 Pickett, Mancini, and Mears, "Vulnerable Victims, Monstrous Offenders, and Unmanageable Risk," 729–759.
8 Ibid.
9 Mustaine, Tewksbury, and Stengel, "Social Disorganization and Residential Locations of Registered Sex Offenders," 329–350.
10 Burchfield, Sample, and Lytle, "Public Interest in Sex Offenders," 96–117.
11 Miller, *The Perils of Federalism*; Miller, "The Invisible Black Victim," 805–842; Miller, "The Local and the Legal," 725–732.
12 Miller, *The Perils of Federalism*; Miller, "The Local and the Legal," 725–732.
13 De Fazio, "Legal Opportunity Structure and Social Movement Strategy in Northern Ireland and Southern United States," 3–22.
14 Vanhala, "Legal Opportunity Structures and the Paradox of Legal Mobilization by the Environmental Movement in the UK," 523–556.
15 Cf. Stojkovic and Farkas, "So You Want to Find a Transitional House for Sexually Violent Persons," 659–682.
16 Planty et al., *Female Victims of Sexual Violence, 1994–2010.*
17 Zimring, Hawkins, and Kamin, *Punishment and Democracy*; Leon, *Sex Fiends, Perverts, and Pedophiles*; Garland, *Culture of Control.*
18 Barker, *The Politics of Imprisonment.*
19 Ibid.; Janus, *Failure to Protect*; Gottschalk, *Caught.*
20 Barnett, "Accountability and Global Governance," 136.

21 Ibid.

22 Fox, "Contextualizing the Policy and Pragmatics of Reintegrating Sex Offenders," 28–50.

23 Cesaroni, "Releasing Sex Offenders into the Community through 'Circles of Support,'" 85–98; Bates, Saunders, and Wilson, "Doing Something about It," 19–42; Wilson, Cortoni, and McWhinnie, "Circles of Support and Accountability," 412–430; Duwe, "Can Circles of Support and Accountability (COSA) Work in the United States?," 143–165; Fox, "Contextualizing the Policy and Pragmatics of Reintegrating Sex Offenders," 28–50.

24 Quick and Feldman, "Distinguishing Participation and Inclusion," 272–290.

25 Ibid., 277.

26 Ibid.

27 Prentky, Barbaree, and Janus, *Sexual Predators*; Janus, *Failure to Protect*.

28 Hudson, *Offending Identities*; Levenson and Tewksbury, "Collateral Damage," 54–68; McAlinden, *The Shaming of Sexual Offenders*.

29 California Sex Offender Management Board, *End of Year Report*.

30 Harris, Levenson, and Ackerman, "Registered Sex Offenders in the United States," 3–33.

31 Harris, Lobanov-Rostovsky, and Levenson, "Widening the Net," 503–519; Harris, Levenson, and Ackerman, "Registered Sex Offenders in the United States," 3–33; Zgoba et al., "The Adam Walsh Act," 722–740.

32 Hanson and Morton-Bourgon, "The Accuracy of Recidivism Risk Assessments for Sexual Offenders," 1–21.

33 Morabito, "Understanding Community Policing as an Innovation," 564–587.

34 Herbert, *Citizens, Cops, and Power*, 13.

35 Maguire, "Structural Change in Large Municipal Police Organizations during the Community Policing Era," 547–576.

36 Herbert, *Citizens, Cops, and Power*.

37 The vast majority of sex offenders are men. Women do perpetrate sexual violence, but on average, their crimes look very different from those I have discussed in this book, so the solutions I offer here are aimed toward sexual violence perpetrated by men.

APPENDIX

1 Luker, *Salsa Dancing into the Social Sciences*.

2 Lofland et al., *Analyzing Social Settings*, 42.

3 Ibid.

4 Stacey, "Can There Be a Feminist Ethnography?," 21–27; Huisman, "'Does This Mean You're Not Going to Come Visit Me Anymore?,'" 372–396.

5 Emerson, Fretz, and Shaw, *Writing Ethnographic Field Notes*, 18.

6 Ibid., 64.

7 Ibid.

8 Weiss, *Learning from Strangers*.

9 Irvine, Drew, and Sainsbury, "'Am I Not Answering Your Questions Properly?,'" 87–106; Novick, "Is There a Bias against Telephone Interviews in Qualitative Research?," 391–398.
10 Weiss, *Learning from Strangers*.
11 Novick, "Is There a Bias against Telephone Interviews in Qualitative Research?," 391–398.
12 Weiss, *Learning from Strangers*.
13 Lofland et al., *Analyzing Social Settings*, 69.
14 Strauss and Corbin, *Basics of Qualitative Research*.
15 Ramakrishnan and Baldassare, *The Ties That Bind*.
16 Lofland et al., *Analyzing Social Settings*.
17 Ibid.
18 Lofland, "History, the City and the Interactionist," 205–223.
19 Lofland et al., *Analyzing Social Settings*.

STATUTES CITED

California Penal Code § 290.46(a)(1). Accessed July 1, 2015. www.leginfo.ca.gov.

California Penal Code § 3003.5(b). Accessed July 1, 2015. leginfo.legislature.ca.gov.

California Welfare and Institutions Code § 6600(a)(1). Accessed July 1, 2015. www.leginfo.ca.gov.

California Welfare and Institutions Code § 6604.9(d). Accessed May 28, 2016. www.leginfo.ca.gov.

California Welfare and Institutions Code § 6608(i). Accessed May 28, 2016. www.leginfo.ca.gov.

California Welfare and Institutions Code §6608.5. Accessed August 14, 2015. www.leginfo.ca.gov.

California Welfare and Institutions Code §6608.5(b)(1). Accessed August 1, 2016. www.leginfo.ca.gov.

California Welfare and Institutions Code §6608.5(f). Accessed August 1, 2016. www.leginfo.ca.gov.

California Welfare and Institutions Code §6609.1(a)(1). Accessed May 28, 2016. www.leginfo.ca.gov.

California Welfare and Institutions Code §6609.2. Accessed May 28, 2016. www.leginfo.ca.gov.

REFERENCES

ABC News. "Mother Who Beat Sex Offender: 'I'd Do It Again.'" *ABC News*, February 28, 2009. Accessed March 2, 2009. abcnews.go.com.

Abrego, Leisy. "Legitimacy, Social Identity, and the Mobilization of Law: The Effects of Assembly Bill 540 on Undocumented Students in California." *Law and Social Inquiry* 33, no. 3 (2008): 709–734.

Action 4 News. "Harlingen Couple Jailed for Beating Convicted Sex Offender." *Action 4 News*, August 22, 2013. Accessed October 8, 2013. www.valleycentral.com.

Aldrich, Daniel. "Location, Location, Location: Selecting Sites for Controversial Facilities." *Singapore Economic Review* 53, no. 1 (2008): 145–172.

———. *Site Fights: Divisive Facilities and Civil Society in Japan and the West*. Ithaca, NY: Cornell University Press, 2008.

Alexander, Michelle. *The New Jim Crow: Mass Incarceration in the Age of Colorblindness*. New York: New Press, 2010.

Allen, Franklin. "Give Sex Offender Chance to Live." *San Diego Union-Tribune*, August 27, 2003.

Anderson, Amy L, and Lisa L Sample. "Public Awareness and Action Resulting from Sex Offender Community Notification Laws." *Criminal Justice Policy Review* 19, no. 4 (2008): 371–396.

Baldassare, Mark. *Improving California's Democracy*. San Francisco: Public Policy Institute of California, October 2012. www.ppic.org.

Bandy, Rachel. "Measuring the Impact of Sex Offender Notification on Community Adoption of Protective Behaviors." *Criminology and Public Policy* 10, no. 2 (2011): 237–263.

Barker, Vanessa. *The Politics of Imprisonment: How the Democratic Process Shapes the Way America Punishes Offenders*. Oxford: Oxford University Press, 2009.

———. "The Politics of Pain: A Political Institutionalist Analysis of Crime Victims' Moral Protests." *Law and Society Review* 41, no. 3 (2007): 619–664.

Barnes, J. C. "Place a Moratorium on the Passage of Sex Offender Residence Restriction Laws." *Criminology and Public Policy* 10, no. 2 (2011): 401–409.

Barnett, Michael. "Accountability and Global Governance: The View from Paternalism." *Regulation and Governance* 10, no. 2 (2016): 134–148.

Bates, Andrew, Rebecca Saunders, and Christopher Wilson. "Doing Something about It: A Follow-Up Study of Sex Offenders Participating in Thames Valley Circles of Support and Accountability." *British Journal of Community Justice* 5, no. 1 (2007): 19–42.

Beamish, Thomas. *Community at Risk: Biodefense and the Collective Search for Security.* Palo Alto, CA: Stanford University Press, 2015.

Becker, Howard. *The Outsiders.* Glencoe, IL: Free Press, 1964.

Beckett, Katherine, Kris Nyrop, and Lori Pfingst. "Race, Drugs, and Policing: Understanding Disparities in Drug Delivery Arrests." *Criminology* 44, no. 1 (2006): 105–137.

Berrey, Ellen, Steve G. Hoffman, and Laura Beth Nielsen. "Situated Justice: A Contextual Analysis of Fairness and Inequality in Employment Discrimination Litigation." *Law and Society Review* 46, no. 1 (2012): 1–36.

Berton, Justin. "Oh, Give Me a Home." *East Bay Express*, March 9, 2005. Accessed December 31, 2009. www.eastbayexpress.com.

Blackstone, Amy, Christopher Uggen, and Heather McLaughlin. "Legal Consciousness and Responses to Sexual Harassment." *Law and Society Review* 43, no. 3 (2009): 631–668.

Bonds, Anne. "Economic Development, Racialization, and Privilege: 'Yes in My Backyard' Prison Politics and the Reinvention of Madras, Oregon." *Annals of the Association of American Geographers* 103, no. 6 (2013): 1389–1405.

Bourdieu, Pierre. "Rethinking the State: Genesis and Structure of the Bureaucratic Field." *Sociological Theory* 12, no. 1 (1994): 1–18.

Bridger, Jeffrey C. "Community Imagery and the Built Environment." *Sociological Quarterly* 37, no. 3 (1996): 353–374.

———. "Community Stories and Their Relevance to Planning." *Applied Behavioral Science Review* 5, no. 1 (1997): 67–80.

Bullard, Robert Doyle. *Dumping in Dixie: Race, Class, and Environmental Quality.* Boulder, CO: Westview Press, 2000.

Bumiller, Kristin. *The Civil Rights Society: The Social Construction of Victims.* Baltimore: Johns Hopkins University Press, 1988.

Burchfield, Keri, Lisa L. Sample, and Robert Lytle. "Public Interest in Sex Offenders: A Perpetual Panic?" *Criminology, Criminal Justice Law, and Society* 15, no. 3 (2014): 96–117.

California Sex Offender Management Board. *End of Year Report.* Sacramento: California Sex Offender Management Board, February 2016. Accessed July 27, 2016. www.casomb.org.

Carr, Patrick J., Laura Napolitano, and Jessica Keating. "We Never Call the Cops and Here Is Why: A Qualitative Examination of Legal Cynicism in Three Philadelphia Neighborhoods." *Criminology* 45, no. 2 (2007): 445–480.

Cesaroni, Carla. "Releasing Sex Offenders into the Community through 'Circles of Support'—A Means of Reintegrating the 'Worst of the Worst.'" *Journal of Offender Rehabilitation* 34, no. 2 (2001): 85–98.

Clear, Todd R. *Imprisoning Communities: How Mass Incarceration Makes Disadvantaged Neighborhoods Worse.* New York: Oxford University Press, 2009.

Clear, Todd R., Dina R. Rose, and Judith A. Ryder. "Incarceration and the Community: The Problem of Removing and Returning Offenders." *Crime and Delinquency* 47, no. 3 (2001): 335–351.

De Fazio, Gianluca. "Legal Opportunity Structure and Social Movement Strategy in Northern Ireland and Southern United States." *International Journal of Comparative Sociology* 53, no. 1 (2012): 3–22.

della Porta, Donatella, and Mario Diani. *Social Movements: An Introduction*. New York: Wiley, 2009.

Devine-Wright, Patrick. *Renewable Energy and the Public: From NIMBY to Participation*. London: Earthscan, 2011.

———. "Rethinking NIMBYism: The Role of Place Attachment and Place Identity in Explaining Place-Protective Action." *Journal of Community and Applied Social Psychology* 19, no. 6 (2009): 426–441.

D'Orazio, Deidre, Steven Arkowitz, Jay Adams, and Wesley Maram. *The California Sexually Violent Predator Statute: History, Description, and Areas for Improvement*. Sacramento: California Coalition on Sexual Offending, January 2009. ccoso.org.

Douard, John, and Pamela D. Schultz. *Monstrous Crimes and the Failure of Forensic Psychiatry*. International Library of Ethics, Law, and the New Medicine. Dordrecht: Springer, 2013.

Driskell, Robyn Bateman, and Larry Lyon. "Are Virtual Communities True Communities? Examining the Environments and Elements of Community." *City and Community* 1, no. 4 (2002): 373–390.

Dum, Christopher. *Exiled in America: Life on the Margins in a Residential Motel*. New York: Columbia University Press, 2016.

Duwe, Grant. "Can Circles of Support and Accountability (COSA) Work in the United States? Preliminary Results from a Randomized Experiment in Minnesota." *Sexual Abuse: A Journal of Research and Treatment* 25, no. 2 (2013): 143–165.

Eason, John. "Mapping Prison Proliferation: Region, Rurality, Race and Disadvantage in Prison Placement." *Social Science Research* 39, no. 6 (2010): 1015–1028.

Edelman, Lauren B., Gwendolyn Leachman, and Doug McAdam. "On Law, Organizations, and Social Movements." *Annual Review of Law and Social Science* 6 (2010): 653–685.

Eliasoph, Nina, and Paul Lichterman. "Culture in Interaction." *American Journal of Sociology* 108, no. 4 (2003): 735–794.

Ellickson, Robert C. *Order without Law: How Neighbors Settle Disputes*. Cambridge, MA: Harvard University Press, 1991.

Emerson, Robert M., Rachel I. Fretz, and Linda L. Shaw. *Writing Ethnographic Field Notes*. Chicago: University of Chicago Press, 1995.

Epstein, Eli. "Community Attacks Detroit Man Accused in Rape." *MSN News*, August 9, 2013. Accessed October 8, 2013. news.msn.com.

Ewick, Patricia, and Susan S. Silbey. *The Common Place of Law*. Chicago: University of Chicago Press, 1998.

Federal Bureau of Investigation. *Uniform Crime Reports*. Washington, DC: U.S. Department of Justice, 2013. Accessed January 1, 2013. www.ucrdatatool.gov.

Fox, Kathryn J. "Contextualizing the Policy and Pragmatics of Reintegrating Sex Offenders." *Sexual Abuse: A Journal of Research and Treatment* 9, no. 1 (2017): 28–50.

Galvan, Eric. "Horn Placement Hits a Road Bump." *Imperial Valley Press*, May 10, 2007. Accessed January 24, 2010. www.ivpressonline.com.

Garland, David. *Culture of Control: Crime and Social Order in Contemporary Society.* Chicago: University of Chicago Press, 2001.

Garriott, William. *Policing Methamphetamine: Narcopolitics in Rural America.* New York: New York University Press, 2011.

Gelman, Andrew, Jeffrey Fagan, and Alex Kiss. "An Analysis of the New York City Police Department's 'Stop-and-Frisk' Policy in the Context of Claims of Racial Bias." *Journal of the American Statistical Association* 102, no. 479 (2007): 813–823.

Gilmore, Ruth Wilson. *Golden Gulag: Prisons, Surplus, Crisis, and Opposition in Globalizing California.* Berkeley: University of California Press, 2007.

Goode, Erich, and Nachman Ben-Yehuda. *Moral Panics: The Social Construction of Deviance.* Malden, MA: Blackwell, 1994.

Goodyear, Charlie, and Erin Hallissy. "Paroled Inmate Loses Lodging Offer; Martinez Landlord Backs Out of Deal on Sexual Predator." *San Francisco Chronicle*, August 15, 2003. www.sfgate.com.

Gottschalk, Marie. *Caught: The Prison State and the Lockdown of American Politics.* Princeton, NJ: Princeton University Press, 2016.

Greenhouse, Carol. *Praying for Justice: Faith, Order, and Community in an American Town.* Ithaca, NY: Cornell University Press, 1986.

Greenhouse, Carol, Barbara Yngvesson, and David Engel. *Law and Community in Three American Towns.* Ithaca, NY: Cornell University Press, 1994.

Guillermo, Emil. "Treating Sexual Predators." *San Francisco Chronicle*, September 11, 2001. Accessed February 15, 2010. articles.sfgate.com.

Hagan, John, and Alberto Palloni. "Sociological Criminology and the Mythology of Hispanic Immigration and Crime." *Social Problems* 46, no. 4 (1999): 617–632.

Hale, Sherry, John Angel, Roger Tang, and Keith Archuleta. "East City: An Island of Poverty in a Sea of Riches." *N.I.A: The Black Magazine*, 1, no. 1 (December 1977/ January 1978): 24–25.

Hanson, R. Karl, and Kelly E. Morton-Bourgon. "The Accuracy of Recidivism Risk Assessments for Sexual Offenders: A Meta-analysis of 118 Prediction Studies." *Psychological Assessment* 21, no. 1 (2009): 1–21.

———. "The Characteristics of Persistent Sexual Offenders: A Meta-analysis of Recidivism Studies." *Journal of Consulting and Clinical Psychology* 73, no. 6 (2005): 1154–1163.

Harris, Andrew J., Jill S. Levenson, and Alissa R. Ackerman. "Registered Sex Offenders in the United States: Behind the Numbers." *Crime and Delinquency* 60, no. 1 (2014): 3–33.

Harris, Andrew J., Christopher Lobanov-Rostovsky, and Jill S. Levenson. "Widening the Net: The Effects of Transitioning to the Adam Walsh Act's Federally Mandated Sex Offender Classification System." *Criminal Justice and Behavior* 37, no. 5 (2010): 503–519.

Harvey, David. "The Right to the City." *International Journal of Urban and Regional Research* 27, no. 4 (2003): 939–941.

Herbert, Steve. *Citizens, Cops, and Power: Recognizing the Limits of Community.* Chicago: University of Chicago Press, 2006.

Herbert, Steve, and Katherine Beckett. "Zoning Out Disorder: Assessing Contemporary Practices of Urban Social Control." In *Special Issue: New Perspectives on Crime and Criminal Justice,* edited by Austin Sarat, 47:1–25. Studies in Law, Politics, and Society. Bingley, UK: Emerald Group, 2009.

Hibbing, John R., and Elizabeth Theiss-Morse. *Stealth Democracy: Americans' Beliefs about How Government Should Work.* Cambridge: Cambridge University Press, 2002.

Hoppe, Trevor. "Punishing Sex: Sex Offenders and the Missing Punitive Turn in Sexuality Studies." *Law and Social Inquiry* 41, no. 3 (2016): 573–594.

Hudak, Stephen. "Sex Offender Village in Sorrento: Moms, Officials to Discuss 'Sex Offender' Village at Town Hall Meeting in Sorrento." *Orlando Sentinel,* October 6, 2011. Accessed October 7, 2011. www.orlandosentinel.com.

Hudson, Kirsty. *Offending Identities: Sex Offenders' Perspectives of Their Treatment and Management.* Portland, OR: Willan Publishing, 2005.

Huebner, Beth M., Kimberly R. Kras, Jason Rydberg, Timothy S. Bynum, Eric Grommon, and Breanne Pleggenkuhle. "The Effect and Implications of Sex Offender Residence Restrictions." *Criminology and Public Policy* 13, no. 1 (2014): 139–168.

Huisman, Kimberly. "'Does This Mean You're Not Going to Come Visit Me Anymore?': An Inquiry into an Ethics of Reciprocity and Positionality in Feminist Ethnographic Research." *Sociological Inquiry* 78, no. 3 (2008): 372–396.

Hunt, Scott A., and Robert D. Benford. "Collective Identity, Solidarity, and Commitment." In *The Blackwell Companion to Social Movements,* edited by David A. Snow, Sarah A. Soule, and Hanspeter Kriesi, 433–457. Malden, MA: Blackwell, 2004.

Irvine, Annie, Paul Drew, and Roy Sainsbury. "'Am I Not Answering Your Questions Properly?' Clarification, Adequacy and Responsiveness in Semi-structured Telephone and Face-to-Face Interviews." *Qualitative Research* 13, no. 1 (2013): 87–106.

Irvine, Janice M. "Emotional Scripts of Sex Panics." *Sexuality Research and Social Policy* 3, no. 3 (2006): 82–94.

Jackson, Rebecca L., and Christmas N. Covell. "Sex Offender Civil Commitment." In *The Wiley-Blackwell Handbook of Legal and Ethical Aspects of Sex Offender Treatment and Management,* edited by Karen Harrison and Bernadette Rainey, 406–423. Chichester, UK: Wiley, 2013.

Janus, Eric. *Failure to Protect.* Ithaca, NY: Cornell University Press, 2006.

Jasper, James. "A Strategic Approach to Collective Action: Looking for Agency in Social-Movement Choices." *Mobilization: An International Quarterly* 9, no. 1 (2004): 1–16.

Jenkins, Philip. *Moral Panic: Changing Concepts of the Child Molester in Modern America.* New Haven, CT: Yale University Press, 1998.

Johnstone, Barbara. *Stories, Community, and Place: Narratives from Middle America.* Bloomington: Indiana University Press, 1990.

Kairys, David. *The Politics of Law: A Progressive Critique.* New York: Basic Books, 1998.

Keller, Suzanne. *Community.* Princeton, NJ: Princeton University Press, 2003.

Kent, Erika, Casey Vaughn, and Joseph Pereira. "Homicide Suspect Calls Victim 'Pedophile' and 'Demon.'" *FOX Carolina 21.* Jonesville, SC, July 29, 2013. Accessed October 8, 2013. www.foxcarolina.com.

Kirk, David S., and Mauri Matsuda. "Legal Cynicism, Collective Efficacy, and the Ecology of Arrest." *Criminology* 49, no. 2 (2011): 443–472.

Kirk, David S., and Andrew V. Papachristos. "Cultural Mechanisms and the Persistence of Neighborhood Violence." *American Journal of Sociology* 116, no. 4 (2011): 1190–1233.

KOMO-TV Staff. "Woman Gets Three Months for Attacking Sex Offender with Bat." *Seattle Post-Intelligencer*, February 27, 2009. Accessed June 21, 2010. www.seattlepi.com.

Krutli, Pius, Michael Stauffacher, Dario Pedolin, Corinne Moser, and Roland W. Scholz. "The Process Matters: Fairness in Repository Siting for Nuclear Waste." *Social Justice Research* 25, no. 1 (2012): 79–101.

Kusenbach, Margarethe. "Patterns of Neighboring: Practicing Community in the Parochial Realm." *Symbolic Interaction* 29, no. 3 (2006): 279–306.

Lancaster, Roger N. *Sex Panic and the Punitive State.* Berkeley: University of California Press, 2011.

Lenz, Nygel. "'Luxuries' in Prison: The Relationship between Amenity Funding and Public Support." *Crime and Delinquency* 48, no. 4 (2002): 499–525.

Leon, Chrysanthi. *Sex Fiends, Perverts, and Pedophiles: Understanding Sex Crime Policy in America.* New York: New York University Press, 2011.

Leonard, Liam, Peter Doran, and Honor Fagan. "A Burning Issue? Governance and Anti-incinerator Campaigns in Ireland, North and South." *Environmental Politics* 18, no. 6 (2009): 896–916.

Levenson, Jill S. "Sex Offender Policies in an Era of Zero Tolerance." *Criminology and Public Policy* 10, no. 2 (2011): 229–233.

———. "Sex Offender Residence Restrictions." In *Sex Offender Laws: Failed Policies, New Directions*, edited by Richard Wright, 267–290. New York: Springer, 2009.

Levenson, Jill S., and Leo P. Cotter. "The Effect of Megan's Law on Sex Offender Reintegration." *Journal of Contemporary Criminal Justice* 21, no. 1 (2005): 49–66.

Levenson, Jill S., and Richard Tewksbury. "Collateral Damage: Family Members of Registered Sex Offenders." *American Journal of Criminal Justice* 34, nos. 1–2 (2009): 54–68.

Leverentz, Andrea. "Narratives of Crime and Criminals: How Places Socially Construct the Crime Problem." *Sociological Forum* 27, no. 2 (2012): 348–371.

Lichterman, Paul. *Elusive Togetherness.* Princeton, NJ: Princeton University Press, 2005.

Littlefield, Dana. "Housing Proposal for Sex Predator Rescinded." *San Diego Union-Tribune*, February 20, 2014. Accessed November 7, 2014. www.utsandiego.com.

Lofland, John, David Snow, Leon Anderson, and Lyn H. Lofland. *Analyzing Social Settings: A Guide to Qualitative Observation and Analysis.* Belmont, CA: Wadsworth/Thomson Learning, 2006.

Lofland, Lyn H. "History, the City and the Interactionist: Anselm Strauss, City Imagery, and Urban Sociology." *Symbolic Interaction* 14, no. 2 (1991): 205–223.

Logan, Wayne A. *Knowledge as Power.* Stanford, CA: Stanford University Press, 2009.

Lovett, Ian. "Building Tiny Parks to Drive Sex Offenders Away." *New York Times,* March 9, 2013. Accessed March 12, 2013. www.nytimes.com.

Luker, Kristin. *Salsa Dancing into the Social Sciences: Research in an Age of Info-Glut.* Cambridge, MA: Harvard University Press, 2008.

Lynch, Mona. "Mass Incarceration, Legal Change, and Locale." *Criminology and Public Policy* 10, no. 3 (2011): 673–698.

———. *Sunbelt Justice: Arizona and the Transformation of American Punishment.* Palo Alto, CA: Stanford University Press, 2009.

Maguire, Edward R. "Structural Change in Large Municipal Police Organizations during the Community Policing Era." *Justice Quarterly* 14, no. 3 (1997): 547–576.

Maliska, Barbara. *Dreams of a City: Creating East City.* VHS, 1997.

Mancini, Christina, J. C. Barnes, and Daniel P. Mears. "It Varies from State to State: An Examination of Sex Crime Laws Nationally." *Criminal Justice Policy Review* 24, no. 2 (2013): 166–198.

Marcuse, Peter. "From Critical Urban Theory to the Right to the City." *City* 13, nos. 2–3 (2009): 185–197.

McAlinden, Anne-Marie. *The Shaming of Sexual Offenders: Risk, Retribution, and Reintegration.* Oxford: Hart, 2007.

McCann, Michael W. *Rights at Work: Pay Equity Reform and the Politics of Legal Mobilization.* Chicago: University of Chicago Press, 1994.

McDowell, Meghan G. "'Becoming a Waste Land Where Nothing Can Survive': Resisting State-Corporate Environmental Crime in a 'Forgotten' Place." *Contemporary Justice Review* 16, no. 4 (2013): 394–411.

Merry, Sally Engle. *Getting Justice and Getting Even: Legal Consciousness among Working-Class Americans.* Chicago: University of Chicago Press, 1990.

Messer, Chris M., Thomas E. Shriver, and Alison E. Adams. "Collective Identity and Memory: A Comparative Analysis of Community Response to Environmental Hazards." *Rural Sociology* 80, no. 3 (2015): 314–339.

Miller, Lisa L. "The Invisible Black Victim: How American Federalism Perpetuates Racial Inequality in Criminal Justice." *Law and Society Review* 44, nos. 3–4 (2010): 805–842.

———. "The Local and the Legal." *Criminology and Public Policy* 10, no. 3 (2011): 725–732.

———. *The Perils of Federalism: Race, Poverty, and the Politics of Crime Control.* New York: Oxford University Press, 2008.

Mohai, Paul, David Pellow, and J. Timmons Roberts. "Environmental Justice." *Annual Review of Environment and Resources* 34, no. 1 (2009): 405–430.

Morabito, Melissa Schaefer. "Understanding Community Policing as an Innovation: Patterns of Adoption." *Crime and Delinquency* 56, no. 4 (2010): 564–587.

Moran, Chris. "Offer to House 2 Sex Predators Rescinded." *San Diego Union-Tribune*, April 29, 2005. www.sandiegouniontribune.com.

Morrill, Calvin, Karolyn Tyson, Lauren B. Edelman, and Richard Arum. "Legal Mobilization in Schools: The Paradox of Rights and Race among Youth." *Law and Society Review* 44, nos. 3–4 (2010): 651–694.

Mustaine, Elizabeth Ehrhardt. "Sex Offender Residency Restrictions." *Criminology and Public Policy* 13, no. 1 (2014): 169–177.

Mustaine, Elizabeth E., Richard Tewksbury, and Kenneth M. Stengel. "Social Disorganization and Residential Locations of Registered Sex Offenders: Is This a Collateral Consequence?" *Deviant Behavior* 27, no. 3 (2006): 329–350.

Nation, Nancy Isles. "Ghilotti Leads Isolated Life in Vacaville." *San Francisco Chronicle*, July 1, 2004.

Novick, Gina. "Is There a Bias against Telephone Interviews in Qualitative Research?" *Research in Nursing and Health* 31, no. 4 (2008): 391–398.

Parent, Dale, and Brad Snyder. *Police-Corrections Partnerships*. Washington, DC: National Institute of Justice, March 1999. Accessed February 2, 2017. www.ncjrs.gov.

Paris, Michael. *Framing Equal Opportunity: Law and the Politics of School Finance Reform*. Palo Alto, CA: Stanford University Press, 2010.

———. "Legal Mobilization and the Politics of Reform: Lessons from School Finance Litigation in Kentucky, 1984–1995." *Law and Social Inquiry* 26, no. 3 (2006): 631–681.

Pastor, Manuel, Jim Sadd, and John Hipp. "Which Came First? Toxic Facilities, Minority Move-In, and Environmental Justice." *Journal of Urban Affairs* 23, no. 1 (2001): 1–21.

Pellow, David Naguib. *Garbage Wars: The Struggle for Environmental Justice in Chicago*. Cambridge, MA: MIT Press, 2004.

Petersilia, Joan. *When Prisoners Come Home: Parole and Prisoner Reentry*. New York: Oxford University Press, 2003.

Pettit, Becky, and Bruce Western. "Mass Imprisonment and the Life Course: Race and Class Inequality in U.S. Incarceration." *American Sociological Review* 69, no. 2 (2004): 151–169.

Pickett, Justin T., Christina Mancini, and Daniel P. Mears. "Vulnerable Victims, Monstrous Offenders, and Unmanageable Risk: Explaining Public Opinion on the Social Control of Sex Crime." *Criminology* 51, no. 3 (2013): 729–759.

Planty, Michael, Lynn Langton, Christopher Krebs, Marcus Berzofsky, and Hope Smiley-McDonald. *Female Victims of Sexual Violence, 1994–2010*. Washington, DC: Bureau of Justice Statistics, March 2013. Accessed September 3, 2013. www.bjs.gov.

Polletta, Francesca, and James Jasper. "Collective Identity and Social Movements." *Annual Review of Sociology* 27 (2001): 283–305.

Prentky, Robert A., Howard E. Barbaree, and Eric S. Janus. *Sexual Predators: Society, Risk, and the Law*. New York: Routledge, 2015.

Purcell, Mark. "Ruling Los Angeles: Neighborhood Movements, Urban Regimes, and the Production of Space in Southern California." *Urban Geography* 18, no. 8 (1997): 684–704.

Putnam, Robert. *Bowling Alone: The Collapse and Revival of American Community.* New York: Simon and Schuster, 2000.

Quick, Kathryn S., and Martha S. Feldman. "Distinguishing Participation and Inclusion." *Journal of Planning Education and Research* 31, no. 3 (2011): 272–290.

Ramakrishnan, Subramanian Karthick, and Mark Baldassare. *The Ties That Bind: Changing Demographics and Civic Engagement in California.* San Francisco: Public Policy Institute of California, 2004. Accessed December 10, 2014. www.ppic.org.

Reed, Dan, and Chakko Kuruvila Matthai. "Jittery Soledad Copes with Freed Molester." *San Jose Mercury News*, August 14, 2003.

Rios, Victor M. *Punished: Policing the Lives of Black and Latino Boys.* New York: New York University Press, 2011.

Robbers, Monica L. P. "Lifers on the Outside: Sex Offenders and Disintegrative Shaming." *International Journal of Offender Therapy and Comparative Criminology* 53, no. 1 (2009): 5–28.

Rocha, Veronica. "Convicted Child Predator's Proposed Home Destroyed in 'Suspicious Fire' in Rural Fresno County." *Los Angeles Times*, January 13, 2017. Accessed January 17, 2017. www.latimes.com.

Ruming, Kristian. "'It Wasn't about Public Housing, It Was about the Way It Was Done': Challenging Planning Not People in Resisting the Nation Building Economic Stimulus Plan, Australia." *Journal of Housing and the Built Environment* 29, no. 1 (2014): 39–60.

Saha, Robin, and Paul Mohai. "Historical Context and Hazardous Waste Facility Siting: Understanding Temporal Patterns in Michigan." *Social Problems* 52, no. 4 (2005): 618–648.

Sample, Lisa L. "The Need to Debate the Fate of Sex Offender Community Notification Laws." *Criminology and Public Policy* 10, no. 2 (2011): 265–274.

Sample, Lisa L., Mary K. Evans, and Amy L. Anderson. "Sex Offender Community Notification Laws: Are Their Effects Symbolic or Instrumental in Nature?" *Criminal Justice Policy Review* 22, no. 1 (2011): 27–49.

Sampson, Robert J., and Stephen W. Raudenbush. "Seeing Disorder: Neighborhood Stigma and the Social Construction of 'Broken Windows.'" *Social Psychology Quarterly* 67, no. 4 (2004): 319–342.

Sexton, Lori. "Penal Subjectivities: Developing a Theoretical Framework for Penal Consciousness." *Punishment and Society* 17, no. 1 (2015): 114–136.

Silbey, Susan S. "After Legal Consciousness." *Annual Review of Law and Social Science* 1 (2005): 323–368.

Simon, Jonathan. *Governing through Crime: How the War on Crime Transformed American Democracy and Created a Culture of Fear.* New York: Oxford University Press, 2007.

———. "Megan's Law: Crime and Democracy in Late Modern America." *Law and Social Inquiry* 25, no. 4 (2000): 1111–1150.

Small, Mario Luis. "'How Many Cases Do I Need?': On Science and the Logic of Case Selection in Field-Based Research." *Ethnography* 10, no. 1 (2009): 5–38.

Snyder, Howard N. *Arrest in the United States, 1990–2010.* Washington, DC: Bureau of Justice Statistics, 2012. www.bjs.gov.

Socia, Kelly M. "Residence Restrictions Are Ineffective, Inefficient, and Inadequate: So Now What?" *Criminology and Public Policy* 13, no. 1 (2014): 179–188.

Soss, Joe, Richard C. Fording, and Sanford F. Schram. *Disciplining the Poor: Neoliberal Paternalism and the Persistent Power of Race.* Chicago: University of Chicago Press, 2011.

Soule, Sarah, and Jennifer Earl. "A Movement Society Evaluated: Collective Protest in the United States, 1960–1986." *Mobilization: An International Quarterly* 10, no. 3 (2005): 345–364.

Stacey, Judith. "Can There Be a Feminist Ethnography?" *Women's Studies International Forum* 11, no. 1 (1988): 21–27.

State of California Department of Justice, Office of the Attorney General. "California Sex Offender Registry." Last modified August 21, 2015. Accessed February 21, 2017. oag.ca.gov.

Stein, Arlene. *The Stranger Next Door: The Story of a Small Community's Battle over Sex, Faith, and Civil Rights.* Boston: Beacon Press, 2001.

Stojkovic, Stan, and Mary Ann Farkas. "So You Want to Find a Transitional House for Sexually Violent Persons: An Account of Political Failure." *Criminal Justice Policy Review* 25, no. 6 (2014): 659–682.

Strauss, Anselm, and Juliet Corbin. *Basics of Qualitative Research: Grounded Theory Procedures and Techniques.* Newbury Park, CA: Sage, 1990.

Tarr, David A. "Turmoil in Turkey Town: Development, Disparity, and Discontent in Ranchito, California, 1954–1994." Master's thesis, San Diego State University, 1997.

Taylor, Dorceta E. *Toxic Communities: Environmental Racism, Industrial Pollution, and Residential Mobility.* New York: New York University Press, 2014.

Terry, Karen J. "What Is Smart Sex Offender Policy?" *Criminology and Public Policy* 10, no. 2 (2011): 275–282.

Tewksbury, Richard. "Collateral Consequences of Sex Offender Registration." *Journal of Contemporary Criminal Justice* 21, no. 1 (2005): 67–81.

———. "Policy Implications of Sex Offender Residence Restrictions Laws." *Criminology and Public Policy* 10, no. 2 (2011): 345–348.

Tewksbury, Richard, and Matthew Lees. "Perceptions of Sex Offender Registration: Collateral Consequences and Community Experiences." *Sociological Spectrum* 26, no. 3 (2006): 309–334.

Thomas, Jeremy. "Lompoc's Most Unwanted." *Santa Maria Sun*, April 14, 2009. Accessed January 21, 2010. www.santamariasun.com.

Tilly, Charles, and Sidney G. Tarrow. *Contentious Politics.* Boulder, CO: Paradigm Publishers, 2007.

Travis, Jeremy. *But They All Come Back: Facing the Challenges of Prisoner Reentry.* Washington, DC: Urban Institute Press, 2005.

Tyler, Tom R. *Why People Obey the Law.* Princeton, NJ: Princeton University Press, 2006.

Unnever, James D., and Francis T. Cullen. "The Social Sources of Americans' Punitiveness: A Test of Three Competing Models." *Criminology* 48, no. 1 (2010): 99–129.

U.S. Census Bureau. *2006–2010 American Community Survey 5-Year Estimates.* 2010. Accessed January 28, 2013. factfinder2.census.gov.

———. *2009–2013 American Community Survey 5-Year Estimates.* 2013. Accessed January 28, 2013. factfinder2.census.gov.

———. *2010 Census.* 2010. Accessed January 28, 2013. factfinder2.census.gov.

Vanhala, Lisa. "Legal Opportunity Structures and the Paradox of Legal Mobilization by the Environmental Movement in the UK." *Law and Society Review* 46, no. 3 (2012): 523–556.

Venkatesh, Sudhir. *American Project: The Rise and Fall of a Modern Ghetto.* Cambridge, MA: Harvard University Press, 2002.

Weber, Max. *Basic Concepts in Sociology.* Translated by H. P. Secher. Westport, CT: Greenwood Press, 1962.

———. *The Theory of Social and Economic Organization.* Edited by Talcott Parsons. Translated by A. M. Henderson and Talcott Parsons. New York: Oxford University Press, 1947.

Weiss, Robert S. *Learning from Strangers: The Art and Method of Qualitative Interview Studies.* New York: Free Press, 1994.

Wheeler, Kelly. "Two Sexually Violent Predators Ordered Released to Home Near Jacumba." *City News Service,* June 20, 2008.

Williams, Monica. "Beyond the Retributive Public: Governance and Public Opinion on Penal Policy." *Journal of Crime and Justice* 35, no. 1 (2012): 93–113.

———. "Constructing Hysteria: Legal Signals as Producers of Siting Conflicts over Sexually Violent Predator Placements." *Law and Social Inquiry.* 2016. Epub ahead of print. doi: 10.1111/lsi.12265.

Wilson, Robin J., Franca Cortoni, and Andrew J. McWhinnie. "Circles of Support and Accountability: A Canadian National Replication of Outcome Findings." *Sexual Abuse: A Journal of Research and Treatment* 21, no. 4 (2009): 412–430.

Wolsink, Maarten, and Jeroen Devilee. "The Motives for Accepting or Rejecting Waste Infrastructure Facilities: Shifting the Focus from the Planners' Perspective to Fairness and Community Commitment." *Journal of Environmental Planning and Management* 52, no. 2 (2009): 217–236.

Wozniak, Kevin H. "American Public Opinion about Prisons." *Criminal Justice Review* 39, no. 3 (2014): 305–324.

Wuthnow, Robert. *Loose Connections: Joining Together in America's Fragmented Communities.* Cambridge, MA: Harvard University Press, 1998.

Young, Michael G. "Necessary but Insufficient: NIMBY and the Development of a Therapeutic Community for Homeless Persons with Co-morbid Disorders." *Local Environment* 17, no. 3 (2012): 281–293.

Zandbergen, Paul A., Jill S. Levenson, and Timothy C. Hart. "Residential Proximity to Schools and Daycares: An Empirical Analysis of Sex Offense Recidivism." *Criminal Justice and Behavior* 37, no. 5 (2010): 482–502.

Zevitz, Richard G. "Sex Offender Community Notification: Its Role in Recidivism and Offender Reintegration." *Criminal Justice Studies: A Critical Journal of Crime, Law and Society* 19, no. 2 (2006): 193–208.

———. "Sex Offender Community Notification and Its Impact on Neighborhood Life." *Crime Prevention and Community Safety* 5, no. 4 (2003): 41–61.

———. "Sex Offender Placement and Neighborhood Social Integration: The Making of a Scarlet Letter Community." *Criminal Justice Studies* 17, no. 2 (2004): 203–222.

Zevitz, Richard G., and Mary Ann Farkas. "Sex Offender Community Notification: Examining the Importance of Neighborhood Meetings." *Behavioral Sciences and the Law* 18, no. 2–3 (2000): 393–408.

Zgoba, Kristen M., Michael Miner, Jill Levenson, Raymond Knight, Elizabeth Letourneau, and David Thornton. "The Adam Walsh Act: An Examination of Sex Offender Risk Classification Systems." *Sexual Abuse: A Journal of Research and Treatment* 28, no. 8 (2016): 722–740.

Zimring, Franklin, Gordon Hawkins, and Sam Kamin. *Punishment and Democracy: Three Strikes and You're Out in California.* Oxford: Oxford University Press, 2001.

INDEX

ABOUT THE AUTHOR

Monica Williams is Assistant Professor of Criminal Justice at Weber State University.